Lucian's
Dialogues of the Courtesans

An Intermediate Greek Reader

Greek Text with Running Vocabulary and Commentary

Evan Hayes
and
Stephen Nimis

Lucian's *Dialogues of the Courtesans* : An Intermediate Greek Reader:
Greek Text with Running Vocabulary and Commentary

First Edition
Updated February 2016

© 2015 by Evan Hayes and Stephen Nimis

ISBN-10: 1940997178

ISBN-13: 9781940997179

Published by Faenum Publishing, Ltd.

Cover Design: Evan Hayes

Fonts: Garamond
         GFS Porson

editor@faenumpublishing.com

TABLE OF CONTENTS

for Erin Wagner Siegfried
discipulae, amicae, magistri

Acknowledgments

The idea for this project grew out of work that we, the authors, did with support from Miami University's Undergraduate Summer Scholars Program, for which we thank Martha Weber and the Office of Advanced Research and Scholarship. Work on the series, of which this volume is a part, was generously funded by the Joanna Jackson Goldman Memorial Prize through the Honors Program at Miami University. We owe a great deal to Carolyn Haynes, and the 2010 Honors & Scholars Program Advisory Committee for their interest and confidence in the project.

The technical aspects of the project were made possible through the invaluable advice and support of Bill Hayes, Christopher Kuo, and Daniel Meyers. The equipment and staff of Miami University's Interactive Language Resource Center were a great help along the way. We are also indebted to the Perseus Project, especially Gregory Crane and Bridget Almas, for their technical help and resources. We also profited greatly from advice and help on the POD process from Geoffrey Steadman. All responsibility for errors, however, rests with the authors themselves.

INTRODUCTION

The aim of this book is to make *The Dialogues of the Courtesans* by Lucian of Samosata (c. 120 CE –190) accessible to intermediate students of Ancient Greek. The running vocabulary and grammatical commentary are meant to provide everything necessary to read each page, so that readers can progress through the text, improving their knowledge of Greek while enjoying one of the most entertaining authors of antiquity. These dialogues are another example of Lucian presenting unusual perspectives on Greek culture and literature, this time by creating amusing dialogues that occur mostly among the professional companions, *hetairai*, who formed a special form of upscale entertainment for elite men in the classical period. The women in these dialogues sometimes interact with male clients, but in most of them we find only women, as they speak of their hopes and fears and the business of love.

The Dialogues of the Courtesans is a great text for intermediate readers. Like many of Lucian's works, they are breezy and fun to read with relatively simple sentence structure. Some were considered too naughty for Victorian readers and were expurgated, particularly the oblique discussion of a night of gay carousing (5). A common theme is the problem of reconciling spontaneous affection and payment for services rendered. The courtesan "performed" love and affection, and as Kate Gilhuly has argued, she is thus also a figure for the sophist himself. Lucian, who regularly acknowledges and embraces his outsider status (as a Syrian), *performs* a version of Greek culture that privileges authentic Greek language and literature. Whatever else these dialogues are about--and there is plenty--they are also emblems of that peculiar moment in Greek literary history we call the Second Sophistic.

Courtesans (ἑταίραι)

Courtesans made up a special class of sexual workers in classical Athens where the *Dialogues* are all set. Since citizen women could not be courtesans, foreigners and *metics* (guest-workers) were the usual source for these women. They tended to be better-educated and more refined than *pornai*, another class of sex-workers who were usually slaves. They are found in various sources as hired guests at drinking parties (*symposia*), where drinking, sex and conversation provided entertainment for elite Athenians. Courtesans also played music and danced for their clients. As non-citizens, courtesans could not marry an

Athenian male and produce legitimate children; but they could be "kept" by admirers as concubines and companions. The line separating legitimate wife and concubine was a strict one, as dramatized in the famous oration of Demosthenes *Against Neaira*. Courtesans appear in a number of literary contexts, most frequently in New Comedy, where desire and civic duty are often pitted against each other. Although consorting with courtesans was not considered ignoble, to waste one's patrimony on one or to refuse the duty of marriage represented serious breeches of proper behavior for young men. The figure of the courtesan was thus a crucial focus for various ethical conflicts.

The literary tradition prior to Lucian provided many instances of courtesans, some of them achieving fame for their beauty or wit. Among the most famous was Aspasia, the companion of Pericles, as well as Phryne, the mistress and model of the sculptor Praxiletes. But other names and stories are also well-known: Lais, the rival of Phryne, and Thais, a companion of Ptolemy Soter, responsible in some accounts for the burning of Persepolis. Courtesans were a valued source of amusement for men, but were also the subject of abuse and moral diatribe. Thus they are often praised for their wit and charm but chastened for their greed and manipulative behavior. The ambivalence of men toward these women is not surprising given the attitudes towards women in general in the ancient world. Lucian's own treatment of these figures from the past betrays considerable more sympathy than the literary tradition he inherited.

The Form and Subject Matter of Lucian's Dialogues of the Courtesans

Lucian's *Dialogues of the Courtesans* are closely connected in subject matter with the New Comedy of Menander (342-290 BCE), whose works were adapted by Plautus and Terence into Latin. This drama was written in verse, of course, with songs and spoken parts interspersed. Lucian's dialogues are not in verse and thus harken back to yet another tradition, the Mimes of Sophron (5th C BCE), which were dialogues in a kind of rhythmical prose that was meant to be more realistic. Their subject matter also presented scenes from daily life, often in a comic vein. Keith Sidwell thus suggests that *The Dialogues of the Courtesans* can be seen to combine the scenarios of New Comedy with a breezy conversational style more like the mime tradition. But prose dialogue is also the chief form of the philosophical works of Plato, who was himself reputed to be a great admirer of Sophron. Indeed, in another work, *You are a Literary Prometheus*, Lucian describes his works as a marriage between comedy and dialogue, where it is clear that the latter is specifically *philosophical* dialogue. Kate Gilhuly (2007) argues persuasively that the *Dialogues of the Courtesans* are best viewed as the very combination that Lucian describes in *You are a Literary Prometheus*, and based on that identification she reads the *Courtesans* as a reflection on literary form and tradition.

Several dialogues present mothers giving advice to their daughters on the finer points of being a *hetaira* (3, 6, 7). These are striking inversions of the kind of counsel a parent would be imagined to give a daughter. The traditional manipulative ruses that play on the weakness of men are in full display here, along with a sense of the demands of poverty and the degradation into which these women are compelled by circumstances. In a similar vein an older *hetaira* gives advice to a younger one (8), where the heat of passion among men is equated with the ferocity of their violence. "Somehow you seem to want me to be beaten" complains the younger courtesan, who finds little solace in her mentor's suggestion. In another dialogue (11), one courtesan details the clever tricks of an older competitor who has beguiled a young man. Two other dialogues feature courtesans complaining about the behavior of rivals (1, 4), in both cases evoking standard accounts of the operations of witches in attracting lovers. In 14, a client gives a detailed account of the modest "gifts" he has provided a courtesan as the basis for his demands for her attention. It is not clear who is more humiliated by these crass calculations. Numbers 2 and 12 deal with the feelings of courtesans who have been inexplicably wronged by the young men for whom they confess real affection; in both cases there has been a misunderstanding based on mistaken identity. So also in 10 a distressed courtesan discovers that her lover has been compelled against his will to study philosophy instead of consorting with her. The boastful warrior, made famous by Plautus' *Miles Gloriosus*, is featured in Dialogue 13. In 9, a soldier returning unexpectedly finds his courtesan already occupied with another rich client, prompting a dispute that threatens to turn violent; and in 15 two courtesans agree that soldiers are a terrible nuissance as lovers, prone as they are to lawsuits and brawls. The most striking and original dialogue is 5, in which a courtesan recounts her night with two other women at a symposium. All but the last of these have precedents of one sort or another in New Comedy.

The New Comedy plays of Menander and his Roman imitators typically revolve around the conflict between desire and duty: specifically, the desire of a young man for a woman who would make an inappropriate wife. An infatuation with a courtesan is an example of such a problematic desire, but courtesans also feature as mediating figures (like the clever slave) who help circumvent the demands of propriety. More precisely, as M. Henry notes, they are outsiders who facilitate the reconstitution of domestic life, a life from which there are legally prohibited. New Comedy plots are typically resolved by some kind of revelation about the status of the love object (she turns out actually to be a good Athenian citizen), eliminating the social conflict by a narrative sleight of hand. Courtesans themselves, however, typically remain outside of proper society and do not usually become legitimate wives.

Lucian's *Dialogues* sound themes similar to New Comedy, but centralize the courtesan point of view and her experience, although this should not be mistaken for some kind of authentic "woman's voice." The author is Lucian of Samasota, after all, and he is a master ventriloquist. To take the example of dialogue 5, the all-woman symposium, the insistent question that Klonarion keeps asking ("What exactly happened? How exactly does it work?") sounds just like what a *man*, for whom sex must involve penetration, would be most curious about in the case of homoerotic relations among women. Indeed, in some cases the figures we meet are the stereotypes familiar from past literary representations of manipulative women, unscrupulously plying their trade without any sign of affection. But we also discover young women with hopes and fears, navigating with difficulty a life on the margins of proper society, subject to the whims of their clients despite their attempts to exercise control over their world.

The most discussed dialogue (and the most fequently expurgated) is number 5, in which Leaina relates to Klonarium her erotic adventure at a symposium with two other women. Two recent articles (Gilhuly 2006 and Bissa 2013) provide complementary analyses that focus respectively on the literary character of the work and on the representational status of the portrayal, and their discussions can serve as a general introduction to the problems and interests of all these dialogues. Gilhuly focuses on the way gender and genre interact in this dialogue, noting that Lucian effects a clever inversion of his literary predecessors, particularly the *Symposium* of Plato. His "phallic Lesbian," an impossible position in the traditional constellation of sex and gender positions, "is a local manifestation of Lucian's invented genre--the uncomfortable mingling of philosophy and comedy" (289). Gilhuly's careful reading of the dialogue's engagement with the literary tradition is a model for reading Lucian and his contemporaries. Equally engaging and persuasive is Bissa'a attempt to mine the dialogue for evidence about female same-sex desire and relationships in the ancient world. She notes the way the dialogue raises very modern-sounding issues, such as the nurture vs. nature debate and the phenomenon of gender dysphoria. She concludes that the presentation of the masculinized Megilla "corresponds to modern gender expressions in the transgender spectrum" and that her relationship with her "wife" Demonassa is "presented as diverging from and replacing the traditional heterosexual standard (100)." The juxtaposition of these two different ways of "looking back" at ancient texts dramatizes the broad interest that Lucian still holds for us.

Proper names in the Dialogues of the Courtesans

Karl Mras (1916) surveyed the provenance of the names of the characters in *The Dialogues of the Courtesans* and has shown that most can be attested in a wide range of literary and non-literary sources, and that even unique names are based on analogies with other formations, especially in the case of diminutives (e.g. Κλωνάριον, Κυμβάλιον). The courtesans tend to have meaningful names like "Sweetie" and "Goldy," but many also appear in inscriptions as real names. About a dozen are also the names of courtesans in New Comedy, but this is not Lucian's only source. The male clients and their fathers tend to have Athenian names attested elsewhere as well; about half of these also occur in New Comedy. Some names of slaves, both male and female, are also attested names for slaves, in addition to being found in New Comedy.

So, for example, in the first dialogue two courtesans, Glykera (addressed with the diminutive Glykerion) and Thais speak, and refer to two other courtesans, Abrotonon and Gorgona. The name Glykera and its diminutive occur frequently in Attic funerary inscriptions, but the name also occurs in three plays of Menander (*Perikeiromene, Andria, Misogynes*). In addition, Menander is himself reputed to have loved a courtesan named Glykera. Thais, who also appears in *Dialogue* 3, and whose name becomes generic for a courtesan in Greek and Latin literature (see for example Ovid, *Remedia Amoris* 383-4 and the *Eunuch* of Terence), is the name of a number of courtesans in the historical tradition and is also attested in an Attic inscription as the name of a slave from Miletus. In Menander, Abrotonon is the name of a flute-player (*Perikeiromene*) and a harp-player (*Epitrepontes*), and although the name does not occur in Attic inscriptions, Plutarch states it is the name of the mother of Themistocles. Gorgona, finally, is not found in comedy at all, but is attested in an Attic dedicatory inscription. The names in this first dialogue show the wide range of sources for Lucian's names, but it is also clear that New Comedy is the single most important one.

Of special interest is the name Megillos/Megilla, the transgender character in Dialogue 5. The only other attested use of this name is in Plato's *Laws*, where the Spartan Megillos is called upon to defend the "deviant" (i.e. un-Athenian) sexual practices of Sparta. Gilhully (2006) and others discuss the significance of the allusion.

See "Appendix on Proper Names" for information about other names.

Lucian of Samosata (c. 120 CE –190)

Little is known about the life of Lucian except what can be deduced from his numerous surviving works. By his own account, he was a professional rhetor, a "sophist," trained in public speaking. As such he is a good representative of the renaissance of Greek literature in the imperial period known as the "second sophistic." His Greek prose is patterned on the best Attic authors, a learned version of Greek that was more prestigious than the living lingua franca of the time, *koine*, the Greek of the New Testament and public administration in the eastern half of the Roman Empire. His seventy works were transmitted in many manuscripts, indicating his continuous popularity in the Greek-speaking world. In the renaissance he was reintroduced to the Latin west and was widely read up to the beginning of the 20th century, when for various reasons he fell out of favor among classicists. Interest in Lucian has grown again, along with a greater interest in prose of the imperial period.

THE GREEK TEXT

The Greek text is that of K. Jacobitz (1896), which has been digitized by the Perseus Project and made available with a Creative Commons license, as is our text. Here and there we have made minor changes to the text in the name of readability. This is not a scholarly edition; for that one should turn to the OCT of Macleod.

SELECT BIBLIOGRAPHY

Bissa, Errietta M. A. (2013) "Man, Woman or Myth?: Gender-bending in Lucian's *Dialogues of the Courtesans.*" *Materiali e discussioni per l'analisi dei testi classici* 70, 79-100.

Blondell, R. and S. Boehringer (Spring, 2014) "Revenge of the *Hetairistria*: the Reception of Plato's *Symposium* in Lucian's Fifth *Dialogue of the Courtesans.*" *Arethusa* 47.2, 231-64.

Boehringer, Sandra (2015) "Sex, Lies, and (Video)trap: The Illusion of Sexual Identity in Lucian's *Dialogues of the Courtesans 5*," in Ruby Blondell and Kirk Ormand (edd.), *Ancient Sex, New Essays* (Columbus, OH: Ohio State University Press), 254-284

Gilhuly, K. (2006) "The Phallic Lesbian : Philosophy, Comedy, and Comic Inversion in Lucian's *Dialogues of the Courtesans*," in *Prostitutes and Courtesans in the Ancient World*, ed. by Christopher A. Faraone and Laura K. McClure. (Madison: University of Wisconsin Press), 274-291.

------------. (2007) "Bronze for Gold: Subjectivity in Lucian's *Dialogues of the Courtesans.*" *American Journal of Philology* 128.1, 59-94.

Henry M. M. (1985) *Menander's Courtesans and the Greek Comic Tradition.* Frankfurt : Lang.

Henry, M. M. and A. Glazebrook (2011) *Greek Prostitutes in the Ancient Mediterranean, 800 BCE-200 CE.* Madison, Wis., University of Wisconsin Press.

McLure, L. H. (2003) *Courtesans at Table: Gender and Greek Liteary Culture in Athenaeus.* New York and London: Routledge.

Mras, K. (1916) "Die Personennamen in Lucians *Hetärengesprächen.*" *Wiener Studien* 38, 308-42.

Peterson, Anna I. (2010) *Laughter in the Exchange: Lucian's Invention of the Comic Dialogue.* Diss.: Ohio State University.

Shreve-Price, Sharada Sue. (2014) *Complicated Courtesans: Lucian's Dialogues of the Courtesans.* Diss., University of Iowa.

Sidwel, Keith, tr. (2004) *Lucian: Chattering Courtesans and Other Sardonic Sketches.* Penguin Books, London.

How to use this book:

The page by page vocabularies gloss all but the most common words. We have endeavored to make these glossaries as useful as possible without becoming fulsome. Words occurring frequently in the text and words that are not glossed in every instance can be found in an appendix in the back, but it is our hope that most readers will not need to use this appendix often. Generally, proper names have not been glossed in the text, since they present no grammatical difficulties. Most occur in the vocative case or with a definite article. Information about the sources and lexical force of proper names can be found in an appendix after the glossary in the back.

The commentary is almost exclusively grammatical, explaining subordinate clauses, unusual verb forms, and idioms. Brief summaries of a number of grammatical and morphological topics are interspersed through the text as well, and there is a list of verbs used by Lucian that have unusual forms in an appendix. The principal parts of verbs are given there rather than in the glossaries. A good strategy is to read a passage in Greek, check the glossary for unusual words and consult the commentary as a last resort.

The commentary is meant to be consulted when needed, not to be read continuously. There is considerable repetition in the identification of clauses and troublesome verb forms, so that explanations are available whenever problems might be encountered. There is also considerable repetition in the vocabulary, again so that it will be available when needed. We have avoided duplication of vocabulary within each dialogue, but not among dialogues.

There is no full-scale literary commentary on the *Dialogues*, but S. S. Shreve-Price (2014) provides a discussion of them organized by themes (relationships with men, with other women, poverty, jealousy, etc.) and provides an up-to-date bibliography. The recent translation of Sidwell (2004) also has explanatory notes.

An Important Disclaimer:

This volume is a self-published "Print on Demand" (POD) book, and it has not been vetted or edited in the usual way by publishing professionals. There are sure to be some factual and typographical errors in the text, for which we apologize in advance. The volume is also available only through online distributors, since each book is printed when ordered online. However, this publishing channel and format also account for the low price of the book; and it is a simple matter to make changes when they come to our attention. For this reason, any corrections or suggestions for improvement are welcome and will be addressed as quickly as possible in future versions of the text.

Please e-mail corrections or suggestions to editor@faenumpublishing.com

About the Authors:

Evan Hayes is a graduate in Classics and Philosophy at Miami University and the 2011 Joanna Jackson Goldman Scholar.

Stephen Nimis is Emeritus Professor of Classics at Miami University and Professor of English and Comparative Literature at the American University in Cairo.

ABBREVIATIONS

abs.	absolute	m.	masculine
acc.	accusative	mid.	middle
act.	active	neg.	negative
adj.	adjective	neut.	neuter
adv.	adverb	nom.	nominative
aor.	aorist	obj.	object
app.	apposition	opt.	optative
artic.	articular	part.	participle
attrib.	attributive	pass.	passive
circum.	circumstantial	perf.	perfect
com.	command	pl.	plural
comp.	comparison	plupf.	pluperfect
dat.	dative	pot.	potential
delib.	deliberative	pred.	predicate
f.	feminine	pres.	present
fut.	future	pron.	pronoun
gen.	genitive	purp.	purpose
i.e.	*id est* ("that is")	quest.	question
imper.	imperative	s.	singular
impf.	imperfect	sc.	*scilicet* ("supply")
ind.	indirect	st.	statement
indic.	indicative	subj.	subjunctive
inf.	infinitive	suppl.	supplementary
intr.	intransitive	voc.	vocative

ΛΟΥΚΙΑΝΟΥ
Ἑταιρικοι Διαλογοι

Lucian's
Dialogues of the Courtesans

1. Glycera and Thais

Glycera complains that her lover has moved on to a rival, but Thais reminds her that there is no honor among courtesans.

ΓΛΥΚΕΡΑ: Τὸν στρατιώτην, Θαΐ, τὸν Ἀκαρνᾶνα, ὃς πάλαι μὲν Ἀβρότονον εἶχε, μετὰ ταῦτα δὲ ἠράσθη ἐμοῦ, τὸν εὐπάρυφον λέγω, τὸν ἐν τῇ χλαμύδι, οἶσθα αὐτόν, ἢ ἐπιλέλησαι τὸν ἄνθρωπον;

ΘΑΙΣ: Οὔκ, ἀλλὰ οἶδα, ὦ Γλυκέριον, καὶ συνέπιε μεθ᾽ ἡμῶν πέρυσιν ἐν τοῖς Ἁλώοις. τί δὲ τοῦτο; ἐῴκεις γάρ τι περὶ αὐτοῦ διηγεῖσθαι.

ΓΛΥΚΕΡΑ: Γοργόνα αὐτὸν ἡ παμπόνηρος, φίλη δοκοῦσα εἶναι, ἀπέσπασεν ἀπ᾽ ἐμοῦ ὑπελθοῦσα.

ΘΑΙΣ: Καὶ νῦν σοὶ μὲν ἐκεῖνος οὐ πρόσεστι, Γοργόναν δὲ ἑταίραν πεποίηται;

Ἀβρότονον, ἡ: Abrotonon, a courtesan	οἶδα: to know (*perf.*)
Ἀκαρνάν, -ᾶνος, ὁ: an Akarnanian	πάλαι: long ago
ἁλώιος, -α, -ον: of the threshing floor	παμπόνηρος, -ον: thoroughly knavish
ἀποσπάω: to drag away from	πέρυσι: (*adv.*) last year
Γοργόνα, ἡ: Gorgona, a courtesan	ποιέω: to make
διηγέομαι: to describe in full	πρόσειμι: to be present
ἔοικα: to seem	στρατιώτης, -ου, ὁ: a soldier
ἐπιλανθάνω: to forget	συμπίνω: to drink together
ἔραμαι: to love, to be in love with	ὑπέρχομαι: to go under, fawn on
ἑταίρα, ἡ: a courtesan	φίλος, -η, -ον: beloved, dear
εὐπάρυφος, -ον: with fine purple border	χλαμύς, -ύδος, ἡ: a short mantle

---

ἠράσθη: aor. pass., "*he became enamoured* of me"
ἐπιλέλησαι: perf. 2 s. mid., "*have you forgotten* the man?"
συνέπιε: aor. of συν-πίνω, "he drank with" + gen.
ἐν τοῖς Ἁλώοις: "at the harvest festival"
ἐῴκεις: plupf., "*you seemed to*" + inf.
δοκοῦσα: pres. part. concessive, "*although appearing* to be a friend"
ἀπέσπασεν: aor., "*she took away* from me"
ὑπελθοῦσα: aor. part. instrumental of ὑπο-έρχομαι, "took away *by fawning*"
ἑταίραν: acc. pred., "made Gorgona *his courtesan*"

3

ΓΛΥΚΕΡΑ: Ναί, ὦ Θαΐ, καὶ τὸ πρᾶγμα οὐ μετρίως μου ἥψατο.

ΘΑΙΣ: Πονηρὸν μέν, ὦ Γλυκέριον, οὐκ ἀδόκητον δέ, ἀλλ' εἰωθὸς γίγνεσθαι ὑφ' ἡμῶν τῶν ἑταιρῶν. οὔκουν χρὴ οὔτε ἀνιᾶσθαι ἄγαν οὔτε μέμφεσθαι τῇ Γοργόνῃ· οὐδὲ γὰρ σὲ Ἀβρότονον ἐπ' αὐτῷ πρότερον ἐμέμψατο, καίτοι φίλαι ἦτε. ἀτὰρ ἐκεῖνο θαυμάζω, τί καὶ ἐπήνεσεν αὐτῆς ὁ στρατιώτης οὗτος, ἐκτὸς εἰ μὴ παντάπασι τυφλός ἐστιν, ὃς οὐχ ἑωράκει τὰς μὲν τρίχας αὐτὴν ἀραιὰς ἔχουσαν καὶ ἐπὶ πολὺ τοῦ μετώπου ἀπηγμένας· τὰ χείλη δὲ πελιδνὰ καὶ τράχηλος λεπτὸς καὶ ἐπίσημοι ἐν αὐτῷ

ἄγαν: very, much	μέμφομαι: to blame, censure
ἀδόκητος, -ον: unexpected	μέτριος, -α, -ον: within measure
ἀνιάω: to grieve, distress	μέτωπον, -ή, τό: the brow, forehead
ἀπάγω: to lead away	ὁράω: to see
ἅπτω: to fasten, overtake	οὔκουν: not therefore, so not
ἀραιός, -α, -ον: thin, narrow	παντάπασι: altogether, wholly
ἀτάρ: but, yet	πελιδνός, -ή, -όν: livid
γίγνομαι: to become	πολύς, πολλά, πολύ: much, many
ἔθω: to be accustomed	πονηρός, -ά, -όν: painful, grievous
ἐπαινέω: to approve, praise	πρᾶγμα, -ατος, τό: a deed, act
ἐπίσημος, -ον: having a mark on	πρότερον: before
ἑταίρα, ἡ: a courtesan	τράχηλος, ὁ: the neck, throat
θαυμάζω: to wonder	τυφλός, -ή, -όν: blind
θρίξ, τρίχος, ἡ: the hair of the head	φιλός, -η, -ον: friendly
καίτοι: and yet	χεῖλος, -εος, τό: a lip
λεπτός, -ή, -όν: scraggly	χρή: it is necessary

ἥψατο: aor. mid., "the matter *overtook* me"

εἰωθὸς: perf. part. of ἔθω, "but it is *customary*" + inf.

ὑφ' ἡμῶν: agency expression, "to happen *at our hands*"

ἐμέμψατο: aor., "Abrotonon *didn't blame* you"

ἐκτὸς εἰ μὴ: "*unless* he is blind"

ἑωράκει: plupf. of ὁράω, "who *hadn't seen*"

αὐτὴν ... ἔχουσαν: pres. part. in ind. st. after ἑωράκει, "seen *that she has*"

ἀραιὰς: acc. pred. "hair that is *thin*"

ἀπηγμένας: part. perf. of ἀπο-άγω, also a predicate of τρίχας, "hair *that has been pulled back from*" + gen.

4

αἱ φλέβες καὶ ῥὶς μακρά. ἓν μόνον, εὐμήκης ἐστὶ καὶ
ὀρθὴ καὶ μειδιᾷ πάνυ ἐπαγωγόν.

ΓΛΥΚΕΡΑ: Οἴει γάρ, ὦ Θαΐ, τῷ κάλλει ἠρᾶσθαι τὸν
Ἀκαρνᾶνα; οὐκ οἶσθα ὡς φαρμακὶς ἡ Χρυσάριόν ἐστιν
ἡ μήτηρ αὐτῆς, Θεσσαλάς τινας ᾠδὰς ἐπισταμένη καὶ
τὴν σελήνην κατάγουσα; φασὶ δὲ αὐτὴν καὶ πέτεσθαι
τῆς νυκτός: ἐκείνη ἐξέμηνε τὸν ἄνθρωπον πιεῖν τῶν
φαρμάκων ἐγχέασα, καὶ νῦν τρυγῶσιν αὐτόν.

ΘΑΙΣ: Καὶ σὺ ἄλλον, ὦ Γλυκέριον, τρυγήσεις, τοῦτον δὲ
χαίρειν ἔα.

ἄλλος, -η, -ον: other, another
ἄνθρωπος, ὁ: person, man
ἐάω: to allow (+ *inf.*)
ἐγχέω: to pour in
ἐκμαίνω: to drive mad
ἐπαγωγός, -όν: attractive
ἐπίσταμαι: to know
ἐράω: to love, become enamoured (*mid.*)
εὐμήκης, -ες: of a good length, tall
Θεσσαλός, -η, -ον: Thessalian
κάλλος, -εος, τό: beauty
κατάγω: to lead down
μακρός, -ά, -ον: long
μειδιάω: to smile
μήτηρ, μήτερος, ἡ: a mother
μόνος, -η, -ον: alone
νύξ, νυκτός, ἡ: the night

οἶδα: to know (*perf.*)
οἴομαι: to suppose, think
ὀρθός, -ή, -όν: straight
πάνυ: altogether, entirely
πέτομαι: to fly
πίνω: to drink
ῥίς, -νος, ἡ: the nose
σελήνη, ἡ: the moon
τρυγάω: to gather in
φαρμακίς, -ίδος, ἡ: a sorceress, witch
φάρμακον, τό: a drug, poison
φημί: to declare, claim
φλέψ, -βος, ἡ: a vein
χαίρω: to rejoice, fare well
Χρυσάριόν, ἡ: Chysarion, the mother of Gorgona
ᾠδή, ἡ: a song, lay, ode

ἐπαγωγόν: adverbial acc., "she smiles very *attractively*"
ἠρᾶσθαι: perf. inf. pass. in ind. st. after οἴει, "do you suppose *that he became enamoured?*"
Θεσσαλάς: "knowing *Thessalian* songs" Thessaly was famous for witchcraft
κατάγουσα: pres. part., "*leading down* the moon" a common power that witches were thought to have
τῆς νυκτός: genitive of time within which, "in the course of the night"
ἐξέμηνε: aor., "she (the mother) drove him mad"
πιεῖν: aor. inf. of purpose, "poured out (for him) *to drink*" + gen.
ἐγχέασα: aor. part. instrumental of ἐν-χέω, "drove him mad *by having poured*"
χαίρειν: inf. complementing ἔα, "allow him *to be well*" i.e. bid him farewell

2. Myrtion, Pamphilos, and Doris

Myrtion confronts her lover Pamphilos with the rumor that he has married someone else. Pamphilos assures her that the rumor is false.

ΜΥΡΤΙΟΝ: Γαμεῖς, ὦ Πάμφιλε, τὴν Φίλωνος τοῦ ναυκλήρου θυγατέρα καὶ ἤδη σε γεγαμηκέναι φασίν; οἱ τοσοῦτοι δὲ ὅρκοι οὓς ὤμοσας καὶ τὰ δάκρυα ἐν ἀκαρεῖ πάντα οἴχεται, καὶ ἐπιλέλησαι Μυρτίου νῦν, καὶ ταῦτα, ὦ Πάμφιλε, ὁπότε κύω μῆνα ὄγδοον ἤδη; τοῦτο γοῦν καὶ μόνον ἐπριάμην τοῦ σοῦ ἔρωτος, ὅτι μου τηλικαύτην πεποίηκας τὴν γαστέρα καὶ μετὰ μικρὸν παιδοτροφεῖν δεήσει, πρᾶγμα ἑταίρᾳ βαρύτατον· οὐ γὰρ ἐκθήσω

ἀκαρής, -ές: very short	μικρός, -ά, -όν: small, little
βαρύς, -εῖα, -ύ: heavy	μόνος, -η, -ον: only, alone
γαμέω: to marry	ναύκληρος, ὁ: a shipowner
γαστήρ, -έρος, ἡ: the belly	νῦν: now
γοῦν: at least then, at any rate	ὄγδοος, -η, -ον: eighth
δάκρυον, τό: a tear	οἴχομαι: to be gone
δεῖ: it is necessary	ὄμνυμι: to swear
ἐκτίθημι: to set out, put away	ὁπότε: when
ἐπιλανθάνω: to forget	ὅρκος, ὁ: an oath
ἔρως, ἔρωτος, ὁ: love	παιδοτροφέω: rear children
ἤδη: already	ποιέω: to make, do
θυγάτηρ, -τέρος, ἡ: a daughter	πρίαμαι: to buy
κύω: to conceive, be pregnant	τηλικοῦτος, -αύτην, -αῦτος: so long, so great
μείς, μῆνος, ἡ: a month	τοσοῦτος, -αύτη, -οῦτο: so large, so tall

---

γεγαμηκέναι: perf. inf. in ind. st. after **φασίν**, "they say *that you have married* already"

ὤμοσας: aor. of **ὄμνυμι**, "which *you swore*"

ἐν ἀκαρεῖ (sc. **χρόνῳ**): "in a very short (time)"

ἐπιλέλησαι: perf. 2 s. mid. of **ἐπι-λανθάνω**, "you have forgotten" + gen.

ἐπριάμην: aor., "I purchased"

ἔρωτος: gen. of value, "purchased *for your love*"

ὅτι ... πεποίηκας: perf. in noun clause in apposition to **τοῦτο**, "this, namely that *you have made* me"

δεήσει: fut. of **δεῖ**, "it will be necessary to" +inf.

ἐκθήσω: fut. of **ἐκ-τίθημι**, "I will not put away" i.e. abort

6

τὸ τεχθέν, καὶ μάλιστα εἰ ἄρρεν γένοιτο, ἀλλὰ Πάμφιλον
ὀνομάσασα ἐγὼ μὲν ἕξω παραμύθιον τοῦ ἔρωτος, σοὶ δὲ
ὀνειδιεῖ ποτε ἐκεῖνος, ὡς ἄπιστος γεγένησαι περὶ τὴν
ἀθλίαν αὐτοῦ μητέρα. γαμεῖς δ' οὐ καλὴν παρθένον·
εἶδον γὰρ αὐτὴν ἔναγχος ἐν τοῖς Θεσμοφορίοις μετὰ
τῆς μητρός, οὐδέπω εἰδυῖα ὅτι δι' αὐτὴν οὐκέτι ὄψομαι
Πάμφιλον. καὶ σὺ δ' οὖν πρότερον ἰδοῦ αὐτὴν καὶ τὸ
πρόσωπον καὶ τοὺς ὀφθαλμοὺς ἰδέ· μή σε ἀνιάτω, εἰ
πάνυ γλαυκοὺς ἔχει αὐτοὺς μηδὲ ὅτι διάστροφοί εἰσι καὶ
ἐς ἀλλήλους ὁρῶσι· μᾶλλον δὲ τὸν Φείδωνα ἑώρακας

ἄθλιος, -α, -ον: miserable
ἀλλήλων: of one another, to one another
ἀνιάω: to grieve, distress
ἄπιστος, -ον: not to be trusted
ἄρρεν, ἄρρενος, τό: the male
γίγνομαι: to become, be
γλαυκός, -ή, -όν: gray, silvery
διάστροφος, -ον: twisted, distorted
εἶδον: to see (*aor.*)
ἔναγχος: (*adv.*) just now, lately
Θεσμοφόρια, -ων, τά: the Thesmophoria festival

καλός, -η, -ον: good, noble
ὀνειδίζω: to reproach
ὀνομάζω: to name
οὐκέτι: no more, no longer
ὀφθαλμός, ὁ: the eye
παραμύθιον, τό: a consolation
παρθένος, ἡ: a maid
πρόσωπον, τό: the face
πρότερον: prior, formerly
τίκτω: to bring into the world, bear

τὸ τεχθέν: aor. part. pass. of τίκτω, "the having been born" i.e. the child
γένοιτο: aor. opt. in future less vivid protasis, "especially *if it were to be* a male"
Πάμφιλον ... παραμύθιον: acc. pred., "name him *Pamphilos* ... keep him *as a consolation*"
ἕξω: fut. of ἔχω, "*I will keep* him"
ὡς ... γεγένησαι: perf. in causal clause, "he will reproach you *because you have been*"
ἐν τοῖς Θεσμοφορίοις: the Thesmophoria was an Athenian festival for Demeter that was attended by married women only
εἰδυῖα: perf. part. fem. of οἶδα, "I, not yet *knowing*"
ὄψομαι: fut. of ὁράω in ind. st. after εἰδυῖα, "knowing *that I would see*"
ἰδοῦ: aor. imper. mid., "look!"
ἰδέ: aor. imper. act., "look!"
μή ἀνιάτω: pres. imper. 3 s. in apodosis, "*may it not annoy* you!" spoken ironically
μηδὲ ὅτι (sc. ἀνιάτω): "nor (let it annoy you) *that* they are"
ἐς ἀλλήλους: "that (her eyes) look *at each other*" i.e. she is cross-eyed
ἑώρακας: perf. of ὁράω, "you have seen"

τὸν πατέρα τῆς νύμφης, τὸ πρόσωπον αὐτοῦ οἶσθα, ὥστε οὐδὲν ἔτι δεήσει τὴν θυγατέρα ἰδεῖν.

ΠΑΜΦΙΛΟΣ: Ἔτι σου ληρούσης, ὦ Μύρτιον, ἀκούσομαι παρθένους καὶ γάμους ναυκληρικοὺς διεξιούσης; ἐγὼ δὲ ἢ σιμήν τινα ἢ καλὴν νύμφην οἶδα; ἢ ὅτι Φείδων ὁ

ἀκούω: to hear	ναυκληρικός, -όν: of or for a shipowner
γάμος, ὁ: a wedding	νύμφη, ἡ: a bride
δεῖ: it is necessary	παρθένος, ἡ: a maid
εἶδον: to see (aor.)	πατήρ, πατέρος, ὁ: a father
ληρέω: to speak foolishly	σιμός, -ή, -όν: snub-nosed

ὥστε ... δεήσει: fut. of δεῖ in result clause, "so that there is not need to" + inf.

ληρούσης: pres. part. circumstantial agreeing with σου, "shall I listen to you *speaking nonsense?*"

διεξιούσης: pres. part. circumstantial of δια-εξ-έρχομαι, also agreeing with σου, "listen to you *describing at length*"

Participles: General Principles

Participles fall into three broad classes of use, with many other distinctions:

1. Attributive participles modify a noun or pronoun like other adjectives. They can occur with an article in the attributive position or with no article:

   οὐ γὰρ ἐκθήσω τὸ τεχθέν: "I will not abort *the one having been born*"

2. Circumstantial participles are added to a noun or pronoun to set forth some circumstance under which an action takes place. Although agreeing with a noun or pronoun, these participles actually qualify the verb in a sentence, indicating time, manner, means, cause, purpose, concession, condition or attendant circumstance. Circumstantial participles can occur in the genitive absolute construction.

   Ἔτι σου ληρούσης, ὦ Μύρτιον, ἀκούσομαι παρθένους καὶ γάμους ναυκληρικοὺς διεξιούσης;: "How long shall I listen to you *speaking nonsense* about maidens and *describing* the weddings of shipowners?" For more examples, see p. 67.

3. Supplementary participles complete the idea of certain verbs. Often it is the participle itself that expresses the main action:

   αἰσχύνεται λεπτὰ ἔχουσα τὰ σκέλη: "she is ashamed at *having* skinny legs."

The participial form of indirect discourse after verbs of showing and perceiving is a special class of supplementary participles.

   ὃς οὐχ ἑωράκει τὰς μὲν τρίχας αὐτὴν ἀραιὰς ἔχουσαν: "who did not see *that she has* thin hair."

Ἀλωπεκῆθεν—οἶμαι γὰρ ἐκεῖνον λέγειν σε—θυγατέρα
ὅλως εἶχεν ὡραίαν ἤδη γάμου; ἀλλ' οὐδὲ φίλος ἐστὶν
οὗτος τῷ πατρί: μέμνημαι γὰρ ὡς πρῴην ἐδικάσατο
περὶ συμβολαίου: τάλαντον, οἶμαι, ὀφείλων γὰρ τῷ
πατρὶ οὐκ ἤθελεν ἐκτίνειν, ὁ δὲ παρὰ τοὺς ναυτοδίκας
ἀπήγαγεν αὐτόν, καὶ μόλις ἐξέτισεν αὐτό, οὐδ' ὅλον, ὡς
ὁ πατὴρ ἔφασκεν. εἰ δὲ καὶ γαμεῖν ἐδέδοκτό μοι, τὴν
Δημέου θυγατέρα τὴν τοῦ πέρυσιν ἐστρατηγηκότος
ἀφείς, καὶ ταῦτα πρὸς μητρὸς ἀνεψιὰν οὖσαν, τὴν Φεί-
δωνος ἐγάμουν ἄν; σὺ δὲ πόθεν ταῦτα ἤκουσας; ἢ τίνας

ἀνεψιά, ἡ: a first-cousin	ὅλως: entirely
ἀπάγω: to lead away	ὀφείλω: to owe
ἀφίημι: to send forth, set aside	πέρυσι: (*adv.*) a year ago, last year
δικάζομαι: to go to law	πόθεν: whence?
ἐθέλω: to be willing	πρῴην: earlier
ἐκτίνω: to pay in full	στρατηγέω: to be general
μιμνήσκω: to remind	συμβόλαιον, τό: a pledge or loan
μόλις: scarcely	τάλαντον, τό: a talant
ναυτοδίκαι, οἱ: judges of the admiralty-court	φάσκω: to say, claim
ὅλος, -η, -ον: whole	ὡραῖος, -α, -ον: produced at the right season

Ἀλωπεκῆθεν: "Pheidon *from Alopece*"

ὅτι ... εἶχεν: ind. st. after οἶδα, "know *whether he has*"

λέγειν: ind. st., "I suppose *that you mean* him"

ὡραίαν: acc. pred., "a daughter *of the proper age for*" + gen.

μέμνημαι: pref. with present meaning, "I remember"

ἐδικάσατο: aor. mid., "remember that *he went to law against*"

ὁ δὲ: "but he" i.e. Pamphilos' father

ἀπήγαγεν: aor. of ἀπο-άγω, "he dragged into court"

ἐξέτισεν: aor. of ἐκ-τίνω, "he scarcely *exacted* it" i.e. the loan

εἰ δὲ καὶ ... ἐδέδοκτό: plupf. of δοκέω in past contrafactual protasis, "*and even if it
  had seemed a good idea* to me" + inf.

τὴν τοῦ ... ἐστρατηγηκότος: perf. part. gen. in attributive phrase, "the daughter *of the
  one having been made general*"

οὖσαν: pres. part. also agreeing with θυγατέρα above, "her *being* the cousin"

ἀφείς: aor. part. of ἀπο-ἵημι, "he, *having set aside*"

ἐγάμουν ἄν: impf. in present contrafactual apodosis, "would I be marrying?"

τίνας: acc. pl. f., "*what* jealousies?"

σεαυτῇ, ὦ Μύρτιον, κενὰς ζηλοτυπίας σκιαμαχοῦσα
ἐξεῦρες;

ΜΥΡΤΙΟΝ: Οὐκοῦν οὐ γαμεῖς, ὦ Πάμφιλε;

ΠΑΜΦΙΛΟΣ: Μέμηνας, ὦ Μύρτιον, ἢ κραιπαλᾷς; καίτοι
χθὲς οὐ πάνυ ἐμεθύσθημεν.

ΜΥΡΤΙΟΝ: Ἡ Δωρὶς αὕτη ἐλύπησέ με: πεμφθεῖσα γὰρ
ὡς ἔρια ὠνήσαιτό μοι ἐπὶ τὴν γαστέρα καὶ εὔξαιτο τῇ
Λοχείᾳ ὡς ὑπὲρ ἐμοῦ, Λεσβίαν ἔφη ἐντυχοῦσαν αὐτῇ —
μᾶλλον δὲ σὺ αὐτῷ, ὦ Δωρί, λέγε ἅπερ ἀκήκοας, εἴ γε
μὴ ἐπλάσω ταῦτα.

ἀκούω: to hear	λοχεῖος, -α, -ον: belonging to childbirth
γαμέω: to marry	λυπέω: to vex, annoy
γαστήρ, -έρος, ἡ: the belly	μαίνομαι: to rage, be furious
ἐντυγχάνω: to encounter (+ dat.)	μεθύσκω: to intoxicate
ἐξευρίσκω: to find out, discover	ὅσπερ, ἥπερ, ὅπερ: the very thing which
ἔριον, τό: wool	οὐκοῦν: therefore, then, accordingly
εὔχομαι: to pray	πάνυ: altogether, entirely
ζηλοτυπία, ἡ: jealousy	πέμπω: to send, despatch
καίτοι: and yet	πλάττω: to form, create
κενός, -ή, -όν: empty	σκιαμαχέω: to fight a shade
κραιπαλάω: to have a sick head-ache	χθές: yesterday
Λεσβία, ἡ: Lesbia, a slave	ὠνέομαι: to buy, purchase

σκιαμαχοῦσα: pres. part. instrumental, "discovered *by fighting shadows*"

ἐξεῦρες: aor. (unagmented) of ἐξ-ευρίσκω, "have you discovered?"

μέμηνας: perf. of μαίνω, "you have gone mad"

ἐμεθύσθημεν: aor. pass. of μεθύσκω in concessive clause, "and yet not much *did we become drunk*"

πεμφθεῖσα: aor. part. pass., "she *having been sent*"

ὡς ... ὠνήσαιτο: aor. opt. in purpose clause in secondary sequence, "in order to buy"

εὔξαιτο: aor. opt. also in purpose clause, and *in order to pray*"

Λοχείᾳ: an epithet of Artemis in her role as protector of those giving birth

ὡς ὑπὲρ ἐμοῦ: "pray *on my behalf*"

ἐντυχοῦσαν: aor. part. circumstantial, agreeing with Λεσβίαν, "she said that Lesbia, *having encountered* her" the indirect statement is left incomplete

μᾶλλον δὲ: "but rather" correcting a statement already made

ἀκήκοας: perf. of ἀκούω in ind. quest., "say what *you have heard*"

ἐπλάσω: aor. 2 s. of πλάττω, "unless *you invented*"

ΔΩΡΙΣ: Ἀλλ᾽ ἐπιτριβείην, ὦ δέσποινα, εἴ τι ἐψευσάμην· ἐπεὶ γὰρ κατὰ τὸ πρυτανεῖον ἐγενόμην, ἐνέτυχέ μοι ἡ Λεσβία μειδιῶσα καὶ φησίν, «ὁ ἐραστὴς ὑμῶν ὁ Πάμφιλος γαμεῖ τὴν Φίλωνος θυγατέρα·» εἰ δὲ ἀπιστοίην, ἠξίου με παρακύψασαν ἐς τὸν στενωπὸν ὑμῶν ἰδεῖν πάντα κατεστεφανωμένα καὶ αὐλητρίδας καὶ θόρυβον καὶ ὑμέναιον ᾁδοντάς τινας.

ΠΑΜΦΙΛΟΣ: Τί οὖν; παρέκυψας, ὦ Δωρί;

ΔΩΡΙΣ: Καὶ μάλα, καὶ εἶδον ἅπαντα ὡς ἔφη.

ᾁδω: to sing
ἀξιόω: to ask
ἀπιστέω: to disbelieve
αὐλητρίς, -ίδος, ἡ: a flute-girl
γαμέω: to marry
γίγνομαι: to become
δέσποινα, ἡ: the mistress, lady of the house
εἶδον: to see (*aor.*)
ἐντυγχάνω: to encounter
ἐπιτρίβω: to rub on the surface, to crush
ἐραστής, -οῦ, ὁ: a lover

θόρυβος, ὁ: an uproar, clamor
θυγάτηρ, -τέρος, ἡ: a daughter
καταστεφανόω: to crown
μάλα: very, very much
μειδιάω: to smile
παρακύπτω: to stoop sideways (in order to peer at something)
πρυτανεῖον, τό: the town-hall
στενωπός, ὁ: street, alley
ὑμέναιος, ὁ: the wedding song
ψεύδομαι: to lie

ἐπιτριβείην: aor. opt. pass. in wish for the future serving as an apodosis, "may I be crushed!"

εἴ τι ἐψευσάμην: aor. in past contrafactual protasis, "if I had lied" i.e. but I didn't

ἐγενόμην: aor. of γίγνομαι, "when I had become" i.e. when I was

ἐνέτυχέ: aor. of ἐν-τυγχάνω, "Lesbia happened upon" + dat.

μειδιῶσα: aor. part., "she *having smiled*" i.e. with a smile

εἰ δὲ ἀπιστοίην: aor. opt. in ind. st. after ἠξίου representing a subjunctive in a future more vivid protasis, "she asked that, *if I disbelieved*"

ἠξίου: impf. of ἀξιόω, "she asked"

παρακύψασαν: aor. part. agreeing with με, "me, *having stooped down*" i.e. in order to peep

ἰδεῖν: aor. inf. of εἶδον in ind. st. after ἠξίου, "asked me *to see*"

κατεστεφανωμένα: perf. part. acc. in ind. st. after ἰδεῖν, "see that all *has been garlanded*"

ᾁδοντάς: pres. part. also in ind. st., "see that some *were singing*"

11

ΠΑΜΦΙΛΟΣ: Μανθάνω τὴν ἀπάτην· οὐ γὰρ πάντα ἡ
Λεσβία, ὦ Δωρί, πρὸς σὲ ἐψεύσατο καὶ σὺ τἀληθῆ
ἀπήγγελκας Μυρτίῳ. πλὴν μάτην γε ἐταράχθητε· οὔτε
γὰρ παρ' ἡμῖν οἱ γάμοι, ἀλλὰ νῦν ἀνεμνήσθην ἀκούσας
τῆς μητρός, ὁπότε χθὲς ἀνέστρεψα παρ' ὑμῶν· ἔφη γάρ,
Ὠ Πάμφιλε, ὁ μὲν ἡλικιώτης σοι Χαρμίδης τοῦ γείτο-
νος Ἀρισταινέτου υἱὸς γαμεῖ ἤδη καὶ σωφρονεῖ, σὺ δὲ
μέχρι τίνος ἑταίρᾳ σύνει; τοιαῦτα παρακούων αὐτῆς ἐς
ὕπνον κατηνέχθην· εἶτα ἔωθεν προῆλθον ἀπὸ τῆς οἰκίας,
ὥστε οὐδὲν εἶδον ὧν ἡ Δωρὶς ὕστερον εἶδεν. εἰ δὲ ἀπιστεῖς, αὖθις ἀπελθοῦσα, ὦ Δωρί, ἀκριβῶς ἰδὲ μὴ τὸν

ἀκούω: to hear
ἀκριβῶς: accurately
ἀληθής, -ές: true
ἀναμιμνήσκω: to remind
ἀναστρέφω: to turn upside down, upset
ἀπαγγέλλω: to report, announce
ἀπάτη, ἡ: a trick, fraud
ἀπέρχομαι: to go away
ἀπιστέω: to disbelieve
αὖθις: back, back again
γαμέω: to marry
γείτων, -ονος, ὁ: a neighbour
εἶτα: then, next
ἑταίρα, ἡ: a courtesan
ἔωθεν: from morn
ἡλικιώτης, -ου, ὁ: a fellow, comrade
ἰδέ: lo, behold

καταφέρω: to carry down, off
μανθάνω: to come to learn
μάτην: in vain, idly
μέχρι: up to (+ *gen.*)
μήτηρ, μήτρος, ἡ: a mother
οἰκία, ἡ: a house
παρακούω: to listen carelessly to (+ *gen.*)
πλήν: but
προέρχομαι: to go forward
σύνειμι: to be with (+ *dat.*)
σωφρονέω: to be sound of mind
ταράττω: to stir up, trouble
τοιοῦτος, -αύτη, -οῦτο: such as this
υἱός, ὁ: a son
ὕπνος, ὁ: sleep, slumber
ὕστερον: later
χθές: yesterday

ἐψεύσατο: aor., "*she lied* not"

ἀπήγγελκας: perf. of ἀπο-αγγέλλω, "she has reported to" + dat.

ἐταράχθητε: aor. pass. of ταράττω, "you have been vexed"

ἀνεμνήσθην: aor. pass. of ἀνα-μιμνήσκω, "I remembered" + part.

μέχρι τίνος (sc. χρόνου): "up to what point of time?" i.e. how long?

σύνει: from συν-εἰμι, "will you be with?" + dat.

κατηνέχθην: aor. pass. of κατα-φέρω, "*I was carried off* to sleep"

ὥστε ... εἶδον: aor. in result clause, "*so I knew* nothing"

ὧν: relative attracted into case of the antecedent, "of the things *which*"

ancient greek capital letters - Bing images

B Beta (bay-tah)	**Γ** Gamma (gam-ah)	**Δ** Delta (del-ta)	**E** Epsilon (ep-si-lon)	**Z** Zeta (zay-tah)	**H** Eta (ay-tah)
K Kappa (cap-pah)	**Λ** Lambda (lamb-dah)	**M** Mu (mew)	**N** Nu (new)	**Ξ** Xi (zie)	**O** Omicron (om-e-cron)
Σ Sigma (sig-mah)	**T** Tau (taw)	**Υ** Upsilon (up-si-lon)	**Φ** Phi (fie)	**X** Chi (kie)	**Ψ** Psi (sigh)

στενωπόν, ἀλλὰ τὴν θύραν, ποτέρα ἐστὶν ἡ κατεστεφανωμένη: εὑρήσεις γὰρ τὴν τῶν γειτόνων.

ΜΥΡΤΙΟΝ: Ἀπέσωσας, ὦ Πάμφιλε: ἀπηγξάμην γὰρ ἄν, εἴ
τι τοιοῦτο ἐγένετο.

ΠΑΜΦΙΛΟΣ: Ἀλλ᾽ οὐκ ἂν ἐγένετο, μηδ᾽ οὕτω μανείην, ὡς
ἐκλαθέσθαι Μυρτίου, καὶ ταῦτα ἤδη μοι κυούσης παιδίον.

ἀπάγχω: to strangle, choke	καταστεφανόω: to garland
ἀποσώζω: to save	κύω: to conceive, to be pregnant
γειτών, -ονος, ὁ: a neighbor	μαίνω: to cause to be mad
ἐκλανθάνομαι: to forget utterly (+ *gen.*)	παιδίον, τό: a child
εὑρίσκω: to find	πότερος, -α, -ον: whether of the two?
θύρα, ἡ: a door	στενωπός, ὁ: street, alley

ἡ κατεστεφανωμένη: perf. part. pred., "see which door is *the one garlanded*"

εὑρήσεις: fut. of εὑρίσκω, "you will find"

ἀπέσωσας: aor., "*you saved* me"

ἀπηγξάμην: aor. mid. in past contrafactual apodosis, "I would have choked myself"

ἐγένετο: aor. in past contrafactual protasis, "if such a thing *had happened*"

οὐκ ἂν ἐγένετο: aor. past contrafactual, "but *it would not have happened*"

μηδ᾽ μανείην: aor. opt. pass. pot. of μαίνω (with ἂν from previous clause), "nor would I be so maddened"

ὡς ἐκλαθέσθαι: aor. inf. in result clause, "so as to forget" + gen.

κυούσης: pres. part. agreeing with Μυρτίου, "the one *carrying* my child"

Result Clauses

ὥστε (sometimes ὡς) introduces result clauses either with an infinitive or with a finite verb.

ὥστε + infinitive indicates a possible or intended result, without emphasizing its actual occurrence. The infinitive does not express time, but only aspect.

> μηδ᾽ οὕτω μανείην, ὡς ἐκλαθέσθαι Μυρτίου: "nor would I be so maddened *that I would forget* Myrtion"

ὥστε + indicative emphasizes the actual occurrence of the result, both in time and aspect. When other moods occur, they retain their usual force.

> εἶτα ἔωθεν προῆλθον, ὥστε οὐδὲν εἶδον ὧν ἡ Δωρὶς ὕστερον εἶδεν: "Then I left early *and so I knew nothing* of what Doris saw later"

3. Philinna and her Mother

Philinna explains to her mother that there are two sides to every story, but her mother warns her about disrespecting her lovers.

ΜΗΤΗΡ: Ἐμάνης, ὦ Φίλιννα, ἢ τί ἔπαθες ἐν τῷ ξυμποσίῳ χθές; ἧκε γὰρ παρ' ἐμὲ Δίφιλος ἔωθεν δακρύων καὶ διηγήσατό μοι ἃ ἔπαθεν ὑπὸ σοῦ· μεμεθύσθαι γάρ σε καὶ ἐς τὸ μέσον ἀναστᾶσαν ὀρχήσασθαι αὐτοῦ διακωλύοντος καὶ μετὰ ταῦτα φιλῆσαι Λαμπρίαν τὸν ἑταῖρον αὐτοῦ, καὶ ἐπεὶ ἐχαλέπηνέ σοι, καταλιποῦσαν αὐτὸν ἀπελθεῖν πρὸς τὸν Λαμπρίαν καὶ περιβαλεῖν ἐκεῖνον, ἑαυτὸν δὲ ἀποπνίγεσθαι τούτων γιγνομένων. ἀλλ' οὐδὲ τῆς

ἀνίστημι: to make to stand up
ἀποπνίγω: to choke, throttle
δακρύω: to weep, shed tears
διακωλύω: to forbid, prevent
διηγέομαι: to describe in full
ἑταῖρος, ὁ: a comrade
ἔωθεν: from morning
ἥκω: to have come
καταλείπω: to leave behind

μεθύσκω: to become drunk
μέσος, -η, -ον: middle, in the middle
ὀρχέομαι: to dance
πάσχω: to suffer
περιβάλλω: to embrace
συμπόσιον, τό: a symposium
φιλέω: to kiss
χαλεπαίνω: to be severe, sore
χθές: yesterday

ἐμάνης: aor. pass. of μαίνομαι, "were you mad?"

ἔπαθες: aor., "what *did you experience*?" i.e. what happened to you?

ὑπὸ σοῦ: the agency expression, "suffered *at your hands*"

μεμεθύσθαι: perf. inf. in ind. st. after διηγήσατο, "reported that *you became drunk*"

ἀναστᾶσαν: aor. part. agreeing with σε, "that you, *having stood up*"

ὀρχήσασθαι: aor. inf. also in ind. st. after διηγήσατο, "reported that *you danced*"

διακωλύοντος: pres. part. in gen. abs., "him *forbidding* you"

φιλῆσαι: aor. inf. also in ind. st., "reported that *you kissed* Lamprias"

ἐχαλέπηνε: aor., "after *he became angry*"

καταλιποῦσαν: aor. part. agreeing with σε, "that you, *having left*"

ἀπελθεῖν ... περιβαλεῖν: aor. inf. in ind. st., "reported that *you left ... you embraced*"

ἀποπνίγεσθαι: pres. inf. in ind. st. with subject ἑαυτὸν, "that he himself was choking" i.e. with rage

γιγνομένων: pres. part. in gen. abs., "while these things *were happening*"

νυκτός, οἶμαι, συνεκάθευδες, καταλιποῦσα δὲ δακρύοντα
μόνη ἐπὶ τοῦ πλησίον σκίμποδος κατέκεισο ᾄδουσα καὶ
λυποῦσα ἐκεῖνον.

ᾄδω: to sing
δακρύω: to shed tears, cry
κατάκειμαι: to lie down, lie outstretched
καταλείπω: to leave behind
λυπέω: to grieve, annoy
μόνος, -η, -ον: alone

νύξ, νυκτός, ἡ: night
οἶμαι: to suppose, think
πλησίον: nearby
σκίμπους, -ποδος, ὁ: a small couch, low bed
συγκαθεύδω: to sleep with

τῆς νυκτός: gen. of time within which, "in the course of the night"

καταλιποῦσα: aor. part., "you *having left* him crying"

κατέκεισο: impf. of **κατά-κειμαι**, "you were reclining"

Indirect Statement

The term indirect statement (ind. st.) is used in this commentary not only for reported speech, but other complements of verbs of perception, belief, etc.

1. Verbs of saying can take **ὅτι** or **ὡς** plus the indicative to express indirect statement:

> οὐδέπω εἰδυῖα ὅτι δι᾽ αὐτὴν οὐκέτι ὄψομαι Πάμφιλον: "not yet knowing *that I will no longer see* Pamphilon on account of her."

When the main verb is a past tense, the indicative in indirect statement can be changed to the corresponding tense of the optative.

> ἡ γυνὴ δὲ αὐτοῦ ἔλεγεν ὡς ὑπὸ φαρμάκων ἐκμήναιμι αὐτόν: "his wife was saying *that I drove him mad* with potions." (for ὡς ... ἐκμήνα)

2. Verbs of knowing, perceiving, hearing or showing take the accusative + participle construction.

> ἰδεῖν πάντα κατεστεφανωμένανους: "to see *that all has been garlanded*"

> ἐπεὶ δὲ χαλεπαίνουσαν εἶδέ με: "then he saw *that I was becoming angry*"

> ὡς δὲ προσιόντα ᾔσθοντο τὸν Λαμπρίαν: "they perceived *that* Lamprias *was approaching.*"

3. Verbs of thinking, believing and saying can take the accusative plus infinitive construction.

> διηγήσατό ... μεμεθύσθαι σε. "he reported *that you became drunk.*"

> οἶμαι γὰρ ἐκεῖνον λέγειν σε. "I suppose *that you mean* him."

ΦΙΛΙΝΝΑ: Τὰ γὰρ αὑτοῦ σοι, ὦ μῆτερ, οὐ διηγήσατο: οὐ
γὰρ ἂν συνηγόρευες αὐτῷ ὑβριστῇ ὄντι, ὃς ἐμοῦ ἀφέμενος ἐκοινολογεῖτο Θαΐδι τῇ Λαμπρίου ἑταίρᾳ, μηδέπω
ἐκείνου παρόντος: ἐπεὶ δὲ χαλεπαίνουσαν εἶδέ με καὶ
διένευσα αὐτῷ οἷα ποιεῖ, τοῦ ὠτὸς ἄκρου ἐφαψάμενος
ἀνακλάσας τὸν αὐχένα τῆς Θαΐδος ἐφίλησεν οὕτω προ-
σφυῶς, ὥστε μόλις ἀπέσπασε τὰ χείλη, εἶτ᾽ ἐγὼ μὲν
ἐδάκρυον, ὁ δὲ ἐγέλα καὶ πρὸς τὴν Θαΐδα πολλὰ πρὸς
τὸ οὖς ἔλεγε κατ᾽ ἐμοῦ δηλαδή, καὶ ἡ Θαῒς ἐμειδίασε

ἄκρος, -α, -ον: at the tip	κοινολογέομαι: to take counsel with
ἀνακλάω: to bend back	μειδιάω: to smile
ἀποσπάω: to drag away from	μηδέπω: not as yet
αὐχήν, -ένος, ὁ: the neck	μόλις: scarcely
ἀφίημι: to send forth, discharge	οἷος, -α, -ον: what sort of
γελάω: to laugh	οὖς, ὠτὸς, τό: auris, the ear
δακρύω: to shed tears, cry	ποιέω: to do
δηλαδή: quite clearly	πολύς, πολλά, πολύ: much, many
διαγέομαι: to narrate	προσφυῶς: firmly
διανεύω: to beckon	συναγορεύω: to join in advocating
εἶτα: then, next	ὑβριστής, -οῦ, ὁ: an insolent man
ἐκεῖνος, -η, -ον: that one	φιλέω; to kiss
ἑταίρα, ἡ: a courtesan	χαλεπαίνω: to be severe, sore
ἐφάπτω: to take hold of (+ gen.)	χεῖλος, -εος, τό: a lip

τὰ ... αὑτοῦ: "the things of himself" i.e. the things he did

ἂν συνηγόρευες: impf. in present contrafactual, "you wouldn't be advocating along
   with" i.e. you would not take the side of + dat.

ὑβριστῇ: dat. pred., "him being *outrageous*"

ἀφέμενος: aor. part. mid., "who *having abandoned*" + gen.

παρόντος: pres. part. in gen. abs., "that one (Lamprias) not yet *being present*"

χαλεπαίνουσαν: pres. part. in ind. st. after εἶδε, "when he saw that I *was becoming
   angry*"

ἐφαψάμενος: aor. part. mid. of ἐπι-ἄπτω, "having taking hold of" + gen.

ἀνακλάσας: aor. part. m. nom., "he, *having bent back*"

ὥστε ... ἀπέσπασε: aor. in result clause, "so that he scarcely removed"

ἐδάκρυον: impf. inceptive, "I began crying"

ἐγέλα ... ἔλεγε: impf. "he began laughing ... he kept speaking"

ἐμειδίασε: aor., "she gave a smile"

βλέπουσα πρὸς ἐμέ. ὡς δὲ προσιόντα ᾔσθοντο τὸν
Λαμπρίαν καὶ ἐκορέσθησάν ποτε φιλοῦντες ἀλλήλους,
ἐγὼ μὲν ὅμως παρ' αὐτὸν κατεκλίθην, ὡς μὴ καὶ τοῦτο
προφασίζοιτο ὕστερον, ἡ Θαῖς δὲ ἀναστᾶσα ὠρχήσατο
πρώτη ἀπογυμνοῦσα ἐπὶ πολὺ τὰ σφυρὰ ὡς μόνη καλὰ
ἔχουσα, καὶ ἐπειδὴ ἐπαύσατο, ὁ Λαμπρίας μὲν ἐσίγα
καὶ εἶπεν οὐδέν, Δίφιλος δὲ ὑπερεπήνει τὸ εὔρυθμον
καὶ τὸ κεχορηγημένον, καὶ ὅτι εὖ πρὸς τὴν κιθάραν ὁ
ποὺς καὶ τὸ σφυρὸν ὡς καλὸν καὶ ἄλλα μυρία, καθάπερ
τὴν Καλάμιδος Σωσάνδραν ἐπαινῶν, ἀλλ' οὐχὶ Θαῖδα,

αἰσθάνομαι: to perceive	ὀρχέομαι: to dance
ἀλλήλων: of one another	παύω: to make to cease
ἀπογυμνόω: to strip quite bare	πούς, ποδός, ὁ: a foot
βλέπω: to look at	προφασίζομαι: to set up as a pretext
ἐπαινέω: to praise	πρῶτος, -η, -ον: first
εὔρυθμος, -ον: rhythmical	σιγάω: to be silent
καθάπερ: just as	σφυρόν, τό: the ankle
κατακλίνω: to lay down	ὑπερεπαινέω: to praise above measure
κιθάρα, ἡ: a cithara	ὕστερον: later
κορέννυμι: to sate	χορηγέω: to outfit a dance, to furnish
μυρίος, -ος, -ον: numberless	

βλέπουσα: pres. part., "*as she was looking* at me"

προσιόντα: pres. part. in ind. st. after ᾔσθοντο, "perceived *that he was approaching*"

ἐκορέσθησαν: aor. pass. of κορέννυμι, "they became sated of" + part.

κατεκλίθην: aor. pass. of κατα-κλίνω, "I reclined"

ὡς μὴ ... προφασίζοιτο: pres. opt. in negative purpose clause, "lest he have a pretext"

ἀναστᾶσα: aor. part. intransitive, "Thais, *having stood up*"

ἀπογυμνοῦσα: aor. part., "she *having stripped*"

ὡς ... ἔχουσα: pres. part. giving an alleged motive, "as though she alone has"

ὑπερεπήνει: impf. of ὑπερ-ἐπι-αινέω, "he was praising excessively"

τὸ κεχορηγημένον: perf. part. "the having been outfitted for the dance" i.e. clothes

εὖ πρὸς: "(saying) the foot is *well towards* the cithara" i.e. in step

ὡς καλὸν: "*how beautiful* the leg!"

καθάπερ ... ἐπαινῶν: pres. part., "as though praising"

Καλάμιδος: Calamis was a famous 5th century BCE sculptor whose statue of Sosandra was famous

Σωσάνδραν: probably an epithet of Aphrodite, but her statue on the Acropolis was famous

ἦν καὶ σὺ οἶσθα συλλουομένην ἡμῖν οἵα ἐστί. Θαῒς δὲ
οἷα καὶ ἔσκωψεν εὐθὺς ἐς ἐμέ: «Εἰ γάρ τις,» ἔφη, «μὴ
αἰσχύνεται λεπτὰ ἔχουσα τὰ σκέλη, ὀρχήσεται καὶ αὐτὴ
ἐξαναστᾶσα.» τί ἂν λέγοιμι, ὦ μῆτερ; ἀνέστην γὰρ καὶ
ὠρχησάμην. ἀλλὰ τί ἔδει ποιεῖν; ἀνασχέσθαι καὶ ἐπαληθεύειν τὸ σκῶμμα καὶ τὴν Θαΐδα ἐᾶν τυραννεῖν τοῦ
συμποσίου;

ΜΗΤΗΡ: Φιλοτιμότερον μέν, ὦ θύγατερ: οὐδὲ φροντίζειν
γὰρ ἐχρῆν: λέγε δ᾿ ὅμως τὰ μετὰ ταῦτα.

αἰσχύνομαι: to be ashamed	ὀρχέομαι: to dance
ἀνέχω: to check	σκέλος, -εος, τό: the leg
ἀνίστημι: to make to stand up, raise up	σκώπτω: to jeer, scoff at
δεῖ: it is necessary	σκῶμμα, -ατος, τό: a gibe, scoff
ἐξανίστημι: to raise up; to make one rise	συλλούομαι: to bathe together
ἐπαληθεύω: to prove	συμπόσιον, τό: a symposium
εὐθύς; immediately	τυραννεύω: to tyrannize
ἔχω: to have	φιλότιμος, -ον: generous
λεπτός, -ή, -όν: scraggly	φροντίζω: to think, consider, reflect
οἶδα: to know (perf.)	χρή: it is necessary

συλλουομένην: pres. part. circumstantial, "Thais whom you know *from bathing with us*"

ἔσκωψεν: aor., "she jeered"

ἔχουσα: pres. part. supplementing αἰσχύνεται, "is ashamed of *having*"

ἐξαναστᾶσα: aor. part. intransitive of ἐξ-ανα-ἵστημι, "she herself, *having stood up*"

ἂν λέγοιμι: pres. opt. pot., "what *could I say?*"

ἀνέστην: aor. intransitive, "I stood up"

ἀνασχέσθαι ... ἐπαληθεύειν ... ἐᾶν: inf. answering the question τί ἔδει, "(necessary) to check myself ... to prove correct ... to allow"

τυραννεῖν: pres. inf. complementing ἐᾶν, "allow her *to tyrannize*" + gen.

φιλοτιμότερον: also answering the question τί ἔδει, "necessary to be *more generous*"

Potential Optatives

The optative with **ἂν** expresses potentiality, with a range of possible meanings:

τί ἂν λέγοιμι: "what could I say?"

ὃν ἐπίδοιμι: "whom I would like to see"

τί ἂν λέγοιμι: "why should I mention?"

ΦΙΛΙΝΝΑ: Οἱ μὲν οὖν ἄλλοι ἐπῄνουν, ὁ Δίφιλος δὲ μόνος ὕπτιον καταβαλὼν ἑαυτὸν ἐς τὴν ὀροφὴν ἀνέβλεπεν, ἄχρι δὴ καμοῦσα ἐπαυσάμην.

ΜΗΤΗΡ: Τὸ φιλῆσαι δὲ τὸν Λαμπρίαν ἀληθὲς ἦν καὶ τὸ μεταβᾶσαν περιπλέκεσθαι αὐτῷ; τί σιγᾷς; οὐκέτι γὰρ ταῦτα συγγνώμης ἄξια.

ΦΙΛΙΝΝΑ: Ἀντιλυπεῖν ἐβουλόμην αὐτόν.

ΜΗΤΗΡ: Εἶτα οὐδὲ συνεκάθευδες, ἀλλὰ καὶ ᾖδες ἐκείνου δακρύοντος; οὐκ αἰσθάνῃ, ὦ θύγατερ, ὅτι πτωχαί ἐσμεν, οὐδὲ μέμνησαι ὅσα παρ' αὐτοῦ ἐλάβομεν ἢ οἷον δὴ τὸν

ᾄδω: to sing
αἰσθάνομαι: to perceive
ἀληθής, -ές: true
ἀναβλέπω: to look up
ἀντιλυπέω: to vex in return
ἄξιος, -ία, -ον: worthy of (+ *gen.*)
ἄχρι: up to the point, until
βούλομαι: to will, wish (+ *inf.*)
δακρύω: to weep
ἐπαίνω; to praise
κάμνω: to be weary
καταβάλλω: to throw down
λαμβάνω: to take

μεταβαίνω: to pass over from one place to another
μιμνήσκομαι: to remember
ὀροφή, ἡ: the roof of a house
ὅσος, -η, -ον: how much
οὐκέτι: no longer
παύομαι: to cease
περιπλέκω: to enfold round, embrace
πτωχός, -ή, -όν: poor
σιγάω: to be silent
συγγνώμη, ἡ: sympathy
συγκαθεύδω: to sleep with
ὕπτιος, -α, -ον: supine

ἐπῄνουν: impf. of ἐπι-αινέω, "while the rest *were praising*"

καταβαλὼν: aor. part., "he, *having thrown himself down*"

ἀνέβλεπεν: impf. "he was looking up" i.e. not paying attention

καμοῦσα: pres. part. causal, "until *because being weary*, I stopped"

τὸ φιλῆσαι ... τὸ περιπλέκεσθαι: articular infinitives, "was *the kissing* true ... and *the embracing?*"

μεταβᾶσαν: aor. part. agreeing with acc. subject of περιπλέκεσθαι, "(you) having passed over"

ᾖδες: impf. of ᾄδω, "you were singing"

δακρύοντος: pres. part. in gen. abs., "with that one *crying*"

ὅσα ... ἐλάβομεν: aor. in ind. quest., "do you remember *how much we received?*"

19

πέρυσι χειμῶνα διηγάγομεν ἄν, εἰ μὴ τοῦτον ἡμῖν ἡ Ἀφροδίτη ἔπεμψε;

ΦΙΛΙΝΝΑ: Τί οὖν; ἀνέχωμαι διὰ τοῦτο ὑβριζομένη ὑπ' αὐτοῦ;

ΜΗΤΗΡ: Ὀργίζου μέν, μὴ ἀνθύβριζε δέ. οὐκ οἶσθα ὅτι ὑβριζόμενοι παύονται οἱ ἐρῶντες καὶ ἐπιτιμῶσιν ἑαυτοῖς; σὺ δὲ πάνυ χαλεπὴ ἀεὶ τῷ ἀνθρώπῳ γεγένησαι, καὶ ὅρα μὴ κατὰ τὴν παροιμίαν ἀπορρήξωμεν πάνυ τείνουσαι τὸ καλῴδιον.

ἀεί: always, for ever
ἀνέχομαι: to endure
ἀνθυβρίζω: to abuse in turn
ἀπορρήγνυμι: to break off
διάγω: to go through
ἐπιτιμάω: to lay a value upon
ἐράω: to love
καλῴδιον, τό: small cord
ὀργίζω: to provoke to anger, irritate

παροιμία, ἡ: a proverb
παύομαι: to cease
πέμπω: to send, despatch
πέρυσι: a year ago, last year
τείνω: to stretch
ὑβρίζω: to abuse
χαλεπός, -ή, -όν: hard to bear, painful
χειμών, -ῶνος, ὁ: winter

οἷον ... διηγάγομεν ἄν: aor. of δια-άγω in ind. quest. and also serving as a past contrafactual apodosis, "remember *how we would have survived?*"

εἰ μὴ ... ἔπεμψε: aor. in past contrafactual protasis, "if Aphrodite had not sent him"

ἀνέχωμαι: pres. subj. in deliberative question, "should I endure?" + part.

ὀργίζου: pres. imper. mid., "become angry!"

μὴ ἀνθύβριζε: pres. imper. of ἀντι-ὑβρίζω, "don't offend in return"

ὑβριζόμενοι: pres. part. pass., "when being wronged"

ἑαυτοῖς: dat. after ἐπιτιμῶσιν, "they honor *themselves*"

γεγένησαι: perf. "*you have become* too harsh"

μὴ ... ἀπορρήξωμεν: aor. subj. in noun clause after verb of caution, "watch out *lest we break*"

κατὰ τὴν παροιμίαν: "according to the proverb"

τείνουσαι: pres. part. instrumental, "break *by stretching*"

Noun Clauses

A clause can perform the function of a noun, most commonly as objects of verbs of caution or effort. The clauses were originally independent of each other:

ὅρα μὴ ἀπορρήξωμεν πάνυ τείνουσαι τὸ καλῴδιον: "watch out *lest we break* the cord by stretching too much" i.e. "Watch out! Let's not break!"

4. Melitta and Bacchis

Melitta asks for the help of Bacchis to regain the affection of her lover. The situation calls for the powers of a witch.

ΜΕΛΙΤΤΑ: Εἴ τινα οἶσθα, Βακχί, γραῦν, οἷαι πολλαὶ Θεττα-
λαὶ λέγονται ἐπᾴδουσαι καὶ ἐρασμίους ποιοῦσαι, εἰ καὶ
πάνυ μισουμένη γυνὴ τυγχάνοι, οὕτως ὄναιο, παραλαβοῦσα ἧκέ μοι· θαἰμάτια γὰρ καὶ τὰ χρυσία ταῦτα προείμην ἡδέως, εἰ μόνον ἴδοιμι ἐπ᾽ ἐμὲ αὖθις ἀναστρέψαντα
Χαρῖνον μισήσαντα Σιμίχην ὡς νῦν ἐμέ.

ἀναστρέφω: to turn back	μισέω: to hate
αὖθις: back, back again	μόνον: only
γραῦς, γραός, ἡ: an old woman	οἷος, -α, -ον: such as
γυνή, ἡ: a woman	ὀνίνημι: to profit, benefit
εἶδον: to see (*aor.*)	πάνυ: altogether, completely
ἐπᾴδω: to sing to or in accompaniment	παραλαμβάνω: to receive from
ἐράσμιος, -ον: lovely	ποιέω: to make
ἡδέως: sweetly	προίημι: to forgo, give up
ἧκω: to come	τυγχάνω: to happen to (+ part.)
Θετταλός, -η, -ον: Thessalian	χρυσίον, τό: a piece of gold
ἱμάτιον, τό: a cloak or mantle	

πολλαὶ: nom. pred. after the personal use of λέγονται, "such as are said to *be many*"

ἐπᾴδουσαι ... ποιοῦσαι: pres. part. circumstantial, "who are *singing ... making*"

εἰ ... τυγχάνοι: pres. opt. in pres. general protasis, "if ever a woman happens to be" + part

μισουμένη: pres. part. supplementing τυγχάνοι, "happens to be very *hated*"

οὕτως ὄναιο: aor. opt. of ὀνίνημι in parenthetical wish for the future, "may you so profit!" i.e. bless you!

παραλαβοῦσα: aor. part., "(you) *having taken* her"

ἧκε: pres. imper., "*come* to me!"

θαἰμάτια (=τά ἱμάτια): "clothing"

προείμην: aor. opt. mid. of προ-ίημι (without ἂν) in future less vivid apodosis, "I would give up"

ἴδοιμι: aor. opt. in future less vivid protasis, "if I were to see"

ἀναστρέψαντα: aor. part. circumstantial, "see Charinos *return*"

μισήσαντα: aor. part. also agreeing with Χαρῖνον, "seeing him *hate* Simiche"

21

ΒΑΚΧΙΣ: Τί φής; οὐκέτι σύνεστε — ἀλλὰ παρὰ τὴν
Σιμίχην, ὦ Μέλιττα, καταλιπὼν οἴχεται Χαρῖνος — δι᾽
ἣν τοσαύτας ὀργὰς τῶν γονέων ἠνέσχετο οὐ βουληθεὶς
τὴν πλουσίαν ἐκείνην γῆμαι πέντε προικὸς τάλαντα,
ὡς ἔλεγον, ἐπιφερομένην; πέπυσμαι γὰρ ταῦτά σου
ἀκούσασα.

ΜΕΛΙΤΤΑ: Ἅπαντα ἐκεῖνα οἴχεται, ὦ Βακχί, καὶ πέμπτην
ταύτην ἡμέραν οὐδ᾽ ἑώρακα ὅλως αὐτόν, ἀλλὰ πίνουσι
παρὰ τῷ συνεφήβῳ Παμμένει αὐτός τε καὶ Σιμίχη.

ΒΑΚΧΙΣ: Δεινά, ὦ Μέλιττα, πέπονθας. ἀλλὰ τί καὶ ὑμᾶς
διέστησεν; ἔοικε γὰρ οὐ μικρὸν τοῦτ᾽ εἶναι.

ἀκούω: to hear
ἀνέχομαι: to endure
ἅπας, ἅπασα, ἅπαν: quite all, the whole
γαμέω: to marry
γονεύς, -έως, ὁ: a parent
δεινός, -ή, -όν: fearful, terrible
διίστημι: to separate
ἔοικα: to seem
ἐπιφέρω: to bring, put or lay upon
ἡμέρα, ἡ: a day
καταλείπω: to leave behind
μικρός, -ά, -όν: small, little
οἴχομαι: to have gone

ὅλως: wholly, entirely
ὀργή, ἡ: anger
πάσχω: to suffer
πέμπτος, -η, -ον: the fifth
πέντε: five
πίνω: to drink
πλούσιος, -α, -ον: rich
προίξ, -κος, ἡ: a gift, dowry
πυνθάνομαι: to learn
σύνειμι: to be together, consort
συνέφηβος, ὁ: a young comrade
τάλαντον, τό: a talant
τοσοῦτος, -αύτη, -οῦτο: so great

δι᾽ ἣν: "on account of whom" i.e. Melitta

ἠνέσχετο: aor. mid. (with double augment) of ἀνα-έχομαι, "he endured"

οὐ βουληθεὶς: aor. part. pass. causal, "because he did not wish" + inf.

προικὸς: gen. of purpose, "five talents *for a dowry*"

ἐπιφερομένην: pres. part. mid. agreeing with πλουσίαν, "that rich girl *bringing with her*"

πέπυσμαι: perf. mid. of πυνθάνω, "*I learned* these things"

ἀκούσασα: aor. part., "I *having heard*" + gen.

οἴχεται: "all that *is gone*"

ἡμέραν: acc. of duration, "for the fifth day"

ἑώρακα: perf., "I have seen"

πέπονθας: perf. of πάσχω, "you have suffered"

διέστησεν: aor. trans. of δια-ίστημι, "what *separated* you?"

22

ΜΕΛΙΤΤΑ: Τὸ μὲν ὅλον οὐδὲ εἰπεῖν ἔχω· πρῴην δὲ
ἀνελθὼν ἐκ Πειραιῶς — κατεληλύθει γάρ, οἶμαι, χρέος
ἀπαιτήσων πέμψαντος τοῦ πατρός — οὔτε προσέβλε-
ψεν ἐσελθὼν οὔτε προσήκατο ὡς ἔθος προσδραμοῦσαν,
ἀποσεισάμενος δὲ περιπλακῆναι θέλουσαν, «Ἄπιθι,»
φησί, «πρὸς τὸν ναύκληρον Ἑρμότιμον ἢ τὰ ἐπὶ τῶν
τοίχων γεγραμμένα ἐν Κεραμεικῷ ἀνάγνωθι, ὅπου

ἀναγιγνώσκω: to read
ἀνέρχομαι: to go up
ἀπαιτέω: to demand back
ἀποσείω: to shake off, wave away
γράφω: to write
ἔθος, -εος, τό: custom, habit
εἰσέρχομαι: to enter
ἔχω: to able to (+ *inf.*)
θέλω: to will, wish
κατέρχομαι: to go down from
ναύκληρος, ὁ: a shipowner

ὅλος, -η, -ον: whole, entire
πατήρ, πατρός, ὁ: a father
Πειραιεύς, -ῶς, ὁ: Peiraeus, the Athenian harbor
περιπλέκω: to enfold round, embrace
προσβλέπω: to look at
προσίημι: to let come to, accept
προστρέχω: to run towards
πρῴην: earlier
τοῖχος, ὁ: a wall
χρέος, τό: an obligation, debt

ἀνελθών: aor. part. of ἀνα-έρχομαι, "he, *having returned* from the Peiraeus"

κατεληλύθει: plupf. of κατα-έρχομαι, "he had gone down" a parenthetical remark

ἀπαιτήσων: fut. part. expressing purpose, "gone down *in order to get back*"

πέμψαντος: aor. part. of πέμπω in gen. abs., "his father *having sent* him"

προσήκατο: aor. mid. of προσ-ἵημι, nor *did he accept* me"

ὡς ἔθος: "as is his custom" i.e. in the usual way

προσδραμοῦσαν: aor. part. of προσ-τρέχω, "me *having run toward* him"

ἀποσεισάμενος: aor. part., "he, *having waved away*"

περιπλακῆναι: aor. inf. pass. of περι-πλέκω, complementing θέλουσαν, "me wishing *to be embraced*"

ἄπιθι: pres. imper. "go away!"

ἐν Κεραμεικῷ: the "potters' quarter" in Athens where an important cemetery with many funerary monuments were located

ἀνάγνωθι: aor. imper. of ἀνα-γιγνώσκω, "go read!"

Translating Participles

Greek has many more participles than English. The aorist participle is quite common and has no parallel in English in most cases. Our "translationese" versions of aorist participles will often sound like perfect participles (παραλαβοῦσα: "having taken her along") because English has no way to indicate simple time with a participle. More idiomatic in these cases would be some kind of periphrasis, such as "once he had taken her along," but our translationese version will indicate the syntactic relations more clearly.

κατεστηλίτευται ὑμῶν τὰ ὀνόματα.» «Τίνα Ἑρμότιμον, τίνα,» ἔφην, «ἢ ποίαν στήλην λέγεις;» ὁ δὲ οὐδὲν
ἀποκρινάμενος οὐδὲ δειπνήσας ἐκάθευδεν ἀποστραφείς.
πόσα οἴει ἐπὶ τούτῳ μεμηχανῆσθαί με περιλαμβάνουσαν,
ἐπιστρέφουσαν, φιλοῦσαν ἀπεστραμμένου τὸ μετάφρενον; ὁ δ' οὐδ' ὁπωστιοῦν ὑπεμαλάχθη, ἀλλ' «Εἴ μοι,»
φησίν, «ἐπὶ πλέον ἐνοχλήσεις, ἄπειμι ἤδη, εἰ καὶ μέσαι
νύκτες εἰσίν.»

ΒΑΚΧΙΣ: Ὅμως ᾔδεις τὸν Ἑρμότιμον;

ἀπέρχομαι: to go away
ἀποκρίνομαι: to answer
ἀποστρέφω: to turn away
δειπνέω: to make a meal
εἶδον: to see (aor.)
ἐνοχλέω: to trouble, annoy
ἐπιστρέφω: to roll over
ἤδη: already
καθεύδω: to sleep
καταστηλιτεύω: to inscribe on a stele
μέσος, -η, -ον: middle, in the middle
μετάφρενον, τό: the back

μηχανάομαι: to contrive
νύξ, νυκτός, ἡ: night
οἴομαι: to suppose
ὄνομα, τό: a name
περιλαμβάνω: to seize around, embrace
πλέων, -ον: more
ποῖος, -α, -ον: of what sort?
πόσος, -η, -ον: how many?
στήλη, ἡ: a block of stone used for
   inscriptions
ὑπομαλάττω: to soften
φιλέω: to kiss

κατεστηλίτευται: perf. of κατα-στηλιτεύω, "your names *have been inscribed on a
   stele*"

ὁ δὲ: "but he" i.e. Charinus

ἀποκρινάμενος: aor. part., "he *having answered*"

ἐκάθευδεν: impf. inceptive, "he began sleeping"

ἀποστραφείς: aor. part. pass. of ἀποστρέφω, "having turned himself over"

μεμηχανῆσθαί: perf. inf. in ind. st. after οἴει, "what do you suppose *that I contrived?*"

περιλαμβάνουσαν, ἐπιστρέφουσαν, φιλοῦσαν: pres. part. instrumental agreeing with
   με, "that I, *by embracing, rolling over, kissing*"

ἀπεστραμμένου: perf. part. gen., "the lower back (of him), *having turned away*"

ὁπωστιοῦν (=ὅπως-τι-οῦν): "in any way whatever"

ὑπεμαλάχθη: aor. pass. of ὑπερ-μαλάττω, "*he was softened* not at all"

εἰ ... ἐνοχλήσεις: fut. in minatory protasis, indicating a threat, "if you shall annoy me"
   (i.e., and you had better not!)

ἄπειμι: fut. of ἀπο-έρχομαι, "*I shall leave* immediately"

ὅμως ᾔδεις: plupf. of οἶδα, "but did you know?" with the expectation of a positive
   answer

ΜΕΛΙΤΤΑ: Ἀλλά με ἴδοις, ὦ Βακχί, ἀθλιώτερον διάγουσαν ἢ νῦν ἔχω, εἴ τινα ἐγὼ ναύκληρον Ἑρμότιμον οἶδα. πλὴν ἀλλ' ὁ μὲν ἔωθεν ἀπεληλύθει τοῦ ἀλεκτρυόνος ᾄσαντος εὐθὺς ἀνεγρόμενος, ἐγὼ δὲ ἐμεμνήμην ὅτι κατὰ τοίχου τινὸς ἔλεγε καταγεγράφθαι τοὔνομα ἐν Κεραμεικῷ:

ᾄδω: to sing
ἄθλιος, -α, -ον: miserable
ἀλεκτρυών, -ονος, ὁ: a cock
ἀνεγείρω: to wake up, rouse
ἀπέρχομαι: to go away, depart from
διάγω: to carry across, live
ἔωθεν: from morning

καταγράφω: to inscribe
Κεραμεικός, ὁ: the potters' quarter, which was a famous cemetery
μιμνήσκομαι: to remember
ναύκληρος, ὁ: merchant, ship-owner
νῦν; now, already
τοῖχος, ὁ: a wall of a house

ἴδοις: aor. opt. in wish for the future acting as apodosis, "but *may you see* me!"

διάγουσαν: pres. part. after ἴδοις, "see me *living* more miserably"

πλὴν ἀλλ': strong adversative, "but rather"

ἀπεληλύθει: plupf., "he had departed"

ᾄσαντος: pres. part. in gen. abs., "the cock *crowing*"

ἀνεγρόμενος: aor. part., "he, *having awakened* immediately"

ἐμεμνήμην: plupf. with imperfect force, "I was remembering"

καταγεγράφθαι: perf. inf. in ind. st. after ἔλεγε, "he kept saying that my name *had been written down*"

Future Conditions

The future less vivid condition indicates a future action as a *possibility*; the future more vivid condition indicates a future action as a *probability*.

More Vivid: ἐάν (Attic contraction = ἤν or ἄν) plus subjunctive in the protasis, future indicative or equivalent in the apodosis: in English "if he does this ... then he will...."

ἄν δ' ἔτι τοιοῦτον ἐραστὴν εὔρωμεν, θῦσαι μὲν δεήσει: "if we find such a lover, it will be necessary to make a sacrifice"

Less Vivid: εἰ plus optative in the protasis, ἄν plus the optative in the apodosis: in English: "If he were to... then he would..."

τὰ χρυσία ταῦτα προείμην ἄν ἡδέως, εἰ μόνον ἴδοιμι Χαρῖνον
"I would give up these gold pieces gladly, if only I were to see Charinus"

The future indicative can be used in the protasis, producing a condition even "more vivid" than the future more vivid conditions, often used in threats. This is called the "future emotional" condition by Smyth, future "minatory" by others.

εἴ μοι ἐπὶ πλέον ἐνοχλήσεις, ἄπειμι ἤδη,: "if you annoy me anymore, I will leave immediately" i.e. so you had better not

ἔπεμψα οὖν Ἀκίδα κατασκεψομένην· ἡ δ' ἄλλο μὲν οὐδὲν
εὗρε, τοῦτο δὲ μόνον ἐπιγεγραμμένον ἐσιόντων ἐπὶ τὰ
δεξιὰ πρὸς τῷ Διπύλῳ, «Μέλιττα φιλεῖ Ἑρμότιμον,»
καὶ μικρὸν αὖθις ὑποκάτω, «Ὁ ναύκληρος Ἑρμότιμος
φιλεῖ Μέλιτταν.»

ΒΑΚΧΙΣ: Ὢ τῶν περιέργων νεανίσκων. συνίημι γάρ.
λυπῆσαί τις θέλων τὸν Χαρῖνον ἐπέγραψε ζηλότυπον
ὄντα εἰδώς· ὁ δὲ αὐτίκα ἐπίστευσεν. εἰ δέ που ἴδοιμι
αὐτόν, διαλέξομαι. ἄπειρός ἐστι καὶ παῖς ἔτι.

ΜΕΛΙΤΤΑ: Ποῦ δ' ἂν ἴδοις ἐκεῖνον, ὃς ἐγκλεισάμενος ἑαυτὸν
σύνεστι τῇ Σιμίχῃ; οἱ γονεῖς δὲ ἔτι παρ' ἐμοὶ ζητοῦσιν

ἄπειρος, -ον: inexperienced
αὐτίκα: forthwith
γονεύς, -έως, ὁ: a parent
δεξιός, -ά, -όν: on the right hand or side
διαλέγω: to relate
δίπυλος, -ον: double-gated
ἐγκλείω: to shut in, close
εἶδον: to see (aor.)
εἰσέρχομαι: to go into
ἐπιγράφω: to inscribe
εὑρίσκω: to find
ζηλότυπος, -ον: jealous
ζητέω: to seek, seek for

θέλω: to will, wish, purpose
κατασκέπτω: to look carefully
λυπέω: to grieve, vex, annoy
μικρός, -η, -ον: small, little
μόνος, -η, -ον: only
νεάνισκος, ὁ: youth
παῖς, παιδός, ὁ: a child
περίεργος, -ον: meddlesome
πιστεύω: to believe in
σύνειμι: to be with, consort with
συνίημι: to understand
ὑποκάτω: below, underneath

κατασκεψομένην: fut. part. of παρα-σκέπτω agreeing with Ἀκίδα and expressing
   purpose, "I sent Alkis *in order to look carefully*"
ἡ δ': "but she" i.e. Alkis
ἄλλο μὲν οὐδὲν ... τοῦτο δὲ μόνον: "nothing else ... but only this"
εὗρε: aor. (unaugmented), "she found"
ἐπιγεγραμμένον: perf. part. agreeing with τοῦτο, "she found this alone *inscribed*"
ἐσιόντων: pres. part. gen., "on the right *of those entering*"
Διπύλῳ: a gate into Athens that the Kerameikos cemetery straddles
λυπῆσαι: aor. inf. complementing θέλων, "someone wishing *to annoy*"
ὄντα: pres. part. in ind. st. after εἰδώς, "knowing *that he is* jealous"
εἰ δέ που ἴδοιμι: aor. opt. in general protasis, "if ever I see him"
ἂν ἴδοις: aor. opt. pot., "where *could you see* him?"
ἐγκλεισάμενος: aor. part. mid., "who, *having locked himself in*"

26

αὐτόν. ἀλλ᾽ εἴ τινα εὕροιμεν, ὦ Βακχί, γραῦν, ὡς ἔφην· ἀποσώσειε γὰρ ἂν φανεῖσα.

ΒΑΚΧΙΣ: Ἔστιν, ὦ φιλτάτη, ὅτι χρησίμη φαρμακίς, Σύρα τὸ γένος, ὠμὴ ἔτι καὶ συμπεπηγυῖα, ἥ μοί ποτε Φανίαν χαλεπαίνοντα κἀκεῖνον εἰκῆ, ὥσπερ Χαρῖνος, διήλλαξε μετὰ μῆνας ὅλους τέτταρας, ὅτε ἐγὼ μὲν ἤδη ἀπεγνώκειν, ὁ δὲ ὑπὸ τῶν ἐπῳδῶν ἧκεν αὖθις ἐπ᾽ ἐμέ.

ΜΕΛΙΤΤΑ: Τί δὲ ἔπραξεν ἡ γραῦς, εἴπερ ἔτι μέμνησαι;

ΒΑΚΧΙΣ: Λαμβάνει μὲν οὐδὲ πολύν, ὦ Μέλιττα, τὸν μισθόν, ἀλλὰ δραχμὴν καὶ ἄρτον· ἐπικεῖσθαι δὲ δεῖ μετὰ

ἀπογιγνώσκω: give up, despair	λαμβάνω: to take
ἀποσώζω: to save	μείς, μῆνος, ἡ: a month
ἄρτος, ὁ: a loaf of bread	μισθός, ὁ: wages, pay, hire
αὖθις: back, back again	ὅλος, -η, -ον: whole, entire
γένος, -ους, τό: race, family	πράττω: to do
γραῦς, ἡ: an old woman, hag	συμπήγνυμι: to construct, frame
δεῖ: it is necessary	Σύρος, -α, -ον: Syrian
διαλλάττω: to change	τέτταρες, -ων, οἱ: four
δραχμή, ἡ: a drachma	φαίνομαι: to appear
εἰκῆ: heedlessly, for not reason	φαρμακίς, -ίδος, ἡ: a sorceress, witch
εἴπερ: if ever	φίλτατος, -η, -ον: dearest
ἐπίκειμαι: to be laid upon	χαλεπαίνω: to sore, angry
ἐπῳδή, ἡ: a charm, spell	χρήσιμος, -η, -ον: useful
ἥκω: to have come	ὠμός, -ή, -όν: raw, savage

εἴ ... εὕροιμεν: aor. opt. in future less vivid protasis, "*if we were to find* some hag"

ἀποσώσειε: aor. opt. in future less vivid apodosis, "she would save him"

φανεῖσα: aor. part. pass. of φαίνομαι representing an aor. opt. in a future less vivid protasis, "if she we were to appear"

τὸ γένος: acc. of respect, "Syrian *by race*"

συμπεπηγυῖα: perf. part. of συν-πήγνυμι, "having been put together" i.e. solid, firm

χαλεπαίνοντα: pres. part. acc. agreeing with Φανίαν, "altered Phanias *when he too was angry* for no reason"

ὥσπερ Χαρῖνος: "*just as Charinus* is"

διήλλαξε: aor. of δια-αλλάττω, "*she altered* Phanias

ἀπεγνώκειν: plupf. of ἀπο-γιγνώσκω, "when *I had despaired*"

ὁ δὲ: "but he" i.e. Phanias

ὑπὸ τῶν ἐπῳδῶν: the agency expression, "at the hands of her songs"

ἐπικεῖσθαι: pres. inf. after δεῖ, "it is necessary *to have in addition*"

τῶν ἁλῶν καὶ ὀβολοὺς ἑπτὰ καὶ θεῖον καὶ δᾷδα. ταῦτα
δὲ ἡ γραῦς λαμβάνει, καὶ κρατῆρα κεκερᾶσθαι δεῖ καὶ
πίνειν ἐκείνην μόνην. δεήσει δέ τι αὐτοῦ ἀνδρὸς εἶναι,
οἷον ἱμάτια ἢ κρηπῖδας ἢ ὀλίγας τῶν τριχῶν ἤ τι τῶν
τοιούτων.

ΜΕΛΙΤΤΑ: Ἔχω τὰς κρηπῖδας αὐτοῦ.

ΒΑΚΧΙΣ: Ταύτας κρεμάσασα ἐκ παττάλου ὑποθυμιᾷ τῷ
θείῳ, πάττουσα καὶ τῶν ἁλῶν ἐπὶ τὸ πῦρ· ἐπιλέγει δὲ
ἀμφοῖν τὰ ὀνόματα καὶ τὸ ἐκείνου καὶ τὸ σόν. εἶτα ἐκ τοῦ
κόλπου προκομίσασα ῥόμβον ἐπιστρέφει, ἐπῳδήν τινα
λέγουσα ἐπιτρόχῳ τῇ γλώττῃ, βαρβαρικὰ καὶ φρικώδη

ἅλς, ἁλός, ἡ: a lump of salt
ἄμφω, οἱ: both
ἀνήρ, ἀνδρὸς, ὁ: man
βαρβαρικός, -ή, -όν: barbaric
γλῶττα, -ης, ἡ: the tongue, language
δαίς, δαιδος, ἡ: a torch
ἐπιλέγω: to say upon
ἐπιστρέφω: to turn about, turn round
ἐπίτροχος, -ον: voluble, babbling
ἑπτά: seven
ἐπῳδή, ἡ: a charm, spell
θεῖον, τό: sulphur
θρίξ, τρίχος, ἡ: the hair of the head
ἱμάτιον, τό: a cloak or mantle
κεράννυμι: to mix
κόλπος, ὁ: the bosom

κρατήρ, -ῆρος, ὁ: a mixing vessel
κρεμάννυμι: to hang, hang up
κρηπίς, -ῖδος, ἡ: a boot
μόνος, -η, -ον: only
ὀβολός, ὁ: an obol
ὀλίγος, -η, -ον: few, little, scanty, small
ὄνομα, τό: name
πάτταλος, ὁ: a peg
πάττω: to sprinkle
προκομίζω: to bring forward, produce
πῦρ, τό: fire
ῥόμβος, ὁ: a spinning-top or wheel
τοιοῦτος, -αύτη, -οῦτο: such as this
ὑποθυμιάω: fumigate
φρικώδης, -ες: horrible

κρατῆρα: cognate acc., "to have mixed *a mixing bowl* (of wine)"

κεκερᾶσθαι: perf. inf. of κεράννυμι, "necessary *to have mixed*"

ἐκείνην: acc. subject of πίνειν, "necessary for *that one* alone to drink"

δεήσει: fut. of δεῖ, "it will be necessary" + inf.

κρεμάσασα: aor. part. of κρεμάννυμι, "she, *having hung* these things"

τῷ θείῳ: dat. of means, "fumigate *with sulfur*"

ἀμφοῖν: gen. dual, "the names *of both*"

ῥόμβον: an object tied to a string which could be spun (ῥέμβω) like a top, used in the worship of certain mystery deities, here being used as a magic device

ἐπιτόχῳ τῇ γλώττῃ: dat. of means, "speaking *with her babbling language*"

28

ὀνόματα. ταῦτα ἐποίησε τότε. καὶ μετ᾽ οὐ πολὺ Φανίας,

ἅμα καὶ τῶν συνεφήβων ἐπιτιμησάντων αὐτῷ καὶ τῆς

Φοιβίδος, ᾗ συνῆν, πολλὰ αἰτούσης, ἧκέ μοι, τί πλέον;

ὑπὸ τῆς ἐπῳδῆς ἀγόμενος. ἔτι δὲ καὶ τοῦτό με σφόδρα

κατὰ τῆς Φοιβίδος τὸ μίσηθρον ἐδιδάξατο, τηρήσασαν

ἄγω: to lead	ὄμομα, -τος, τό: name, word
αἰτέω: to ask, beg	πλέων, πλέον: more
ἅμα: at the same time	πολύς, πολλά, πολύ: much, many
διδάσκω: to teach	σύνειμι: to consort with
ἐπιτιμάω: to censure	συνέφηβος, ὁ: a young comrade
ἐποιδή, ἡ: spell, enchantment	σφόδρα: very, very much
ἥκω; to come	τηρέω: to watch
μίσηθρον, τό: charm for producing hatred	τότε: at that time, then

---

μετ᾽ οὐ πολὺ (sc. χρόνον): "after a short while"

ἐπιτιμησάντων: aor. part. in gen. abs., "his friends *having censured* him"

ᾗ συνῆν: impf. of σύνειμι in rel. clause, "and Phoibis, *with whom he was consorting*"

αἰτούσης: pres. part. in gen. abs., "with Phoibis *begging*"

τί πλέον: parenthetical, "what more (is there to say)?"

ἀγόμενος: pres. part. pass., "he (Phanias) *being led*"

κατὰ τῆς Φοιβίδος: "a hatred *against Phoibis*"

τηρήσασαν: aor. part. agreeing with με, "me *having observed* her footprint"

Note the different meanings of the word αὐτός:

1. The nominative forms of the word without the definite article are always intensive (= Latin *ipse*): αὐτὸς: he himself, αὐτοί, they themselves.

   πίνουσι αὐτός τε καὶ Σιμίχη: "*he himself* and Simiche are drinking"

   The other cases of the word are also intensive when they modify a noun or pronoun, either without the definite article or in predicative position:

   δεήσει δέ τι αὐτοῦ ἀνδρὸς εἶναι: "it will be necessary to have something *of the man himself*"

2. Oblique cases of the word, when used without a noun or a definite article, are the unemphatic third person pronouns: him, them, etc.

   τὰς κρηπῖδας αὐτοῦ: *his* boots; ἴδοιμι αὐτόν: if I see *him*

3. Any case of the word with an article in attributive position means "the same":

   καὶ σὺ χρῶ ἐπὶ τὸν Γοργίαν τῷ αὐτῷ φαρμάκῳ. "use *the same drug* on Gorgias"

τὸ ἴχνος, ἐπὰν ἀπολίποι, ἀμαυρώσασαν ἐπιβῆναι μὲν τῷ ἀριστερῷ ἐκείνης τὸν ἐμὸν δεξιόν, τῷ δεξιῷ δὲ τὸν ἀριστερὸν ἔμπαλιν καὶ λέγειν, «Ἐπιβέβηκά σοι καὶ ὑπεράνω εἰμί·» καὶ ἐποίησα ὡς προσέταξε.

ΜΕΛΙΤΤΑ: Μὴ μέλλε, μὴ μέλλε, ὦ Βακχί, κάλει ἤδη τὴν Σύραν. σὺ δέ, ὦ Ἀκί, τὸν ἄρτον καὶ τὸ θεῖον καὶ τὰ ἄλλα πάντα πρὸς τὴν ἐπῳδὴν εὐτρέπιζε.

ἀμαυρόω: to rub away	εὐτρεπίζω: to make ready, get ready
ἀπολείπω: to leave behind	ἤδη: already
ἀριστερός, -ον: on the left	ἴχνος, -εος, τό: a footstep
δεξιός, -ά, -όν: on the right	καλέω: to call, summon
ἔμπαλιν: backwards, back	μέλλω: to be about to do
ἐπιβαίνω: to go upon	προστάττω: to instruct
ἐπῳδή, ἡ: a charm, spell	ὑπεράνω: over, above

ἐπὰν ἀπολίποι: aor. opt. of ἀπο-λείπω in secondary sequence (after ἐδιδάξατο) representing a subjunctive in a general temporal clause, where we would expect ἐπὰν to change to ἐπεί, "whenever she left"

ἀμαυρώσασαν: aor. part. also agreeing with με, "me, *having rubbed it away*"

ἐπιβῆναι: aor. inf. in ind. st. after ἐδιδάξατο, "taught me *to step upon*"

ἀριστερῷ: dat. after ἐπιβῆναι, "to step my right foot *on the left* of that one"

λέγειν: pres. inf. also in ind. st., "and taught me *to say*"

ἐπιβέβηκα: perf. of ἐπι-βαίνω, "*I have stepped upon* you"

προσέταξε: aor. of προσ-τάττω, "I did as *she instructed*"

μὴ μέλλε: pres. imper., "don't be about to!" i.e. don't delay!

The Particles δή and γε

These post-positive particles confer on Lucian's dialogues the liveliness of actual conversation. Their force can be difficult to ascertain, but in general, γε concentrates our focus on the word that precedes it. This focus can be restrictive ("in this case at least") or intensive ("this indeed").

For the first use, note the expression τά γε ἄλλα: "the other things at least" (i.e. apart from what had been mentioned) and in cases where it is attached to pronouns like ἔγωγε, "I at least" (i.e. even if no one else).

The more common intensive use can be seen in εὖ γε ("well done!") and in sarcastic expressions like αὐτοῦ ἀξία γε οὖσα (you being especially worthy of him).

The particle δή can also be intensive, but it emphasizes the reality of the word it follows ("verily," "actually," "indeed"): εἰ δὴ καὶ σὺ ταῦτα ἐκμάθοις: "if you actually were to learn these things.

5. Clonarium and Leaina

Leaina recounts to her disbelieving friend her experience with another woman, but refuses to go into too much detail.

ΚΛΩΝΑΡΙΟΝ: Καινὰ περὶ σοῦ ἀκούομεν, ὦ Λέαινα, τὴν Λεσβίαν Μέγιλλαν τὴν πλουσίαν ἐρᾶν σου ὥσπερ ἄνδρα καὶ συνεῖναι ὑμᾶς οὐκ οἶδ᾽ ὅ τι ποιούσας μετ᾽ ἀλλήλων. τί τοῦτο; ἠρυθρίασας; ἀλλ᾽ εἰπὲ εἰ ἀληθῆ ταῦτά ἐστιν.

ΛΕΑΙΝΑ: Ἀληθῆ, ὦ Κλωνάριον· αἰσχύνομαι δέ, ἀλλόκοτον γάρ τί ἐστι.

ΚΛΩΝΑΡΙΟΝ: Πρὸς τῆς κουροτρόφου τί τὸ πρᾶγμα, ἢ τί βούλεται ἡ γυνή; τί δὲ καὶ πράττετε, ὅταν συνῆτε; ὁρᾷς; οὐ φιλεῖς με· οὐ γὰρ ἂν ἀπεκρύπτου τὰ τοιαῦτα.

αἰσχύνομαι: to be ashamed
ἀκούω: to hear
ἀληθής, -ές: true
ἀλλήλων: of one another
ἀλλόκοτος, -ον: strange
ἀποκρύπτω: to hide
βούλομαι: to will, wish
γυνή, γυναικός, ἡ: a woman
ἐράω; to love

ἐρυθριάω: to blush, to color up
καινός, -ή, -όν: new, fresh
κουροτρόφος, -ον: rearing boys
ὁράω: to see
πλούσιος, -α, -ον: rich, wealthy, opulent
πρᾶγμα, -ατος, τό: a deed, act
πράττω: to do
σύνειμι: to consort with
φιλέω: to love, regard with affection

ἐρᾶν: pres. inf. in ind. st. after ἀκούομεν, "hear *that Megilla loves you*"

Λεσβίαν: a citizen of Lesbos, home of the famous poetess Sappho, and hence like our English word "lesbian," a gay female

συνεῖναι: also in ind. st. after ἀκούομεν, "hear that you *consort together*"

οὐκ οἶδ᾽ ὅ τι: the phrase functions as the object of ποιούσας, "having done *I don't know what*"

ἠρυθρίασας: aor., "did you blush?"

πρὸς τῆς κουροτρόφου: "in the name of the child-rearer!" an epithet of a number of goddesses, including Hecate, Artemis and Aphrodite

ὅταν συνῆτε: pres. subj. in general temporal clause, "whenever you consort"

ὁρᾷς: "do you notice?" a rhetorical question linked with the next clause

ἂν ἀπεκρύπτου: impf. in present contrafactual apodosis, "(if not) you wouldn't be hiding"

ΛΕΑΙΝΑ: Φιλῶ μέν σε, εἰ καί τινα ἄλλην. ἡ γυνὴ δὲ δεινῶς ἀνδρική ἐστιν.

ΚΛΩΝΑΡΙΟΝ: Οὐ μανθάνω ὅ τι καὶ λέγεις, εἰ μή τις ἑταιρίστρια τυγχάνει οὖσα: τοιαύτας γὰρ ἐν Λέσβῳ λέγουσι γυναῖκας ἀρρενωπούς, ὑπ’ ἀνδρῶν μὲν οὐκ ἐθελούσας αὐτὸ πάσχειν, γυναιξὶ δὲ αὐτὰς πλησιαζούσας ὥσπερ ἄνδρας.

ΛΕΑΙΝΑ: Τοιοῦτόν τι.

ΚΛΩΝΑΡΙΟΝ: Οὐκοῦν, ὦ Λέαινα, τοῦτο αὐτὸ καὶ διήγησαι, ὅπως μὲν ἐπείρα τὸ πρῶτον, ὅπως δὲ καὶ σὺ συνεπείσθης καὶ τὰ μετὰ ταῦτα.

ΛΕΑΙΝΑ: Πότον τινὰ συγκροτοῦσα αὐτή τε καὶ Δημώνασσα ἡ Κορινθία. πλουτοῦσα δὲ καὶ αὐτὴ καὶ ὁμότεχνος οὖσα

ἀνδρικός, -ή, -όν: masculine, manly
ἀρρενωπός, -όν: masculine, manly
δεινῶς: terribly, remarkably
διηγέομαι: to describe in full
ἐθέλω: to will, wish, purpose
ἑταιρίστρια, ἡ: fem. form of ἑταιριστής, a courtesan for ladies
Κορίνθιος, -α, -ον: Corinthian
Λέσβος, ἡ: the island of Lesbos, home of Sappho
μανθάνω: to learn

ὁμότεχνος, -ον: practising the same craft with (+ dat.)
οὐκοῦν: therefore, then, accordingly
πάσχω: to suffer
πειράω: to attempt, endeavour, try
πλησιάζω: to bring near, consort with
πλουτέω: to be rich, wealthy
πότος, ὁ: a drinking-bout
συγκροτέω: to strike together, compose
συμπείθω: to assist in persuading
τυγχάνω: to happen

ἑταιρίστρια: pred. nom., "to be some sort of *courtesan for ladies*" the only other occurrence of the word is in Plato, *Symposium* 191e.

οὖσα: pres. part. supplementing τυγχάνει, "unless she happens *to be*"

ὑπ’ ἀνδρῶν: the agency expression with πάσχειν, "to suffer nothing *at the hands of men*"

πλησιαζούσας: pres. part. acc. pl. f., "but themselves *consorting with*" + dat.

διήγησαι: aor. imper. "do tell!"

ὅπως ... ἐπείρα: impf. inceptive in ind. quest., "tell *how she began trying*"

ὅπως ... συνεπείσθης: aor. pass. in ind. quest., "tell *how you were persuaded*"

συγκροτοῦσα: pres. part., "she herself (i.e. Megilla) *composing* a drinking party"

πλοτοῦσα ... αὐτὴ: "she herself (i.e. Demonassa) also being wealthy"

τῇ Μεγίλλῃ, παρέλαβον κἀμὲ κιθαρίζειν αὐταῖς: ἐπεὶ δὲ
ἐκιθάρισα καὶ ἀωρὶ ἦν καὶ ἔδει καθεύδειν, καὶ ἐμέθυον,
Ἄγε δή, ἔφη, ὦ Λέαινα, ἡ Μέγιλλα, κοιμᾶσθαι γὰρ ἤδη
καλόν, ἐνταῦθα κάθευδε μεθ᾽ ἡμῶν μέση ἀμφοτέρων.

ΚΛΩΝΑΡΙΟΝ: Ἐκάθευδες; τὸ μετὰ ταῦτα τί ἐγένετο;

ΛΕΑΙΝΑ: κατεφίλουν με τὸ πρῶτον ὥσπερ οἱ ἄνδρες, οὐκ
αὐτὸ μόνον προσαρμόζουσαι τὰ χείλη, ἀλλ᾽ ὑπανοίγουσαι
τὸ στόμα, καὶ περιέβαλλον καὶ τοὺς μαστοὺς ἔθλιβον:

ἀμφότερος, -α, -ον: both of two	μεθύω: to be drunk
ἀωρί: at an untimely hour, too early	μέσος, -η, -ον: middle, in the middle
δεῖ: it is necessary	μόνον: only
θλίβω: to press, fondle	παραλαμβάνω: to invite along
καθεύδω: to lie down to sleep	περιβάλλω: to throw round, embrace
καταφιλέω: to kiss tenderly	προσαρμόζω: to fit to, attach closely to
κιθαρίζω: to play the cithara	στόμα, τό: the mouth
κοιμάω: to put to sleep	ὑπανοίγω: to open slightly
μαστός, ὁ: a breast	χεῖλος, -εος, τό: a lip

παρέλαβον: aor., "*they invited* me too"
κιθαρίζειν: inf. of purpose, "invited me *to play the cithara*"
ἄγε δὴ: "come now!" a colloquial expression in the classical period
κοιμᾶσθαι: pres. inf. epexegetic after καλόν, "already ready *to go to sleep*"
τὸ μετὰ ταῦτα: "the after these things" i.e. what happened next?
καταφιλοῦσα: pres. part. with μεταξὺ, "in the middle of *kissing*"

Uses of the Infinitive

Besides complementing verbs and being used in indirect statements, infinitives can be used...

1. with the neuter case of the definite article to form a verbal noun.

   ἄχρι τοῦ καγχάζειν:
   "up to the point *of laughing out loud*"

2. epexegetically with adjectives or nouns.

   ἄξιον γὰρ αὐτὴν παρεῖναι ταῖς σπονδαῖς:
   "for it is worthy for her *to be present*"

3. to express purpose after certain verbs.

   ὁ πατὴρ γὰρ παρέδωκέ με φιλοσοφεῖν:
   "my father handed me over to him in order *to philosophize* me"

ἡ Δημώνασσα δὲ καὶ ἔδακνε μεταξὺ καταφιλοῦσα· ἐγὼ
δὲ οὐκ εἶχον εἰκάσαι ὅ τι τὸ πρᾶγμα εἴη. χρόνῳ δὲ ἡ
Μέγιλλα ὑπόθερμος ἤδη οὖσα τὴν μὲν πηνήκην ἀφείλετο τῆς κεφαλῆς, ἐπέκειτο δὲ πάνυ ὁμοία καὶ προσφυής,
καὶ ἐν χρῷ ὤφθη αὐτὴ καθάπερ οἱ σφόδρα ἀνδρώδεις
τῶν ἀθλητῶν ἀποκεκαρμένη· καὶ ἐγὼ ἐταράχθην

ἀθλητής, ὁ: an athlete	μεταξύ: between
ἀνδρώδης, -ες: manly	ὅμοιος, -α, -ον: like, resembling
ἀποκείρω: to clip or cut off	πάνυ: altogether, entirely
ἀφαιρέω: to remove X (acc.) from Y (gen.)	πηνήκη, ἡ: false hair, wig
δάκνω: to bite	προσφυής, -ες: firmly attached
εἰκάζω: to calculate	σφόδρα: very
ἐπίκειμαι: to be laid upon	ταράττω: to disturb, trouble
καθάπερ: just as	ὑπόθερμος, -ον: somewhat hot or passionate
καταφιλέω: to kiss tenderly	χρόνος, ὁ: time
κεφαλή, ἡ: the head	χρώς, ὁ: the skin

οὐκ εἶχον: impf., "I wasn't able to" + inf.

ὅ τι ... εἴη: pres. opt. in ind. quest. in secondary sequence, "to calculate *what it was*"

χρόνῳ δὲ: "but in time" i.e. eventually

ἀφείλετο: aor. mid. of ἀπο-αίρέω, "*she removed* her wig"

ἐπέκειτο: "impf., "it was situated" i.e. when she was wearing it

πάνυ ὁμοία: "very realistic"

ἐν χρῷ: "close to the skin" i.e. clean-shaven

ὤφθη: aor. pass. of ὁράω, "was seen" i.e. became visible

αὐτὴ: "(the head) *itself*"

ἀποκεκαρμένη: perf. part., "(the head) *having been shaved*"

ἐταράχθην: aor. pass., "I was disturbed"

Indirect Question

Indirect question in Greek follows the same rules as indirect statement, but is introduced by an interrogative word. The indicative can be changed to the optative in secondary sequence.

> ἐγὼ δὲ οὐκ εἶχον εἰκάσαι ὅ τι τὸ πρᾶγμα εἴη. I wasn't able to calculate *what the matter was*."

> ἐροῦ τὴν μητέρα, εἴ ποτε λέλουται μετ' αὐτῆς. "Ask your mother *whether she has washed* with her."

> ἡ δέσποινα δὲ ἐπυνθάνετο ἀεὶ τί πράττοιτε καὶ ἔνθα εἴητε. "The mistress was always asking *what you were doing and where you were*."

ἰδοῦσα. ἡ δέ, «Ὦ Λέαινα,» φησίν, «ἑώρακας ἤδη οὕτω καλὸν νεανίσκον;» «Ἀλλ' οὐχ ὁρῶ,» ἔφην, «ἐνταῦθα νεανίσκον, ὦ Μέγιλλα.» «Μὴ καταθήλυνέ με,» ἔφη, «Μέγιλλος γὰρ ἐγὼ λέγομαι καὶ γεγάμηκα πρόπαλαι ταύτην τὴν Δημώνασσαν, καὶ ἔστιν ἐμὴ γυνή.» ἐγέλασα, ὦ Κλωνάριον, ἐπὶ τούτῳ καὶ ἔφην, «Οὐκοῦν σύ, ὦ Μέγιλλε, ἀνήρ τις ὢν ἐλελήθεις ἡμᾶς, καθάπερ τὸν Ἀχιλλέα φασὶν κρυπτόμενον ἐν ταῖς παρθένοις, καὶ τὸ ἀνδρεῖον ἐκεῖνο ἔχεις καὶ ποιεῖς τὴν Δημώνασσαν ἅπερ οἱ ἄνδρες;» «Ἐκεῖνο μέν,» ἔφη, «ὦ Λέαινα, οὐκ ἔχω:

ἀνδρεῖος, -α, -ον: masculine
Ἀχιλλεύς, ὁ: Achilles
γαμέω: to marry
γελάω: to laugh
καλὸς, -ή, -ὸν: handsome, beautiful
καταθηλύνω: to make womanish
κρύπτω: to hide

λανθάνω: to escape notice
Μέγιλλα, ἡ: Megilla
Μέγιλλος, ὁ: Megillus
νεανίσκος, ὁ: youth
οὐκοῦν: therefore, then, accordingly
παρθένος, ἡ: a maid
πρόπαλαι: very long ago

ἰδοῦσα: aor. part. instrumental, "disturbed *by seeing* it"

ἡ δέ: "*but she* says" i.e. Megilla

ἑώρακας: perf., "have you ever seen?"

μὴ καταθήλυνε: pres. imper., "*don't feminize* me"

λέγομαι: pres. pass., "*I am called* Megillus" i.e. the masculine form of her name. Megillus is a Spartan interlocutor in Plato's *Laws*. See Gilhuly 2006.

γεγάμηκα: perf., "I have married" using the active (and normally male) form of the verb

ἀνήρ τις: nom. pred. after ὤν, "being *a man*"

ἐλελήθεις: plupf. of λανθάνω, "had you escaped our notice?" + part.

Ἀχιλλέα: "just like Achilles," Achilles' mother Thetis tried to hide him among the women of Scyros, but he was exposed by Odysseus

φασὶν: parenthetical, "as they say"

κρυπτόμενον: pres. part. circumstantial, "Achilles, *when he was being hidden*"

τὸ ἀνδρεῖον ἐκεῖνο: "that manly thing" i.e. a penis

ἅπερ οἱ ἄνδρες: "do you do *just what men* do?"

ἐκεῖνο: "*that* (i.e. what men have) I do not have"

δέομαι δὲ οὐδὲ πάνυ αὐτοῦ· ἴδιον δέ τινα τρόπον ἡδίω

παρὰ πολὺ ὁμιλοῦντα ὄψει με.» «Ἀλλὰ μὴ Ἑρμαφρόδι-

τος εἶ,» ἔφην, «οἷοι πολλοὶ εἶναι λέγονται ἀμφότερα

ἔχοντες;» ἔτι γὰρ ἠγνόουν, ὦ Κλωνάριον, τὸ πρᾶγμα.

«Οὔ,» φησίν, «ἀλλὰ τὸ πᾶν ἀνήρ εἰμι.» «Ἤκουσα,»

ἔφην ἐγώ, «τῆς Βοιωτίας αὐλητρίδος Ἰσμηνοδώρας

διηγουμένης τὰ ἐφέστια παρ' αὐτοῖς, ὡς γένοιτό τις ἐν

Θήβαις ἐκ γυναικὸς ἀνήρ, ὁ δ' αὐτὸς καὶ μάντις ἄρι-

στος, οἶμαι, Τειρεσίας τοὔνομα. μὴ οὖν καὶ σὺ τοιοῦτόν

τι πέπονθας;»   «Οὔκουν, ὦ Λέαινα,» ἔφη, «ἀλλὰ

ἀγνοέω: not to know	Θῆβαι, -ῶν, αἱ: Thebes
ἀμφότερος, -α, -ον: both of two	ἴδιος, -α, -ον: one›s own
ἄριστος, -η, -ον: best	μάντις, -εως, ὁ: a seer, prophet
αὐλητρίς, -ίδος, ἡ: a flute-girl	οἶμαι: to suppose, think
Βοιωτίος, -α, -ον: Boeotian	οἷος, -α, -ον: such as
δέομαι: to need, lack (+ gen.)	ὁμιλέω: to consort with
ἐφέστιος, -ον: at one's own fireside	οὔκουν: not therefore, so not
ἡδύς, εῖα, ῦ: sweet	τρόπος, ὁ: a way, manner

αὐτοῦ: gen. after δέομαι, "I have no need *of that*"

ἴδιον τρόπον: acc. of respect, "consorting *in our own way*"

ἡδίω: (= ἡδίο[ν]α), acc. comparative agreeing with τρόπον, "a way *sweeter* by far"

ὁμιλοῦντα: pres. part. agreeing with με, "see me *consorting*"

ὄψει: fut. of ὁράω, "you will see"

Ἑρμαφρόδιτος: the son of Hermes and Aphrodite who had the genitals of both sexes

λέγονται: pres. in personal form of ind. st., "many *are said* to be"

ἠγνόουν: impf., "for *I was still ignorant*"

τὸ πᾶν: acc. adverbial, "completely"

αὐλητρίδος: gen. of source after ἤκουσα, "I heard the *fluteplayer*"

διηγουμένης: pres. part. circumstantial, "heard the flute-player Ismenodora *relating*"

τὰ ἐφέστια: "relating *homespun tales*"

ὡς γένοιτο: aor. opt. in ind. st., "relating *that someone had become* a man"

Τειρεσίας: Tiresias the famous Theban prophet was first turned from a man to a woman because of Hera's anger, and then turned back to a man

τοὔνομα: acc. of respect, "by name"

πέπονθας: perf. of πάσχω with μὴ expecting a negative answer, "you haven't suffered such, have you?"

ἐγεννήθην μὲν ὁμοία ταῖς ἄλλαις ὑμῖν, ἡ γνώμη δὲ καὶ ἡ
ἐπιθυμία καὶ τἆλλα πάντα ἀνδρός ἐστί μοι.» «Καὶ ἱκανὴ
γοῦν σοι,» ἔφην, «ἐπιθυμία;» «Πάρεχε γοῦν, ὦ Λέαινα,
εἰ ἀπιστεῖς,» ἔφη, «καὶ γνώσῃ οὐδὲν ἐνδέουσάν με τῶν
ἀνδρῶν: ἔχω γάρ τι ἀντὶ τοῦ ἀνδρείου. ἀλλὰ πάρεχε,
ὄψει γάρ.» παρέσχον, ὦ Κλωνάριον, ἱκετευούσης πολλὰ
καὶ ὅρμον τινά μοι δούσης τῶν πολυτελῶν καὶ ὀθόνας
τῶν λεπτῶν. εἶτ᾽ ἐγὼ μὲν ὥσπερ ἄνδρα περιελάμβανον,
ἡ δὲ ἐποίει τε καὶ ἐφίλει καὶ ἤσθμαινε καὶ ἐδόκει μοι ἐς
ὑπερβολὴν ἤδεσθαι.

ἀνδρεῖος, -α, -ον: of or for a man
ἀπιστέω: to disbelieve
ἀσθμαίνω: to gasp for breath
γεννάω: to beget, engender
γιγνώσκω: to learn to know
γνώμη, ἡ: mind
γοῦν: at least then, at any rate
δίδωμι: to give
ἐνδέω: to lack, fall short
ἐπιθυμία, ἡ: desire, longing
ἤδομαι: to enjoy oneself

ἱκανός, -η, -ον: sufficing
ἱκετεύω: to beg
λεπτός, -ή, -όν: elegant
ὀθόνη, ἡ: fine linen
ὅμοιος, -α, -ον: like, resembling (+ *dat.*)
ὅρμος, ὁ: a chain, necklace
παρέχω: to furnish, provide, supply
περιλαμβάνω: to seize around, embrace
πολυτελής, -ές: very expensive, very costly
ὑπερβολή, ἡ: a throwing beyond, utmost

ἐγεννήθην: aor. pass. of γεννάω, "I was born"
ὑμῖν: dat. after ὁμοία, "similar *to you* all"
ἀνδρός: gen. pred. "all are *a man's*"
ἱκανὴ: "is desire *enough*?" i.e. do you have the desire but do not act on it?
πάρεχε: pres. imper., "provide (an opportunity)!" i.e. give me a chance
γνώσῃ: fut., "you will come to know"
ἐνδέουσαν: pres. part. in ind. st. after γνώσῃ, "know *that I am lacking*"
ὄψει: fut. mid., "you will see"
παρέσχον: aor., "I provided (an opportunity)"
ἱκετευούσης: pres. part. in gen. abs., "with her *begging*"
δούσης: aor. part. also in gen. abs., "with her *having given* a necklace"
τῶν πολυτελῶν ... τῶν λεπτῶν: gen. of description, "necklace *of expensive (stones)* ... clothing *of elegant (material)*"
ἐγὼ μὲν ... ἡ δὲ: "*while I* was embracing ... *she* was doing"
ὥσπερ ἄνδρα: "embracing her *as though she were a man*"
ἐς ὑπερβολὴν: "enjoy *to the utmost*"
ἤδεσθαι: aor. inf. complementing ἐδόκει, "she seemed *to enjoy*"

ΚΛΩΝΑΡΙΟΝ: Τί ἐποίει, ὦ Λέαινα, ἢ τίνα τρόπον; τοῦτο γὰρ μάλιστα εἰπέ.

ΛΕΑΙΝΑ: Μὴ ἀνάκρινε ἀκριβῶς, αἰσχρὰ γάρ: ὥστε μὰ τὴν οὐρανίαν οὐκ ἂν εἴποιμι.

αἰσχρός, -ά, -όν: causing shame
ἀκριβῶς: exactly, carefully
ἀνακρίνω: to examine closely

μάλιστα: especially
οὐράνιος, -ον: heavenly
τρόπος, ὁ: a turn, manner

μὰ τὴν οὐρανίαν: "no, by the heavenly (Aphrodite)" another reference to Plato's *Symposium*

ὥστε ... ἂν εἴποιμι: aor. opt. pot. in result clause, "so that I wouldn't like to say"

Defective Verbs

The principal parts of some verbs come from completely different words. Sometimes there are more than one form for a specific tense, in which case one will usually be preferred. Here are some important examples:

Present	Future	Aorist	Perfect	Aorist Passive	Translation
ἔρχομαι	εἶμι				to go
	ἐλεύσομαι	ἦλθον	ἐλήλουθα		
αἱρέω	αἱρήσω	εἷλον	ᾕρηκα	ᾑρέθην	to take
φέρω	οἴσω	ἤνεγκα	ἐνήνοχα	ἠνέχθην	to bear, carry
		ἤνεγκον			
ὁράω			ἑώρακα		to see
		εἶδον	οἶδα		*perf.* to know
	ὄψομαι		ὄπωπα	ὤφθην	
τρέχω	δραμοῦμαι	ἔδραμον	δεδράμηκα		to run

38

6. Crobyle and Corinna

A mother gives advice to her daughter, a newly-initiated courtesan.

ΚΡΩΒΥΛΗ: Ὦ Κόριννα, ὡς μὲν οὐ πάνυ δεινὸν ἦν, ὃ ἐνόμιζες, τὸ γυναῖκα γενέσθαι ἐκ παρθένου, μεμάθηκας ἤδη,
μετὰ μειρακίου μὲν ὡραίου γενομένη, μνᾶν δὲ τὸ πρῶτον
μίσθωμα κομισαμένη, ἐξ ἧς ὅρμον αὐτίκα ὠνήσομαί σοι.

ΚΟΡΙΝΝΑ: Ναί, μαννάριον. ἐχέτω δὲ καὶ ψήφους τινὰς
πυραυγεῖς οἷος ὁ Φιλαινίδος ἐστίν.

ΚΡΩΒΥΛΗ: Ἔσται τοιοῦτος. ἄκουε δὲ καὶ τἆλλα παρ' ἐμοῦ
ἅ σε χρὴ ποιεῖν καὶ ὅπως προσφέρεσθαι τοῖς ἀνδράσιν:

ἀκούω: to hear	ὅρμος, ὁ: a necklace, chain
ἀνήρ, ἀνδρός, ὁ: a man	πάνυ: altogether, entirely
αὐτίκα: forthwith, straightway, at once	παρθένος, ἡ: a virgin, girl
δεινός, -ή, -όν: fearful, terrible	προσφέρω: to carry to
κομίζω: to take care of, provide for	πυραυγής, -ες: fiery bright
μανθάνω: to learn	τοιοῦτος, -αύτη, -οῦτο: such as this
μαννάριον, τό: «mommy dear»	Φιλαινίς, -ίδος, ἡ: Philainis, a courtesan
μειράκιον, τό: a boy, lad	χρή: it is necessary
μίσθωμα, -ατος, τό: the price	ψῆφος, ὁ: a pebble, bead
μνᾶ, ἡ: a mna (a weight)	ὠνέομαι: to buy, purchase
νομίζω: to believe, suppose	ὡραῖος, -α, -ον: youthful, ripe

ὡς ... ἦν: ind. st. after **μεμάθηκας**, "you have learned *that it was*"

ἐνόμιζες: impf. habitual, "which *you used to suppose*"

τὸ γυναῖκα γενέσθαι: aor. articular inf., the subject of ἦν "the becoming a woman"

μεμάθηκας: perf. of **μανθάνω**, "you have learned"

γενομένη: aor. part., "you, *having been* with a lad"

κομισαμένη: aor. part., "you, *having brought home*"

μνᾶν: a mna is about 100 drachma

ὠνήσομαι: fut., "*I will buy* for you"

ἐχέτω: pres. imper. 3 s., "let it (i.e. the necklace) have!"

Φιλαινίδος: gen., "like (the necklace) *of Philainis*"

ἔσται: fut., "*it will be* such"

ὅπως προσφέρεσθαι (sc. χρή): ind. quest., "hear *how (it is necessary) to carry yourself towards*" + inf.

ἄλλη μὲν γὰρ ἡμῖν ἀποστροφὴ τοῦ βίου οὐκ ἔστιν, ὦ
θύγατερ, ἀλλὰ δύο ἔτη ταῦτα ἐξ οὗ τέθνηκεν ὁ μακαρίτης
σου πατήρ, οὐκ οἶσθα ὅπως ἀπεζήσαμεν; ὅτε δὲ ἐκεῖνος
ἔζη, πάντα ἦν ἡμῖν ἱκανά: ἐχάλκευε γὰρ καὶ μέγα ἦν
ὄνομα αὐτοῦ ἐν Πειραιεῖ, καὶ πάντων ἐστὶν ἀκοῦσαι
διομνυμένων ἦ μὴν μετὰ Φιλῖνον μηκέτι ἔσεσθαι ἄλλον
χαλκέα. μετὰ δὲ τὴν τελευτὴν τὸ μὲν πρῶτον ἀποδομένη τὰς πυράγρας καὶ τὸν ἄκμονα καὶ σφῦραν δύο
μνῶν, μῆνας ἀπὸ τούτων ἑπτὰ διετράφημεν: εἶτα νῦν
μὲν ὑφαίνουσα, νῦν δὲ κρόκην κατάγουσα ἢ στήμονα

ἄκμων, -ονος, ὁ: an anvil	μακαρίτης, ὁ: one blessed
ἀποδίδωμι: to give back, sell (mid.)	μείς, μῆνος, ἡ: a month
ἀποζάω: to live off	μηκέτι: no longer
ἀποστροφή, ἡ: a turning back	μνᾶ, ἡ: a weight
βίος, ὁ: life	πατήρ, ὁ: a father
διατρέφω: to sustain continually	Πειραιεύς, ὁ: Peiraeeus, Athens' harbor
διόμνυμι: to swear solemnly	πυράγρα, ἡ: a pair of fire-tongs
ἑπτά: seven	στήμων, -ονος ὁ: the warp of a loom
ἔτος, -εος, τό: a year	σφῦρα, ἡ: a hammer
ζάω: to live	τελευτή, ἡ: a completion, death
θυγάτηρ, -τερος, ἡ: a daughter	ὑφαίνω: to weave
ἱκανός,-η, -ον: sufficing	Φιλῖνος, ὁ: Philinos, the husband of Krobyle
κατάγω: to lead down	χαλκεύς, -έως: a coppersmith
κρόκη, ἡ: a weaving thread	χαλκεύω: to work as a coppersmith

ἐξ οὗ: "from which (time)"

τέθνηκεν: perf. of θνήσκω, "he has been dead"

ὅπως ἀπεζήσαμεν: aor. in ind. quest., "know *how we lived poorly*"

ἀκοῦσαι: aor. inf. complementing ἐστὶν, "it is possible *to hear*" + gen.

διομνυμένων: pres. part. gen. of source, "to hear all *swearing*"

ἦ μὴν: introducing an oath in ind. st., "swearing that *verily*"

μηκέτι ἔσεσθαι: fut. inf. in ind. st. after διομνυμένων, "swearing that another *will never be*"

ἀποδομένη: aor. part. mid. instrumental, "I, *by having sold*"

δύο μνῶν: gen. of price, "for two *mna*"

μῆνας ... ἑπτά: acc. of duration, "we were sustained *for seven months*"

διετράφημεν: aor. pass. of διατρέφω, "we were sustained"

ὑφαίνουσα: pres. part. instrumental, "I, *by weaving*"

κρόκην ... στήμονα: "the warp ... the woof" i.e. the lengthwise and crosswise threads of a garment

κλώθουσα ἐποριζόμην τὰ σιτία μόλις· ἔβοσκον δὲ σέ, ὦ
θύγατερ, τὴν ἐλπίδα περιμένουσα.

ΚΟΡΙΝΝΑ: Τὴν μνᾶν λέγεις;

ΚΡΩΒΥΛΗ: Οὔκ, ἀλλὰ ἐλογιζόμην ὡς τηλικαύτη γενομένη
θρέψεις μὲν ἐμέ, σεαυτὴν δὲ κατακοσμήσεις ῥαδίως καὶ
πλουτήσεις καὶ ἐσθῆτας ἕξεις ἁλουργεῖς καὶ θεραπαίνας.

ΚΟΡΙΝΝΑ: Πῶς ἔφης, μῆτερ, ἢ τί λέγεις;

ΚΡΩΒΥΛΗ: Συνοῦσα μὲν τοῖς νεανίσκοις καὶ συμπίνουσα
μετ᾽ αὐτῶν καὶ συγκαθεύδουσα ἐπὶ μισθῷ.

ΚΟΡΙΝΝΑ: Καθάπερ ἡ Δαφνίδος θυγάτηρ Λύρα;

ΚΡΩΒΥΛΗ: Ναί.

ΚΟΡΙΝΝΑ: Ἀλλ᾽ ἐκείνη ἑταίρα ἐστίν.

ἁλουργής, -ές: sea-purple	μόλις: scarcely
βόσκω: to feed, tend	νεάνισκος, ὁ: youth, young man
Δαφνίς, -ίδος, ἡ: Daphnis, Lyra's mother	περιμένω: to await
ἐλπίς, -ίδος, ἡ: hope, expectation	πλουτέω: to be rich
ἐσθής, -ῆτος, ἡ: dress, clothing	πορίζω: to to furnish, provide
θεράπαινα, ἡ: a handmaid	ῥαδίως: easily
καθάπερ:, just as	σιτίον, τό: grain, food
κατακοσμέω: to adorn	συγκαθεύδω: to lie down with
κλώθω: to twist by spinning, spin	συμπίνω: to join in a drinking bout
λογίζομαι: to calculate, compute	σύνειμι: to consort with
Λύρα, ἡ: Lyra, a courtesan	τηλικοῦτος, -αύτη, -οῦτο: such an age
μισθός, ὁ: wages, pay	τρέφω: to nourish

τὴν ἐλπίδα: "awaiting *the hope*" i.e. the fulfillment of the hope

λέγεις: "do you mean?" i.e. is the *mna* what she was expecting

ὡς ... θρέψεις: fut. (like the following verbs) of τρέφω in ind. st. after ἐλογιζόμην, "I
  was calculating *that you will nourish* me"

γενομένη: aor. part., "you, *once you became*"

ἕξεις: fut. of ἔχω also in ind. st., "calculating *that you will have*"

συνοῦσα: pres. part. instrumental, "by consorting with" + dat.

ἐπὶ μισθῷ: "for a fee"

ΚΡΩΒΥΛΗ: Οὐδὲν τοῦτο δεινόν· καὶ σὺ γὰρ πλουτήσεις ὡς ἐκείνη καὶ πολλοὺς ἐραστὰς ἕξεις. τί ἐδάκρυσας, ὦ Κόριννα; οὐχ ὁρᾷς ὁπόσαι καὶ ὡς περισπούδαστοί εἰσιν αἱ ἑταῖραι καὶ ὅσα χρήματα λαμβάνουσι; τὴν Δαφνίδος γοῦν ἐγὼ οἶδα, ὦ φίλη Ἀδράστεια, ῥάκη, πρὶν αὐτὴν ἀκμάσαι τὴν ὥραν, περιβεβλημένην· ἀλλὰ νῦν ὁρᾷς οἷα πρόεισι, χρυσὸς καὶ ἐσθῆτες εὐανθεῖς καὶ θεράπαιναι τέτταρες.

ΚΟΡΙΝΝΑ: Πῶς δὲ ταῦτα ἐκτήσατο ἡ Λύρα;

ΚΡΩΒΥΛΗ: Τὸ μὲν πρῶτον κατακοσμοῦσα ἑαυτὴν εὐπρεπῶς καὶ εὐσταλὴς οὖσα καὶ φαιδρὰ πρὸς ἅπαντας, οὐκ ἄχρι

Ἀδράστεια, ἡ: the Inevitable one
ἀκμάζω: to be in full bloom
ἄχρι: up to the point (+ gen.)
γοῦν: at any rate
δακρύω: to weep
δεινός, -ή, -όν: terrible, dreadful
ἐραστής, -οῦ, ὁ: a lover
εὐανθής, -ές: blooming, budding
εὐπρεπής, -ές: well-looking, comely
εὐσταλής, -ές: well-behaved
θεράπαινα, ἡ: a handmaid
κατακοσμέω: to set in order, arrange
κτάομαι: to acquire
λαμβάνω: to take
οἶδα: to know (perf.)

οἷος, -α, -ον: what sort of
ὁπόσος, -η, -ον: how many
ὅσος, -η, -ον: how much
περιβάλλω: to throw round, wear
περισπούδαστος, -ον: much desired
πλουτέω: to be wealthy
πρίν: before (+ inf.)
προέρχομαι: to proceed
ῥάκος, τό: a rag
τέσσαρες, οἱ: four
φαιδρός, -ά, -όν: bright, beaming
φίλος, -η, -ον: beloved, dear
χρῆμα, -ατος: a thing, money (pl.)
χρυσός, ὁ: gold
ὥρα, ἡ: season, time

οὐδὲν: acc. of respect, "terrible *not at all*"
ἐδάκρυσας: aor., "why *did you burst out crying*?"
ὁπόσαι καὶ ὡς: introducing ind. quest., "do you not see *how many and how* desired?"
τὴν Δαφνίδος: "the (daughter) of Daphnis"
Ἀδράστεια: an epithet of Nemesis, the goddess of retribution
ῥάκη: neuter plural acc. object of περιβεβλημένην, "she has worn *rags*"
πρὶν ... ἀκμάσαι: aor. inf., "before having matured"
περιβεβλημένην: perf. part. in ind. st. after οἶδα, "I know *that she has worn*"
οἷα πρόεισι: ind. quest. "you see *how she proceeds*"
ἐκτήσατο: aor., "how *did she acquire*?"
κατακοσμοῦσα: pres. part. instrumental, "she, *by adorning* herself"
εὐσταλὴς: nom. pred., "by being *well-behaved*"

τοῦ καγχάζειν ῥᾳδίως καθάπερ σὺ εἴωθας, ἀλλὰ μειδιῶσα ἡδὺ καὶ ἐπαγωγόν, εἶτα προσομιλοῦσα δεξιῶς
καὶ μήτε φενακίζουσα, εἴ τις προσέλθοι ἢ προπέμψειε,
μήτε αὐτὴ ἐπιλαμβανομένη τῶν ἀνδρῶν. ἢν δέ ποτε καὶ
ἀπέλθῃ ἐπὶ δεῖπνον λαβοῦσα μίσθωμα, οὔτε μεθύσκεται
— καταγέλαστον γὰρ καὶ μισοῦσιν οἱ ἄνδρες τὰς τοι-

ἀνήρ, ἀνδρὸς, ὁ: man	μεθύσκω: to make drunk
δεῖπνον, τό: a dinner	μειδιάω: to smile
δεξιῶς: deftly	μισέω: to hate
ἔθω: to be accustomed	μίσθωμα, -ατος, τό: a price, fee
ἐπαγωγός, όν: attractive, seductive	προπέμπω: to summon
ἐπιλαμβάνω: to lay hold of, seize	προσέρχομαι: to approach
ἡδύς, -εῖα, -ύ: sweet	προσομιλέω: to converse with
καγχάζω: to laugh out loud	ῥᾴδιος, -α, -ον: easy
καταγέλαστος, -ον: ridiculous, absurd	φενακίζω: to cheat

εἴωθας: perf. with present meaning of ἔθω, "as you are accustomed"

τοῦ καγχάζειν: pres. inf. articular gen. after ἄχρι, "up to the point *of laughing out loud*"

προσέλθοι ἢ προπέμψειε: aor. opt. in present general protasis, "if someone (ever) *approaches or summons*"

ἐπιλαμβανομένη: pres. part. mid., "she, never *throwing herself at*" + gen.

ἢν ... ἀπέλθῃ: aor. subj. in present general protasis, "if (ever) she attends"

λαβοῦσα: aor. part., "she, *having taken* a fee"

καταγέλαστον: nom. pred. "for that is *ridiculous*"

General Conditions

A **present general condition** has ἐάν (Attic ἤν) + subj. in the protasis; present indicative in the apodosis:

> ἢν δέ ποτε καὶ ἀπέλθῃ, οὔτε μεθύσκεται: "And if (ever) she approaches, she neither becomes drunk..."

However, Lucian often uses the optative in the protasis of such conditions, especially when the premise is unlikely to be fulfilled:

> εἶτα προσομιλοῦσα δεξιῶς εἴ τις προσέλθοι ἢ προπέμψειε: "then smiling deftly *if anyone approaches or summons*"

A **past general condition** has εἰ + the optative in the protasis; imperfect indicative in the apodosis:

> ἀλλ᾽ ἠπείλησε Χαιρέας ἀποσφάξειν ἀμφοτέρους, εἰ λάβοι μέ ποτε μετ᾽ αὐτοῦ: "but Chaereas threatened to slaughter both, if ever he caught me with him"

αὔτας — οὔτε ὑπερεμφορεῖται τοῦ ὄψου ἀπειροκάλως, ἀλλὰ προσάπτεται μὲν ἄκροις τοῖς δακτύλοις, σιωπῇ δὲ τὰς ἐνθέσεις οὐκ ἐπ᾽ ἀμφοτέρας παραβύεται τὰς γνάθους, πίνει δὲ ἠρέμα, οὐ χανδόν, ἀλλ᾽ ἀναπαυομένη.

ΚΟΡΙΝΝΑ: Κἂν εἰ διψῶσα, ὦ μῆτερ, τύχῃ;

ΚΡΩΒΥΛΗ: Τότε μάλιστα, ὦ Κόριννα. καὶ οὔτε πλέον τοῦ δέοντος φθέγγεται οὔτε ἀποσκώπτει ἔς τινα τῶν παρόντων, ἐς μόνον δὲ τὸν μισθωσάμενον βλέπει· καὶ διὰ τοῦτο ἐκεῖνοι φιλοῦσιν αὐτήν. καὶ ἐπειδὰν κοιμᾶσθαι δέῃ, ἀσελγὲς οὐδὲν οὐδὲ ἀμελὲς ἐκείνη ἄν τι ἐργάσαιτο,

---

ἄκρος, -α, -ον: at the furthest point, tip
ἀμελής, -ές: careless, heedless, negligent
ἀμφότερος, -α, -ον: each or both of two
ἀναπαύομαι: to cease, to pause
ἀπειρόκαλος, -ον: tasteless, vulgar
ἀποσκώπτω: to banter, rally
ἀσελγής, -ές: licentious, wanton
βλέπω: to look at
γνάθος, ἡ: the jaw
δάκτυλος, ὁ: a finger
δεῖ: it is necessary
δέον, -οντος, τό: that which is necessary
διψάω: to thirst
ἔνθεσις, -εως, ἡ: a mouthful
ἐπειδάν: whenever (+ subj.)
ἐργάζομαι: to work
ἠρέμος, -α, -ον: gentle
κοιμάω: to sleep

μάλιστα: (adv.) especially
μήτηρ, μήτερος, ἡ: a mother
μισθόμαι: to hire for a fee
μόνος, -η, -ον: alone, only
ὄψον, τό: cooked meat
παραβύω: to stuff in, insert
πάρειμι: to be present
πίνω: to drink
πλέων, -ον: more
προσάπτω: to fasten on, touch
σιωπή, ἡ: silence
τότε: at that time, then
τυγχάνω: to happen to (+ part.)
ὑπερεμφορέομαι: to be filled
φθέγγομαι: to utter a sound
φιλέω: to love, regard with affection
χανδόν: with mouth wide open, greedily

ἀπειροκάλως: adv., "ignorant of beauty" i.e. tastelessly

ἄκροις: "with the tips of her fingers"

ἀναπαυομένη: pres. part. mid., "she drinks pausing" i.e. not continuously

κἂν (=καὶ ἂν) εἰ: "even if" + subjunctive

διψῶσα: aor. part. supplementing τύχῃ, "happens to become thirsty"

τύχῃ: aor. subj. of τυγχάνω in present general protasis, "even if someone happens to"

τοῦ δέοντος: gen. of comparison, "more than is necessary"

τὸν μισθωσάμενον: aor. part. attributive, "only at the one who paid"

ἐπειδὰν ... δέῃ: pres. subj. of δεῖ in general temporal clause, "when(ever) it is necessary" + inf.

ἄν τι ἐργάσαιτο: aor. opt. pot., "that one would do"

ἀλλὰ ἐξ ἅπαντος ἓν τοῦτο θηρᾶται, ὡς ὑπαγάγοιτο καὶ
ἐραστὴν ποιήσειεν ἐκεῖνον· ταῦτα γὰρ αὐτῆς ἅπαντες
ἐπαινοῦσιν. εἰ δὴ καὶ σὺ ταῦτα ἐκμάθοις, μακάριαι καὶ
ἡμεῖς ἐσόμεθα· ἐπεὶ τά γε ἄλλα παρὰ πολὺ αὐτῆς—
ἀλλ' οὐδέν, ὦ φίλη Ἀδράστεια, φημί, ζῴοις μόνον.

ΚΟΡΙΝΝΑ: Εἰπέ μοι, ὦ μῆτερ, οἱ μισθούμενοι πάντες τοι-
οῦτοί εἰσιν οἷος ὁ Εὔκριτος, μεθ' οὗ χθὲς ἐκάθευδον;

ΚΡΩΒΥΛΗ: Οὐ πάντες, ἀλλ' ἔνιοι μὲν ἀμείνους, οἱ δὲ καὶ
ἤδη ἀνδρώδεις, οἱ δὲ καὶ οὐ πάνυ μορφῆς εὐφυῶς ἔχοντες.

Ἀδράστεια, ἡ: the Inevitable one (Nemesis)
ἀμείνων, -ον: better, abler
ἀνδρώδης, -ες: manly
εἶπον: to speak, say (*aor.*)
ἐκμανθάνω: to learn thoroughly
ἔνιοι, -α: some
ἐπαινέω: to approve, praise
εὐφυής, -ές: well-grown, abundant

ζάω: to live
θηράω: to hunt, seek
μακάριος, -α, -ον: blessed, happy
μισθόμαι: to hire for a fee
μορφή, ἡ: form, appearance
ποιέω: to make
ὑπάγω: to lead or bring under
χθές: (*adv.*) yesterday

ὡς ὑπαγάγοιτο ... ποιήσειεν: aor. opt. in purpose clauses instead of subjunctive indicating an alleged purpose, "seeks this one thing, *namely to acquire ... to make*"

ἐραστὴν: acc. pred., "make him *her lover*"

εἰ ... ἐκμάθοις: aor. opt. in future less vivid protasis, "if you were to learn"

ἐσόμεθα: fut. in future more vivid apodosis, "then *we will be*"

τά γε ἄλλα: acc. of respect, "in other ways at least"

αὐτῆς: gen. of comparison, "(you are) better *than her*"

οὐδέν ... φημί: an example of aposiopesis, deciding *not* to say something to avoid the jealous retribution of Nemesis (Adrasteia)

ζῴοις: pres. opt. in wish for the future, "may you live!" i.e. live well!

τοιοῦτοι ... οἷος: correlatives, "are all *such ... as* Eukritos"

μεθ' οὗ: "with whom"

ἔνιοι μὲν ... οἱ δὲ: "while some ... but others"

ἀμείνους: nom. pl. pred., "some are *better*"

μορφῆς: gen. after ἔχοντες, "not having abundantly (good) *appearance*"

ΚΟΡΙΝΝΑ: Καὶ τοιούτοις συγκαθεύδειν δεήσει;

ΚΡΩΒΥΛΗ: Μάλιστα, ὦ θύγατερ· οὗτοι μέν τοι καὶ πλείονα
διδόασιν· οἱ καλοὶ δὲ αὐτὸ μόνον καλοὶ θέλουσιν εἶναι.
καὶ σοὶ δὲ μελέτω ἀεὶ τοῦ πλείονος, εἰ θέλεις ἐν βραχεῖ
λέγειν ἁπάσας ἐνδειξάσας σε τῷ δακτύλῳ, «Οὐχ ὁρᾷς
τὴν Κόρινναν τὴν τῆς Κρωβύλης θυγατέρα ὡς ὑπερπλουτεῖ καὶ τρισευδαίμονα πεποίηκε τὴν μητέρα; τί
φῄς; ποιήσεις ταῦτα; ποιήσεις, οἶδα ἐγώ, καὶ προέξεις
ἁπασῶν ῥᾳδίως. νῦν δ᾽ ἄπιθι λουσομένη, εἰ ἀφίκοιτο καὶ
τήμερον τὸ μειράκιον ὁ Εὔκριτος· ὑπισχνεῖτο γάρ.

ἀεί: (adv.) always, for ever	μειράκιον, τό: a boy, lad, stripling
ἄπιθι: go away!	μέλω: to be an object of care or thought
ἀφικνέομαι: to arrive	προέχω: to surpass (+ gen.)
βραχύς, -εῖα, -ύ: short	ῥᾳδίως: (adv.) easily
δάκτυλος, ὁ: a finger	τήμερον: (adv.) today
δίδωμι: to give	τοι: let me tell you, surely
ἐνδείκνυμι: to mark, point out	τρισευδαίμων, -ον: thrice-happy
θέλω: to will, wish	ὑπερπλουτέω: to be exceeding rich
λούω: to wash	ὑπισχνέομαι: to promise
μάλιστα: especially	

δεήσει: fut.. "will it be necessary to?" + inf.

πλείονα: neut. pl. acc. "they give *more things*"

μόνον καλοί: nom. pred., "to be *handsome only*" i.e. without paying

μελέτω: pres. imper. 3 s., "let it be a care!" + gen.

ἐν βραχεῖ: "in a short (time)"

ἁπάσας: acc. fem. subject of λέγειν, "wish *all* to say"

ἐνδειξάσας: aor. part., acc. pl. agreeing with ἁπάσας, "all *having pointed* you *out*"

ὡς ὑπερπλουτεῖ: ind. st. after ὁρᾷς, "see *that she is very rich*"

τρισευδαίμονα: acc. pred., "made her mother *thrice blessed*"

πεποίηκε: perf., "see that *she has made*"

προέξεις: fut. of προ-έχω, "you will surpass" + gen.

λουσομένη: fut. part. nom. expressing purpose, "go away *in order to wash*"

εἰ ἀφίκοιτο: aor. opt. in future less vivid protasis, "if he were to come" with apodosis
  unexpressed

7. Musarium and her Mother

Mousarion insists on being faithful to her lover, even though he pays only with promises, much to the consternation of her mother.

ΜΗΤΗΡ: Ἂν δ' ἔτι τοιοῦτον ἐραστὴν εὕρωμεν, ὦ Μουσάριον, οἷος ὁ Χαιρέας ἐστί, θῦσαι μὲν τῇ πανδήμῳ δεήσει
λευκὴν μηκάδα, τῇ οὐρανίᾳ δὲ τῇ ἐν κήποις δάμαλιν,
στεφανῶσαι δὲ καὶ τὴν πλουτοδότειραν, καὶ ὅλως
μακάριαι καὶ τρισευδαίμονες ἐσόμεθα. νῦν ὁρᾷς παρὰ
τοῦ νεανίσκου ἡλίκα λαμβάνομεν, ὃς ὀβολὸν μὲν οὐδέπο-
τε σοι δέδωκεν, οὐκ ἐσθῆτα, οὐχ ὑποδήματα, οὐ μύρον,
ἀλλὰ προφάσεις ἀεὶ καὶ ὑποσχέσεις καὶ μακραὶ ἐλπίδες

δάμαλις, -εως, ὁ: a heifer	μηκάς, -άδος, ἡ: a goat
δίδωμι; to give	μύρον, τό: unguent, perfume
ἐλπίς, -ίδος, ἡ: hope, expectation	ὀβολός, ὁ: an obol, a penny
ἐσθής, -ῆτος, ἡ: dress, clothing	ὅλως: (*adv.*) completely
εὑρίσκω: to find	οὐράνιος, -ον: heavenly
ἡλίκος, -η, -ον: how much	πάνδημος, -ον: common
θύω: to sacrifice	πρόφασις, -εως, ἡ: an excuse
κῆπος, ὁ: a garden	στεφανόω: to crown with a garland
λευκός, -ή, -όν: white	τρισευδαίμων, -ον: thrice-happy
μακάριος, -α, -ον: blessed, happy	ὑπόδημα, -ατος, τό: a sandal
μακρός, -ά, -ον: long	ὑπόσχεσις, -εως, ἡ: a promise

ἂν ... εὕρωμεν: aor. subj. in future more vivid protasis, "if you find"

τοιοῦτον ... οἷος: correlatives, "*such* a lover *as* Chaereas"

θῦσαι: aor. inf. after δεήσει, "necessary *to sacrifice*"

τῇ πανδήμῳ ... τῇ οὐρανίᾳ (sc. Ἀφροδίτη): dat. ind. obj., "*to the common* Aphrodite ... *to the heavenly* Aphrodite" governing the two kinds of love, one physical, the other spiritual. See Plato, *Symposium* 180d.

ἐν κήποις: "in the gardens" referring to a statue in a district of Athens. See Pausanias *Description of Greece* 1.19.2

στεφανῶσαι: aor. inf. also after δεήσει, "will be necessary *to crown*"

τὴν πλουτοδότειραν: "the giver of wealth," an epithet of Artemis

ἐσόμεθα: fut. in future more vivid apodosis along with δεήσει, "and we shall be"

ἡλίκα λαμβάνομεν: ind. quest. after ὁρᾷς, "you see *how much we take*"

δέδωκεν: perf. of δίδωμι, "who *has given*"

ἀλλὰ προφάσεις: nom. "but (there are) *excuses*" note the change of construction

καὶ πολὺ τό, ἐὰν ὁ πατὴρ ..., καὶ κύριος γένωμαι τῶν
πατρῴων, καὶ πάντα σά. σὺ δὲ καὶ ὀμωμοκέναι αὐτὸν
φῇς ὅτι νόμῳ γαμετὴν ποιήσεταί σε.

ΜΟΥΣΑΡΙΟΝ: Ὤμοσε γάρ, ὦ μῆτερ, κατὰ ταῖν θεοῖν καὶ
τῆς Πολιάδος.

ΜΗΤΗΡ: Καὶ πιστεύεις δηλαδή: καὶ διὰ τοῦτο πρῴην
οὐκ ἔχοντι αὐτῷ καταθεῖναι συμβολὴν τὸν δακτύλιον
δέδωκας ἀγνοούσης ἐμοῦ, ὁ δὲ ἀποδόμενος κατέπιε, καὶ
πάλιν τὰ δύο περιδέραια τὰ Ἰωνικά, ἕλκοντα ἑκάτερον
δύο δαρεικούς, ἅ σοι ὁ Χῖος Πραξίας ὁ ναύκληρος ἐκόμισε

ἀγνοέω: not to know
ἀποδίδωμαι: to sell
γαμετή, ἡ: a wife
δακτύλιος, ὁ: a ring, seal-ring
δαρεικός, ὁ: a Daric (coin)
δηλαδή: (adv.) quite clearly, manifestly
δύο: two
ἑκάτερος: each of two
ἕλκω: to draw, drag
Ἰωνικός, -ή, -όν: Ionic, Ionian
καταπίνω: to gulp down
κατατίθημι: to put down
κομίζω: to bring

κύριος: a lord, master
ναύκληρος, ὁ: a ship-master
νόμος, ὁ: a law
ὄμνυμι: to swear
πάλιν: (adv.) back, backwards
πατρῷος, -α, -ον: inherited from one›s father
περιδέραιον, τό: a necklace
πιστεύω: to trust, believe in
Πολιάς, -άδος, ἡ: guardian of the city, an
   epithet of Athena
πρῴην: (adv.) earlier
συμβολή, ἡ: a contribution
Χῖος, -α, -ον: Chian, of or from Chios

ἐὰν ὁ πατὴρ (sc. ἀποθάνῃ): aor. subj. in future more vivid protasis, "if ever his father
(dies)" she hesitates to say the unlucky word
γένωμαι: aor. subj. also in future more vivid protasis, "*if I become* master"
σά: nom. pred. "all (will be) *yours*"
ὀμωμοκέναι: perf. inf. in ind. st. after φῇς, "you say *that he has sworn*"
γαμετὴν: acc. pred. "make you *his bride*"
ταῖν θεοῖν: gen. dual, "according to *the two goddesses*" i.e. Demeter and Persephone
Πολιάδος: gen., "the protectress" i.e. Athena
ἔχοντι: pres. part. agreeing with αὐτῷ, "to him not *being able to*" + inf.
καταθεῖναι: aor. inf. of κατα-τίθημι, "being able *to put down*"
δέδωκας: perf., "*you gave* to him"
ἀγνοούσης: pres. part. in gen. abs., "me *not knowing*"
ἀποδόμενος: aor. part. mid., "he *having sold* it"
κατέπιε: aor. of κατα-πίνω, "he drank it away"
ἕλκοντα: pres. part., "each one *weighing*" from the idea of *drawing down* a scale

ποιησάμενος ἐν Ἐφέσῳ: ἐδεῖτο γὰρ Χαιρέας ἔρανον συνεφήβοις ἀπενεγκεῖν. ὀθόνας γὰρ καὶ χιτωνίσκους τί ἂν λέγοιμι; καὶ ὅλως ἕρμαιόν τι ἡμῖν καὶ μέγα ὄφελος ἐμπέπτωκεν οὗτος.

ΜΟΥΣΑΡΙΟΝ: Ἀλλὰ καλὸς καὶ ἀγένειος, καὶ φησὶν ἐρᾶν καὶ δακρύει καὶ Δεινομάχης καὶ Λάχητος υἱός ἐστι τοῦ Ἀρεοπαγίτου καὶ φησὶν ἡμᾶς γαμήσειν καὶ μεγάλας ἐλπίδας ἔχομεν παρ' αὐτοῦ, ἢν ὁ γέρων μόνον καταμύσῃ.

ΜΗΤΗΡ: Οὐκοῦν, ὦ Μουσάριον, ἐὰν ὑποδήσασθαι δέῃ, καὶ ὁ σκυτοτόμος αἰτῇ τὸ δίδραχμον, ἐροῦμεν πρὸς αὐτόν,

---

ἀγένειος, -ον: beardless
αἰτέω: to ask, beg
ἀποφέρω: to carry off or away
Ἀρεοπαγίτης, -ου, ὁ: a member of the Areopagus
γέρων, -οντος, ὁ: an old man
δακρύω: to weep, shed tears
Δεινομάχη, ἡ: Dinomache
δέομαι: to need to (+ *inf.*)
δίδραχμος, -ον: worth two drachms
ἐλπίς, -ίδος, ἡ: hope, expectation
ἐμπίπτω: to fall upon
ἔρανος, ὁ: a meal to which each contributed his share
ἐράω: to love

ἕρμαιον, τό: a god-send, wind-fall
Ἔφεσος, ἡ: Ephesus
καταμύω: to close the eyes
Λάχης, -τος, ὁ: Laches
μόνον: only
ὀθόνη, ἡ: fine linen
ὅλως: wholely
οὐκοῦν: therefore, then, accordingly
ὄφελος, τό: furtherance, advantage, help
ποιέω: to make
σκυτοτόμος, ὁ: a cobbler
συνέφηβος, ὁ: a young comrade
υἱός, ὁ: a son
ὑποδέω: to fasten under
χιτωνίσκος, ὁ: a short frock

ποιησάμενος: aor. part. mid., "he *having caused it to be made*" i.e. earned it
ἀπενεγκεῖν: aor. inf. of ἀπο-φέρω complementing ἐδεῖτο, "he needed *to pay back*"
ἂν λέγοιμι: pres. opt. pot., "why should I mention?"
ἕρμαιόν ... ὄφελος: nom. pred. "as a godsend and advantage" (ironic)
ἐμπέπτωκεν: perf. of ἐν-πίπτω, "*he has fallen on* us"
ἐρᾶν: pres. inf. in ind. st., "says *that he loves* me"
γαμήσειν: fut. inf. in ind. st., "he says *that he will marry*"
ἢν ... καταμύσῃ: aor. subj. in present general protasis, "*if ever* his father *closes his eyes*"
ἐὰν ... δέῃ: pres. subj. 2 s. mid. in future more vivid protasis, "if you need" + inf.
ὑποδήσασθαι: aor. inf. mid., "needs *to be fastened underneath* (his feet)" i.e. to be shod
αἰτῇ: pres. subj. also in future more vivid protasis, "and (if) he asks"
ἐροῦμεν: fut. of λέγω, "then *we will say*"

«Ἀργύριον μὲν οὐκ ἔχομεν, σὺ δὲ τῶν ἐλπίδων ὀλίγας
παρ' ἡμῶν λαβέ:» καὶ πρὸς τὸν ἀλφιτοπώλην τὰ αὐτά:
καὶ ἢν τὸ ἐνοίκιον αἰτώμεθα, «Περίμεινον,» φήσομεν,
«ἔστ' ἂν Λάχης ὁ Κολυττεὺς ἀποθάνῃ: ἀποδώσω γάρ
σοι μετὰ τοὺς γάμους.» οὐκ αἰσχύνῃ μόνη τῶν ἑταιρῶν
οὐκ ἐλλόβιον οὐχ ὅρμον οὐ ταραντινίδιον ἔχουσα;

αἰσχύνομαι: to be ashamed
ἀλφιτοπώλης, -ου, ὁ: seller of barley
ἀποδίδωμι: to give back, return
ἀποθνήσκω: to die off, die
ἀργύριον: a silver coin
γάμος, ὁ: a wedding, wedding-feast
ἐλλόβιον, τό: an earring
ἐλπίς, -ίδος, ἡ: hope, expectation

ἐνοίκιον, τό: the rent for a home
ἔστε: until (+ *subj.*)
ἑταίρα, ἡ: a courtesan
λαμβάνω: to take
ὀλίγος, -η, -ον: few
ὅρμος, ὁ: a cord, chain
περιμένω: to wait for, await
ταραντινίδιον, τό: a lace wrap

τὰ αὐτά: "the same things"

ἢν ... αἰτώμεθα: pres. subj. pass. in future more vivid protasis, "if we are asked"

περίμεινον: aor. imper., "we will say '*wait!*'"

ἔστ' ἂν ... ἀποθάνῃ: aor. subj. in general temporal clause, "until he has died" i.e.
    whenever that may be

ἔχουσα: pres. part. supplementing αἰσχύνῃ, "are you not ashamed at *having*"

Perfect with Present Meaning

The present perfect tense describes a completed action which produces a new state
of affairs in the present: τέθνηκε: he has died (and is now dead). Some verbs in
Greek are perfect in form but emphasize the present state produced.

> μέμνημαι: "I remember" (I have called to mind)
> δέδια: "I am afraid" (I have been made afraid)
> οἶδα: "I know" (I have seen)
> ἕστηκα: "I stand" (I have set myself up)
> ἔοικα: "I am like" (I have been made like)

Note that the pluperfect form of these verbs is often used as the past continuous
(i.e. imperfect tense) of these verbs:

> ἐμέμνητο: "she was remembering" (she had called to mind)
> ᾔδειν: "I knew" (I had seen)
> εἱστήκει: "she was standing" (she had set herself up)
> ἐῴκεις: "you seemed" (you had been made like)

ΜΟΥΣΑΡΙΟΝ: Τί οὖν, ὦ μῆτερ; ἐκεῖναι εὐτυχέστεραί μου καὶ καλλίους εἰσίν;

ΜΗΤΗΡ: Οὔκ, ἀλλὰ συνετώτεραι καὶ ἴσασιν ἑταιρίζειν, οὐδὲ πιστεύουσι ῥηματίοις καὶ νεανίσκοις ἐπ᾿ ἄκρου τοῦ χείλους τοὺς ὅρκους ἔχουσι: σὺ δὲ ἡ πιστὴ καὶ φίλανδρος οὐδὲ προσίῃ ἄλλον τινὰ ὅτι μὴ μόνον Χαιρέαν: καὶ πρῴην μὲν ὅτε ὁ γεωργὸς ὁ Ἀχαρνεὺς ἧκε δύο μνᾶς κομίζων, ἀγένειος καὶ αὐτός — οἴνου δὲ τιμὴν ἀπειλήφει τοῦ πατρὸς πέμψαντος — σὺ δὲ ἐκεῖνον μὲν ἀπεμύκτισας, καθεύδεις δὲ μετὰ τοῦ Ἀδώνιδος Χαιρέου.

ἀγένειος, -ον: beardless	νεάνισκος, ὁ: youth, young man
Ἄδωνις, -ιος, ὁ: Adonis	οἶνος, ὁ: wine
ἄκρος, -α, -ον: at the furthest point, tip	ὅρκος, ὁ: an oath
ἀπολαμβάνω: to receive	πέμπω: to send, despatch
ἀπομυκτίζω: to disdain	πιστεύω: to trust (+ *dat.*)
γεωργός, -όν: tilling the ground	πιστός, -η, -ον: trusting
ἑταιρίζω: to be a courtesan	προσίζω: to cleave to
εὐτυχής, -ές: well off, fortunate	πρῴην: earlier
ἥκω: to have come	ῥημάτιον, τό: a pet phrase
καθεύδω: to lie down with	συνετός, -ή, -όν: intelligent, wise
καλλίων, -ον: more beautiful	τιμή: the price
κομίζω: to bring	φίλανδρος, -ον: loving men
μνᾶ, ἡ: a mna (a coin)	χεῖλος, -ους, τό: a lip

μου: gen. of comparison after εὐτυχέστεραι: "luckier *than me*"

καλλίους (=καλλίο[ν]ες): nom. pl. fem. pred., "they are luckier and *more beautiful*"

ἑταιρίζειν: pres. inf. complementing ἴσασιν, "they know how *to be courtesans*"

ἔχουσι: pres. part. dat. agreeing with νεανίσκοις, "young men *having*"

προσίῃ: fut. mid. of προσ-ίζω, "nor *do you cleave to*"

ὅτι μὴ: "*except* Chaereas alone"

ἀπειλήφει: plupf. of ἀπο-λαμβάνω, "he had received"

πέμψαντος: aor. part. in gen. abs., "his father *having sent* him" i.e. in order to sell

ἀπεμύκτισας: aor., "*you disdained* him"

τοῦ Ἀδώνιδος: "with your *Adonis*" the beautiful lover of Aphrodite

ΜΟΥΣΑΡΙΟΝ: Τί οὖν; ἐχρῆν Χαιρέαν καταλείψασαν παραδέξασθαι τὸν ἐργάτην ἐκεῖνον κινάβρας ἀπόζοντα; λεῖός μοι, φασί, Χαιρέας καὶ χοιρίσκος Ἀχαρνικός.

ΜΗΤΗΡ: Ἔστω: ἐκεῖνος ἀγροῖκος καὶ πονηρὸν ἀποπνεῖ. τί καὶ Ἀντιφῶντα τὸν Μενεκράτους μνᾶν ὑπισχνούμενον οὐδὲ τοῦτον ἐδέξω; οὐ καλὸς ἦν καὶ ἀστεῖος καὶ ἡλικιώτης Χαιρέου;

ΜΟΥΣΑΡΙΟΝ: Ἀλλ' ἠπείλησε Χαιρέας ἀποσφάξειν ἀμφοτέρους, εἰ λάβοι μέ ποτε μετ' αὐτοῦ.

ΜΗΤΗΡ: Πόσοι δὲ καὶ ἄλλοι ταῦτα ἀπειλοῦσιν; οὐκοῦν ἀνέραστος σὺ μενεῖς διὰ τοῦτο καὶ σωφρονήσεις

ἀγροῖκος, -η, -ον: rustic	καταλείβω: to pour down;
ἀμφότερος, -α, -ον: both of two	κινάβρα, ἡ: the rank smell of a he-goat
ἀνέραστος, -ον: not loved	λεῖος, -α, -ον: smooth
ἀπειλέω: to threaten (+ inf.)	μένω: to remain
ἀπόζω: to smell of	οὐκοῦν: therefore, then, accordingly
ἀποπνέω: to breathe	παραδέχομαι: to receive from
ἀποσφάζω: to cut the throat of	πονηρός, -ά, -όν: grievous
ἀστεῖος, -α, -ον: urbane, sophisticated	πόσος, -η, -ον: how many?
δέχομαι: to take, accept, receive	σωφρονέω: to be chaste
ἐργάτης, -ου, ὁ: a workman	ὑπισχνέομαι: to promise
ἡλικιώτης, -ου, ὁ: an equal in age	χοιρίσκος, ὁ: a piglet

ἐχρῆν: impf. with contrafactual sense, "was it necessary?" i.e. surely it was not

καταλείψασαν: aor. part. acc. agreeing with the subject of παραδέξασθαι (=με), "me, *having poured out* Chaereas" i.e. having set him aside

παραδέξασθαι: aor. inf. after ἐχρῆν, "necessary for me *to receive*"

κινάβρας: gen. after ἀπόζοντα, "giving off *the smell of a he-goat*"

φασί: parenthetical, indicating that what follows is well known, "as they say"

καὶ χοιρίσκος Ἀχαρνικός: "even (if) he were an Acharnean piglet" an obscure expression, perhaps containing an obscenity

ἔστω: imper. 3 s., "let it be!" i.e. never mind!

πονηρὸν ἀποπνεῖ: "he breathes nastily" i.e. has bad breath

τί ... ἐδέξω: aor. 2 s. mid., "why didn't you receive?"

οὐ καλὸς ἦν: expecting an affirmative, "was he not handsome?"

ἠπείλησε: aor., "he threatened to" + inf.

εἰ λάβοι: aor. opt. in past general protasis, "*if ever he caught* me"

μενεῖς: fut., "will you remain?"

καθάπερ οὐχ ἑταίρα, τῆς δὲ Θεσμοφόρου ἱερειά τις οὖσα;
ἐῶ τἆλλα. τήμερον Ἀλῶά ἐστι. τί δέ σοι δέδωκεν ἐς τὴν
ἑορτήν;

ΜΟΥΣΑΡΙΟΝ: Οὐκ ἔχει, ὦ μαννάριον.

ΜΗΤΗΡ: Μόνος οὗτος οὐ τέχνην εὕρηκεν ἐπὶ τὸν πατέρα,
οὐκ οἰκέτην καθῆκεν ἐξαπατήσοντα, οὐκ ἀπὸ τῆς μητρὸς
ᾔτησεν ἀπειλήσας ἀποπλευσεῖσθαι στρατευσόμενος, εἰ
μὴ λάβοι, ἀλλὰ κάθηται ἡμᾶς ἐπιτρίβων μήτε αὐτὸς
διδοὺς μήτε παρὰ τῶν διδόντων ἐῶν λαμβάνειν; σὺ δὲ

αἰτέω: to ask, beg
Ἀλῶα, -ων, τά: the feast of the threshing
    floor
ἀποπλέω: to sail off
ἐάω: to allow to (+ *inf.*)
ἐξαπατάω: to deceive thoroughly
ἑορτή: a feast
ἐπιτρίβω: to rub, to weary (someone)
εὑρίσκω: to find
θεσμοφόρος, -ον: law-giving

ἱέρεια, ἡ: a priestess
κάθημαι: to sit down
καθίημι: to send down
μαννάριον, τό: mommy dear
μόνος, -η, -ον: alone
οἰκέτης, -ου, ὁ: a house-slave, menial
στρατεύω: to serve in war
τέχνη, ἡ: art, ruse
τήμερον: today

καθάπερ ... οὖσα: pres. part., "*as though* not *being* a courtesan"

τῆς δὲ Θεσμοφόρου: "but being a priestess *of the lawgiver*" an epithet of Demeter

ἐῶ: "I allow" i.e. I concede

Ἀλῶα: a festival which only women were expected to attend, and men were expected
    to provide expense money

δέδωκεν: perf., "what *has he given?*"

εὕρηκεν: perf. (unreduplicated), "has he alone found?"

ἐπὶ τὸν πατέρα: "found no ruse *against his father*"

καθῆκεν: perf. of κατα-ἵημι: "has he not employed" i.e. by setting in motion

ἐξαπατήσοντα: fut. part. agreeing with οἰκέτην and expressing purpose, "employed a
    servant *to trick* him"

ᾔτησεν: aor., "did he not ask?"

ἀπειλήσας: aor. part. instrumental, "ask *by having threatened*" + inf.

ἀποπλευσεῖσθαι: fut. inf. after ἀπειλήσας, "threatened *to sail away*"

στρατευσόμενος: fut. part. expressing purpose, "to sail away *in order to join the army*"

εἰ μὴ λάβοι: aor. opt. in future less vivid protasis, "unless he would receive"

διδοὺς: pres. part., "he, neither *giving*"

τῶν διδόντων: pres. part., "to take from *those who are giving*"

οἴει, ὦ Μουσάριον, ὀκτωκαίδεκα ἐτῶν ἀεὶ ἔσεσθαι; ἢ τὰ αὐτὰ φρονήσειν Χαιρέαν, ὅταν πλουτῇ μὲν αὐτός, ἡ δὲ μήτηρ γάμον πολυτάλαντον ἐξεύρῃ αὐτῷ; μνησθήσεται ἔτι, οἴει, τότε τῶν δακρύων ἢ τῶν φιλημάτων ἢ τῶν ὅρκων πέντε ἴσως τάλαντα προικὸς βλέπων;

ΜΟΥΣΑΡΙΟΝ: Μνησθήσεται ἐκεῖνος· δεῖγμα δέ· οὐδὲ νῦν γεγάμηκεν, ἀλλὰ καταναγκαζόμενος καὶ βιαζόμενος ἠρνήσατο.

ΜΗΤΗΡ: Γένοιτο μὴ ψεύδεσθαι. ἀναμνήσω δέ σε, ὦ Μουσάριον, τότε.

ἀεί: always, for ever	μιμνήσκομαι: to remember
ἀναμιμνήσκω: to remind	ὀκτωκαίδεκα: eighteen
ἀρνέομαι: to deny, refuse	πέντε: five
βιάζω: to constrain	πλουτέω: to be rich, wealthy
βλέπω: to look at	πολυτάλαντος, -ον: worth many talants
γαμέω: to marry	προίξ, -κος, ἡ: a present, dowry
δάκρυον, τό: a tear	τάλαντον, τό: a talant (a) measure
δεῖγμα, -ατος, τό: a proof	φίλημα, -ατος, τό: a kiss
ἐξευρίσκω: to discover	φρονέω: to think
ἔτος, -ους, τό: a year	ψεύδομαι: to lie
καταναγκάζω: to force, compel	

ἔσεσθαι: fut. inf. after **οἴει**, "do you suppose *that you will be*"

φρονήσειν: fut. inf. also after **οἴει**, "suppose that Chaereas *will think*"

ὅταν πλουτῇ: pres. subj. in general temporal clause, "when(ever) he becomes rich"

ἐξεύρῃ: aor. subj. also in general temporal clause, "when *she* (the mother) *finds*"

αὐτῷ: dat. of advantage, "marriage *for him*"

μνησθήσεται: fut., "will he remember?" + gen.

προικὸς: gen. of purpose, "five talants *for a dowry*"

γεγάμηκεν: perf., "*he has* not now *married*"

καταναγκαζόμενος καὶ βιαζόμενος: pres. part., concessive, "he refused *despite being compelled and forced*"

ἠρνήσατο: aor. of **ἀρνέομαι**, "he refused"

γένοιτο: aor. opt. in wish for the future, "may it be!"

μὴ ψεύδεσθαι: pres. inf. in result clause, "may it be *that he is not lying*"

ἀναμνήσω: fut., "*I will remind* you"

τότε: "then" i.e. when he lies

8. Ampelis and Chrysis

Ampelis gives a younger cortesan advice about love: it is the jealous lover who is the true lover.

ΑΜΠΕΛΙΣ: ῞Οστις δέ, ὦ Χρυσί, μήτε ζηλοτυπεῖ μήτε ὀργίζεται μήτε ἐρράπισέ ποτε ἢ περιέκειρεν ἢ τὰ ἱμάτια περιέσχισεν, ἔτι ἐραστὴς ἐκεῖνός ἐστιν;

ΧΡΥΣΙΣ: Οὐκοῦν ταῦτα μόνα ἐρῶντος, ὦ Ἀμπελί, δείγματα;

ΑΜΠΕΛΙΣ: Ναί, ταῦτ᾽ ἀνδρὸς θερμοῦ· ἐπεὶ τἆλλα, φιλήματα καὶ δάκρυα καὶ ὅρκοι καὶ τὸ πολλάκις ἥκειν ἀρχομένου ἔρωτος σημεῖον καὶ φυομένου ἔτι· τὸ δὲ πῦρ ὅλον ἐκ τῆς ζηλοτυπίας ἐστίν. ὥστε εἰ καὶ σέ, ὡς φῄς, ὁ Γοργίας

ἄρχω: to be first, begin	ὅλος, -η, -ον: whole
Γοργίας, ὁ: Gorgias, a young man	ὀργίζομαι: to be angry
δάκρυον, τό: a tear	ὅρκος, ὁ: an oath
δεῖγμα, -ατος, τό: a sign, proof	περικείρω: to cut all round
ἐραστής, -οῦ, ὁ: a lover	περισχίζω: to slit and tear off
ἐράω: to love	πολλάκις: many times
ζηλοτυπέω: to be jealous	πῦρ, τό: fire
ζηλοτυπία, ἡ: jealousy, rivalry	ῥαπίζω: to beat, flog
ἥκω: to have come, be present	σημεῖον, τό: a sign, a mark, token
θερμός, -ή, -όν: hot, warm	φίλημα, -ατος, τό: a kiss
ἱμάτιον, τό: an outer garment	φύομαι: to be blooming

ὅστις: relative clause in apposition to ἐκεῖνός below, "is that one your lover, *who(ever)* is not jealous?"

ἐρράπισε: aor. of ῥαπίζω, "he who never *struck* you"

ἐρῶντος: pres. part. gen., "are these signs *of one loving?*"

τἆλλα (=τὰ ἄλλα): nom. subject, "*the rest*, kisses etc."

ἀρχομένου: pres. part. mid. gen. agreeing with ἔρωτος, "of a love *that is beginning*"

σημεῖον: nom. pred., "frequent visits are *a sign*"

τὸ πολλάκις ἥκειν: articular inf. nom, "the many times having come"

ὥστε εἰ καὶ: introducing a condition as a result, "*and so even if* he strikes you"

55

ῥαπίζει καὶ ζηλοτυπεῖ, χρηστὰ ἔλπιζε καὶ εὔχου ἀεὶ τὰ αὐτὰ ποιεῖν.

ΧΡΥΣΙΣ: Τὰ αὐτά; τί λέγεις; ἀεὶ ῥαπίζειν με;

ΑΜΠΕΛΙΣ: Οὐχί, ἀλλ’ ἀνιᾶσθαι, εἰ μὴ πρὸς μόνον αὐτὸν βλέποις, ἐπεὶ εἰ μὴ ἐρᾷ γε, τί ἂν ὀργίζοιτο, εἰ σύ τινα ἕτερον ἐραστὴν ἔχεις;

ΧΡΥΣΙΣ: Ἀλλ’ οὐδὲ ἔχω ἔγωγε· ὁ δὲ μάτην ὑπέλαβε τὸν πλούσιόν μου ἐρᾶν, διότι ἄλλως ἐμνημόνευσά ποτε αὐτοῦ.

ΑΜΠΕΛΙΣ: Καὶ τοῦτο ἡδὺ τὸ ὑπὸ πλουσίων οἴεσθαι σπουδάζεσθαί σε· οὕτω γὰρ ἀνιάσεται μᾶλλον καὶ φιλοτιμήσεται, ὡς μὴ ὑπερβάλοιντο αὐτὸν οἱ ἀντερασταί.

ἀνιάω: to grieve, distress
ἀντεραστής, -οῦ, ὁ: a rival in love
βλέπω: to see
διότι: for the reason that, since
ἐλπίζω: to look for, expect
εὔχομαι: to pray
ἡδύς, -εῖα, ύ: sweet
μάτην: in vain, idly, fruitlessly
μνημονεύω: to call to mind, mention (+ gen.)

οἴομαι: to suppose, think
ὀργίζομαι: to be angry
πλούσιος, -α, -ον: rich, wealthy, opulent
ῥαπίζω: to beat, flog
σπουδάζω: to pursue
ὑπερβάλλω: to throw beyond, outdo
ὑπολαμβάνω: to suppose
φιλοτιμέομαι: to be jealous
χρηστός, -ή, -όν: useful, serviceable

ποιεῖν: pres. inf. after εὔχου, "pray *that he does* the same things"
ῥαπίζειν: inf. in ind. st. after λέγεις, "what do you mean? *that he will beat?*"
ἀνιᾶσθαι: pres. inf. pass. also in ind. st., "no, I mean *that he will be grieved*"
εἰ μὴ ... βλέποις: pres. opt. in present general apodosis, "unless you look"
τί ἂν ὀργίζοιτο: pres. opt. pot. serving as the apodosis for two protases, "unless he loves you, *why would he be angry* if you have?"
ὁ δὲ: "but he" i.e. her lover
ὑπέλαβε: aor., "he supposed"
ἐρᾶν: pres. inf. in ind. st. after ὑπέλαβε, "he supposed *that* the rich man *loves me*"
ἄλλως: "randomly"
τὸ ... οἴεσθαι: pres. inf. articular in apposition to τοῦτο, "this, *namely the thinking that*"
σπουδάζεσθαι: pres. inf. pass. in ind. st. after οἴεσθαι, "thinking *that you are pursued*"
ὡς μὴ ὑπερβάλοιντο: aor. opt. in negative purpose clause, "*lest* the rivals *outdo* him"

ΧΡΥΣΙΣ: Καὶ μὴν οὗτός γε μόνον ὀργίζεται καὶ ῥαπίζει, δίδωσι δὲ οὐδέν.

ΑΜΠΕΛΙΣ: Ἀλλὰ δώσει· ζηλότυποι γάρ καὶ μάλιστα λυπη- θήσονται.

ΧΡΥΣΙΣ: Οὐκ οἶδ᾽ ὅπως ῥαπίσματα λαμβάνειν βούλει με, ὦ Ἀμπελίδιον.

ΑΜΠΕΛΙΣ: Οὔκ, ἀλλ᾽, ὡς οἶμαι, οὕτως οἱ μεγάλοι ἔρωτες γίγνονται, καὶ εἰ πύθοιτο ἀμελεῖσθαι, εἰ δὲ πιστεύσαι μόνος ἔχειν, ἀπομαραίνεταί πως ἡ ἐπιθυμία. ταῦτα λέγω πρὸς σὲ εἴκοσιν ὅλοις ἔτεσιν ἑταιρήσασα, σὺ δὲ ὀκτω- καιδεκαέτις, οἶμαι, ἢ ἔλαττον οὖσα τυγχάνεις. εἰ βούλει δέ, καὶ διηγήσομαι ἃ ἔπαθόν ποτε οὐ πάνυ πρὸ πολλῶν

ἀμελέω: to have no care for	λαμβάνω: to take, receive
ἀπομαραίνω: to lessen	λυπέω: to distress, vex, annoy
βούλομαι: to will, wish	μεγάς, μεγάλη, μεγά: great
δίδωμι: to give	ὀκτωκαιδεκαέτις: eighteen years old
διηγέομαι: to describe in full	ὀργίζω: to make angry, irritate
εἴκοσι: twenty	πάνυ: altogether, entirely
ἐλάττων, -ον: smaller, less	πάσχω: to suffer
ἐπιθυμία, ἡ: desire, longing	πιστεύω: to trust, believe in
ἑταιρέω: to be a courtesan	πυνθάνομαι: to learn
ἔτος, -εος, τό: a year	ῥάπισμα, τό: a stroke, a slap on the face
ζηλότυπος, -ον: jealous	τυγχάνω: to happen to (+ *part.*)

καὶ μὴν ... γε: indicating agreement in general, but with an exception in *this case*, "yes but this one"

λυπηθήσονται: fut. pass., "they will be grieved"

οὐκ οἶδ᾽ ὅπως: parenthetical, "I don't know how..." i.e. somehow

με: acc. subj. of λαμβάνειν, "you wish *me* to receive"

εἰ πύθοιτο: aor. opt. in present general protatis, "if (ever) someone learns"

ἀμελεῖσθαι: pres. inf. in ind. st., "learns *that you do not care*"

εἰ πιστεύσαι: aor. opt. also in present general protatis, "if (ever) he believes"

μόνος ἔχειν: pres. inf. in ind. st., "believes *that he alone possesses*"

ἔτεσιν: dat. of duration, where the acc. would be normal, "for twenty *years*"

οὖσα: pres. part. complementing τυγχάνεις, "you happen *to be*"

πρὸ: adverbial, "a few years *before*"

ἐτῶν: ἦρα μου Δημόφαντος ὁ δανειστὴς ὁ κατόπιν οἰκῶν τῆς Ποικίλης. οὗτος οὐδεπώποτε πλέον πέντε δραχμῶν δέδωκε καὶ ἠξίου δεσπότης εἶναι. ἦρα δέ, ὦ Χρυσί, ἐπιπόλαιόν τινα ἔρωτα οὔτε ὑποστένων οὔτε δακρύων οὔτε ἀωρὶ παραγιγνόμενος ἐπὶ τὰς θύρας, ἀλλ' αὐτὸ μόνον συνεκάθευδέ μοι ἐνίοτε, καὶ τοῦτο διὰ μακροῦ. ἐπειδὴ δὲ ἐλθόντα ποτὲ ἀπέκλεισα — Καλλίδης γὰρ ὁ γραφεὺς ἔνδον ἦν δέκα δραχμὰς πεπομφώς — τὸ μὲν πρῶτον ἀπῆλθέ μοι λοιδορησάμενος: ἐπεὶ δὲ πολλαὶ μὲν διῆλθον ἡμέραι, ἐγὼ δὲ οὐ προσέπεμπον, ὁ Καλλίδης

ἀξιόω: to demand
ἀπέρχομαι: to go away, depart from
ἀποκλείω: to shut out
ἀωρί: (adv.) at an untimely hour, too early
γραφεύς, -έως, ὁ: a painter
δακρύω: to weep, shed tears
δανειστής, -οῦ, ὁ: a money-lender
δέκα: ten
δεσπότης, -ου: a master, lord
διέρχομαι: to pass through
δραχμή, ἡ: a drachma (a coin)
ἔνδον: in the house
ἐνίοτε: sometimes
ἐπιπόλαιος, -ον: on the surface, superficial

ἡμέρα, ἡ: a day
θύρα, ἡ: a door
Καλλίδης, ὁ: Kallides
κατόπιν: (adv.) behind
λοιδορέω: to abuse, revile
μακρός, -ά, -ον: long
οἰκέω: to inhabit, occupy
οὐδεπώποτε: never
παραγίγνομαι: to be near, show up
πέμπω: to send, despatch
πλέων, -ον: more
προσπέμπω: to send for
συγκαθεύδω: to sleep with
ὑποστένω: to groan in a low tone

ἦρα: impf. of ἐράω, "*he was in love* with me"
κατόπιν: adverb used attributively, "the one dwelling *behind*"
τῆς Ποικίλης (sc. στόας): the "painted stoa" on the north side of the *agora*
δέδωκε: perf., "*he has* never *given*"
ἠξίου: impf., "he was demanding" + inf.
ἦρα ... ἔρωτα: internal acc., "he loved a love" i.e. he felt a love
ἐπὶ τὰς θύρας: "nor lingering *at the door*" a cliche of lovesick behavior
συνεκάθευδέ: in apposition to αὐτό, "on this, namely *that he would sleep with* me"
διὰ μακροῦ: "with a great interval (of time)"
ἐλθόντα: aor. part. acc. agreeing with object of ἀπέκλεισα, "I locked out him, *after having come*"
πεπομφώς: perf. part. nom., "Kallides was inside *after having sent along* 10 drachma""
λοιδορησάμενος: aor. part. nom., "he, *after having abused* me, left"
διῆλθον: aor., "many days *passed*"
οὐ προσέπεμπον: impf., "I wasn't sending for him"

58

δὲ ἔνδον ἦν, ὑποθερμαινόμενος ἤδη τότε ὁ Δημόφαντος
καὶ αὐτὸς ἀναφλέγεται ἐς τὸ πρᾶγμα καὶ ἐπιστάς ποτε
ἀνεῳγμένην τηρήσας τὴν θύραν ἔκλαεν, ἔτυπτεν, ἠπείλει
φονεύσειν, περιερρήγνυε τὴν ἐσθῆτα, ἅπαντα ἐποίει, καὶ
τέλος τάλαντον δοὺς μόνος εἶχεν ὀκτὼ ὅλους μῆνας. ἡ
γυνὴ δὲ αὐτοῦ πρὸς ἅπαντας ἔλεγεν ὡς ὑπὸ φαρμάκων
ἐκμήναιμι αὐτόν. τὸ δὲ ἦν ἄρα ζηλοτυπία τὸ φάρμακον. ὥστε, Χρυσί, καὶ σὺ χρῶ ἐπὶ τὸν Γοργίαν τῷ αὐτῷ
φαρμάκῳ· πλούσιος δὲ ὁ νεανίσκος ἔσται, ἤν τι ὁ πατὴρ
αὐτοῦ πάθῃ.

ἀναφλέγω: to light up, rekindle	ὀκτώ: eight
ἀνοίγνυμι: to open	περιρρήγνυμι: to rend, tear
ἀπειλέω: to threaten	πρᾶγμα, -ατος, τό: a deed, act
ἄρα: then	τάλαντον, τό: a talant
Γοργίας, ὁ: Gorgias	τέλος: finally
γυνή, ἡ: a woman, wife	τηρέω: to watch over, protect, guard
ἐκμαίνω: to drive mad	τύπτω: to beat, strike, smite
ἐσθής, -ῆτος, ἡ: dress, clothing	ὑποθερμαίνω: to heat a little
ἐφίστημι: to set or place upon	φάρμακον, τό: a drug, medicine
κλάω: to weep, lament, wail	φονεύω: to murder, kill, slay
μείς, μῆνος, ἡ: a month	χράομαι: to use (+ *dat.*)

ἐπιστάς: aor. part. intransitive of ἐπι-ίστημι, "having stationed himself"

ἀνεῳγμένην: perf. part. acc. in ind. st. after τηρήσας, "having observed that the door *had been opened*"

ἔκλαεν, ἔτυπτεν, etc.: impf. inceptives, "he began crying, striking, etc."

φονεύσειν: fut. inf. in ind. st., "threatening *that he would kill*"

δοὺς: aor. part., "he *having given* a talant"

ὑπὸ φαρμάκων: the agency expression, "I drove him mad *at the hands of drugs*"

μῆνας: acc. of duration, "for 8 months"

ὡς ... ἐκμήναιμι: aor. opt. in ind. st. in secondary sequence, "was saying *that I drove him mad*"

τὸ δὲ ... τὸ: emphatic repetition, "*and that* drug"

ζηλοτυπία: nom. pred. "that drug was *jealousy*"

χρῶ: pres. mid. imper., "you use!" + dat.

ἤν ... πάθῃ: aor. subj. of πάσχω in future more vivid protasis, "if his father suffers something"

9. Dorcas, Pannychis, Philostratus, and Polemo

The unexpected return of a rich soldier puts Pannychis in a difficult situation, since she has taken up with another client in his absence.

ΔΟΡΚΑΣ: Ἀπολώλαμεν, ὦ κεκτημένη, ἀπολώλαμεν, ὁ
Πολέμων ἀπὸ στρατιᾶς ἀνέστρεψε πλουτῶν, ὥς φασιν·
ἑώρακα δὲ κἀγὼ αὐτὸν ἐφεστρίδα περιπόρφυρον ἐμπεπορπημένον καὶ ἀκολούθους ἅμα πολλούς. καὶ οἱ φίλοι
ὡς εἶδον, συνέθεον ἐπ᾽ αὐτὸν ἀσπασόμενοι· ἐν τοσούτῳ
δὲ τὸν θεράποντα ἰδοῦσα κατόπιν ἑπόμενον, ὃς συναποδεδημήκει μετ᾽ αὐτοῦ, ἠρόμην καί, «Εἰπέ μοι,» ἔφην,
«ὦ Παρμένων,» ἀσπασαμένη πρότερον αὐτόν, «πῶς
ἡμῖν ἐπράξατε καὶ εἴ τι ἄξιον τῶν πολέμων ἔχοντες
ἐπανεληλύθατε.»

ἀκόλουθος, -ον: following, attending on	κατόπιν: (*adv.*) behind, after
ἀναστρέφω: to return	κτάομαι: to gain, acquire
ἄξιος, -ία, -ον: worthy of (+ *gen.*)	περιπόρφυρος, -ον: edged with purple
ἀπόλλυμι: to destroy utterly	πλουτέω: to be rich, wealthy
ἀσπάζομαι: to welcome kindly	πόλεμος, ὁ: battle, fight, war
ἐμπορπάω: to fasten with a brooch	πράττω: to do
ἐπανέρχομαι: to go back, return	πρότερον: prior
ἕπομαι: to follow	στρατιά, ἡ: army
ἐρωτάω: to ask, enquire	συναποδημέω: to be abroad together
ἐφεστρίς, -ίδος, ἡ: an upper garment	συνθέω: to run together with, flock to
θεράπων, -οντος, ὁ: an attendant	τοσοῦτος, -αύτη, -οῦτο: so large, so tall

---

ἀπολώλαμεν: perf. of ἀπόλλυμι with present meaning, "we are lost"

κεκτημένη: perf. part. mid., "O you *having acquired*" i.e. O mistress

πλουτῶν: pres. part. circumstantial, "he returned *being rich*"

ἑώρακα: perf. or ὁράω, "I have seen"

ἐμπεπορπημένον: perf. part., "having been fastened with a brooch" a sign of wealth

ἀσπασόμενοι: fut. part. expressing purpose, "they flocked to him *in order to greet him*"

συναποδεδημήκει: plupf. of συν-ἀπο-δημέω: "he had traveled abroad with"

ἠρόμην: aor., " I asked"

εἴ ... ἐπανεληλύθατε: perf. of ἐπι-ἀνα-έρχομαι in ind. quest. after εἰπέ, "tell me *whether you have returned* having anything"

ΠΑΝΝΥΧΙΣ: Οὐκ ἔδει τοῦτο εὐθύς, ἀλλ' ἐκεῖνα, «ὅτι μὲν ἐσώθητε, πολλὴ χάρις τοῖς θεοῖς, καὶ μάλιστα τῷ ξενίῳ Διὶ καὶ Ἀθηνᾷ στρατίᾳ· ἡ δέσποινα δὲ ἐπυνθάνετο ἀεὶ τί πράττοιτε καὶ ἔνθα εἴητε.» εἰ δὲ καὶ τοῦτο προσέθηκας, ὡς καὶ ἐδάκρυε καὶ ἀεὶ ἐμέμνητο Πολέμωνος, ἄμεινον ἦν παρὰ πολύ.

ΔΟΡΚΑΣ: Προεῖπον εὐθὺς ἐν ἀρχῇ ἅπαντα· πρὸς δὲ σὲ οὐκ ἂν εἶπον, ἀλλὰ ἃ ἤκουσα ἐβουλόμην εἰπεῖν. ἐπεὶ πρός γε Παρμένοντα οὕτως ἠρξάμην· «Ἦ που, ὦ Παρμένων, ἐβόμβει τὰ ὦτα ὑμῖν; ἀεὶ γὰρ ἐμέμνητο ἡ κεκτημένη μετὰ

ἀεί: always, for ever
ἀκούω: to hear
ἀμείνων, -ον: better
ἀρχή, ἡ: a beginning
ἄρχομαι: to begin
βομβέω: to hum
δέσποινα, ἡ: the mistress, lady of the house
εὐθύς, -εῖα, -ύ: straight
ἦ: in truth, surely

μιμνήσκομαι: to remember
ξένιος, -α, -ον: belonging to a guest
οὖς, ὠτός, τό: the ear
Παρμένων, ὁ: Parmenos
προεῖπον: to tell or state before (*aor.*)
προστίθημι: to put in addition, add
πυνθάνομαι: to learn by inquiry
στράτιος, -α, -ον: warlike
χάρις, ἡ: grace, thanks

οὐκ ἔδει: "this was not necessary" i.e. this you should not (have said)

ἀλλ' ἐκεῖνα: "but rather these things" introducing direct speech of what she should have said

ἐσώθητε: aor. pass. of σώζω in causal clause, "thanks *because you were saved*"

ξενίῳ Διὶ: dat.,"especially *to Zeus, protector of guests*" a traditional title of Zeus

Ἀθηνᾷ στρατίᾳ: dat., "and to Athena the warlike"

τί πράττοιτε: pres. opt. in ind. quest. after ἐπυνθάνετο, "was asking *what you were doing*"

ἔνθα εἴητε: pres. opt. also in ind. question, "asking *where you were*"

προσέθηκας: aor. in past contrafactual protasis, " if you had added"

ἐμέμνητο: plupf. with impf. sense, "that she was remembering" + gen.

ἄμεινον ἦν: contrafactual apodosis without ἄν, "it would have been better"

οὐκ ἂν εἶπον: aor. in past potential, "I wouldn't have said" i.e. I wouldn't have repeated that part to you

ἠρξάμην: aor., "I made a beginning"

ἦ που: expecting an affirmative answer, "*surely* your ears were burning?"

ἐμέμνητο: plupf. with imperfect force, "she (i.e. Pannychis) was remembering"

61

δακρύων, καὶ μάλιστα εἴ τις ἐληλύθει ἐκ τῆς μάχης καὶ πολλοὶ τεθνάναι ἐλέγοντο, ἐσπάραττε τότε τὰς κόμας καὶ τὰ στέρνα ἐτύπτετο καὶ ἐπένθει πρὸς τὴν ἀγγελίαν ἑκάστην.»

ΠΑΝΝΥΧΙΣ: Εὖ γε, ὦ Δορκάς, οὕτως ἐχρῆν.

ΔΟΡΚΑΣ: Εἶτα ἑξῆς μετ' οὐ πολὺ ἠρόμην ἐκεῖνα. ὁ δέ, «Πάνυ λαμπρῶς,» φησίν, «ἀνεστρέψαμεν.»

ΠΑΝΝΥΧΙΣ: Οὕτως κἀκεῖνος οὐδὲν προειπών, ὡς ἐμέμνητό μου ὁ Πολέμων ἢ ἐπόθει ἢ ηὔχετο ζῶσαν καταλαβεῖν;

ΔΟΡΚΑΣ: Καὶ μάλα πολλὰ τοιαῦτα ἔλεγε. τὸ δ' οὖν κεφάλαιον ἐξήγγειλε πλοῦτον πολύν, χρυσόν, ἐσθῆτα,

---

ἀγγελία, ἡ: a message, tidings, news
ἀναστρέφω: to upset, return
δάκρυον, τό: a tear
ἕκαστος, -η, -ον: each, each one
ἐξαγγέλλω: to proclaim
ἑξῆς: one after another
ἐρωτάω: to ask, enquire
εὔχομαι: to pray, make a vow
ζάω: to live
καταλαμβάνω: to lay hold of
κεφάλαιον, τό: the main thing
κόμη, ἡ: the hair of the head
λαμπρός, -ά, -όν: bright, brilliant, radiant

μάχη, ἡ: battle, combat
μιμνήσκομαι: to remember
πάνυ: very
πενθέω: to bewail, lament, mourn for
πλοῦτος, ὁ: wealth
ποθέω: to long for, yearn after
προεῖπον: to tell or state before (aor.)
σπαράττω: to tear, rend in pieces
στέρνον, τό: the breast, chest
τοιοῦτος, -αύτη, -οῦτο: such as this
τύπτω: to beat, strike, smite
χρή: it is necessary
χρυσός, ὁ: gold

εἴ τις ἐληλύθει: plupf. of ἔρχομαι, "especially *if anyone returned*"

τεθνάναι: perf. inf. of θνήσκω in ind. st. after ἐλέγοντο, "were said *to have died*"

ἐλέγοντο: pass. used personally, "if many *were said* to have died"

μετ' οὐ πολὺ: "after not much (time)" i.e. a little later

ἠρόμην: aor. of ἐρωτάω, "I asked"

ἐκεῖνα: "those (questions)" i.e. the ones already mentioned above

κἀκεῖνος (=καὶ ἐκεῖνος): "*and he*" (Polemon) was just so, having first said nothing?"

ὡς ἐμέμνητό: plupf. in ind. st. after προειπών, "having first said nothing about *how he remembered* me?"

ζῶσαν: pres. part. agreeing with the object of καταλαβεῖν, "come upon (me) *living*"

καταλαβεῖν: aor. inf. in ind. st. after ηὔχετο, "or how he was praying *to come upon* me?"

ἀκολούθους, ἐλέφαντα: τὸ μὲν γὰρ ἀργύριον μηδὲ
ἀριθμῷ ἄγειν αὐτόν, ἀλλὰ μεδίμνῳ ἀπομεμετρημένον
πολλοὺς μεδίμνους. εἶχε δὲ καὶ αὐτὸς Παρμένων
δακτύλιον ἐν τῷ μικρῷ δακτύλῳ, μέγιστον, πολύγωνον,
καὶ ψῆφος ἐνεβέβλητο τῶν τριχρώμων, ἐρυθρά τε ἦν
ἐπιπολῆς. εἴασα δ' οὖν αὐτὸν ἐθέλοντά μοι διηγεῖσθαι
ὡς τὸν Ἅλυν διέβησαν καὶ ὡς ἀπέκτειναν Τιριδάταν
τινὰ καὶ ὡς διέπρεψεν ὁ Πολέμων ἐν τῇ πρὸς Πισίδας
μάχῃ: ἀπέδραμόν σοι ταῦτα προσαγγελοῦσα, ὡς περὶ
τῶν παρόντων σκέψαιο. εἰ γὰρ ἐλθὼν ὁ Πολέμων —
ἥξει γὰρ πάντως ἀποσεισάμενος τοὺς γνωρίμους —

ἀκόλουθος, ὁ: follower, servant
Ἅλυς, ὁ: the Halys river in Anatolia
ἀποκτείνω: to kill, slay
ἀπομετρέω: to measure out
ἀποσείω: to shake off
ἀργύριον, τό: silver
ἀριθμός, ὁ: number
γνώριμος, -ον: well-known, familiar
δακτύλιον, τό: a ring
δάκτυλος, ὁ: a finger
διαβαίνω: to ford
διαπρέπω: to distinguish oneself
διηγέομαι: to set out in detail, describe in full
ἐάω: to allow (+ *inf.*)

ἐθέλω: to wish to (+ *inf.*)
ἐλέφας, -αντος, ὁ: ivory
ἐμβάλλω: to throw in, put in
ἐπιπολή, ἡ: a surface, top layer
ἐρυθρός, -ά, -όν: red
μέδιμνος, ὁ: the medimnus, a bushel
μικρός, -ά, -όν: small, little
πάντως: altogether
Πισιδες, οἱ: the Pisidians in Anatolia
πολύγωνος, -ον: many-sided
προσαγγέλλω: to announce
σκέπτομαι: to look about, look carefully
τρίχρωμος, -ον: three-colored
ψῆφος, ἡ: a small stone

ἀριθμῷ ... μεδίμνῳ: dat. instrumental, "measured not *by number* but *by the bushel*"
ἄγειν: pres. inf. in ind. st., "reported *that he was bringing*"
ἐνεβέβλητο: plupf. of ἐν-βάλλω, "a stone *had been placed into*"
εἴασα (sc. χαίρειν): aor. part., "I *having bid* him (farewell)"
ἐθέλοντα: pres. part. agreeing with αὐτὸν, "I left him *wishing* to tell"
ὡς ... διέβησαν: aor. in ind. st. after διηγεῖσθαι, "to tell *how they forded*"
ὡς ἀπέκτειναν: aor. in ind. st., "tell *how they had killed*"
ἀπέδραμόν: aor. of ἀπο-τρέχω, "I ran off"
προσαγγελοῦσα: fut. part. expressing purpose, "ran off *in order to report*"
ὡς ... σκέψαιο: aor. opt. in result clause, "so you might look carefully at" + gen.
εἰ ... εὕροι: aor. opt. in future less vivid protasis, "*if he were to find* Philostratus"
ἥξει: fut. of ἥκω, "he will come"
ἀποσεισάμενος: aor. part., "*once he has shaken off* his companions he will come"

ἀναπυθόμενος εὕροι τὸν Φιλόστρατον ἔνδον παρ' ἡμῖν, τί οἴει ποιήσειν αὐτόν;

ΠΑΝΝΥΧΙΣ: Ἐξευρίσκωμεν, ὦ Δορκάς, ἐκ τῶν παρόντων σωτήριον: οὔτε γὰρ τοῦτον ἀποπέμψαι καλὸν τάλαντον ἔναγχος δεδωκότα καὶ τἆλλα ἔμπορον ὄντα καὶ πολλὰ ὑπισχνούμενον, οὔτε Πολέμωνα τοιοῦτον ἐπανήκοντα χρήσιμον μὴ παραδέχεσθαι: προσέτι γὰρ καὶ ζηλότυπός ἐστιν, ὃς καὶ πενόμενος ἔτι πολὺ ἀφόρητος ἦν: νῦν δὲ τί ἐκεῖνος οὐκ ἂν ποιήσειεν;

ΔΟΡΚΑΣ: Ἀλλὰ καὶ προσέρχεται.

ἀναπυνθάνομαι: to inquire closely into
ἀποπέμπω: to send off or away, to dismiss
ἀφόρητος, -ον: intolerable, insufferable
ἔμπορος, ὁ: a merchant
ἔναγχος: (adv.) just now, lately
ἐξευρίσκω: to find out, discover
ἐπανήκω: to have come back, to return
εὑρίσκω: to find
ζηλότυπος, -ον: jealous

οἴομαι: to suppose, think, deem, imagine
παραδέχομαι: to receive from
πένομαι: to work for one's daily bread
ποιέω: to do
προσέρχομαι: to approach
προσέτι: (adv.) over and above, besides
σωτήριον, τό: deliverance
ὑπισχνέομαι: to promise or
χρήσιμος, -η, -ον: useful, serviceable

ἀναπυθόμενος: aor. part., "if he were to find *once he has enquired*"

ποιήσειν: fut. inf. in ind. st., "what do you suppose *he will do?*"

ἐξευρίσκωμεν: aor. subj. hortatory, "let's discover!"

ἀποπέμψαι: aor. inf. epexegetic after καλὸν, "it is not fair *to send away*"

δεδωκότα: perf. part. of δίδωμι agreeing with τοῦτον, "this one (Φιλόστρατος) *having just given*"

τἆλλα (= τὰ ἄλλα): acc. of respect, "also *in other matters*"

ὄντα ... ὑπισχνούμενον: pres. part. also agreeing with τοῦτον, "this one *being* a merchant ... *promising* many things"

ἐπανήκοντα: pres. part. of ἐπι-ανα-ήκω agreeing with Πολέμωνα, the object of παραδέχεσθαι, "to receive Polemon *having returned*"

μὴ παραδέχεσθαι: pres. inf. epexegetic after καλὸν, "nor is it fair *not to receive*"

πενόμενος: pres. part., "he is jealous *even while working*" i.e. when he was poor

οὐκ ἂν ποιήσειεν: aor. opt. potential, "what would he not do?"

ΠΑΝΝΥΧΙΣ: Ἐκλύομαι, ὦ Δορκάς, ἀπὸ τῆς ἀπορίας καὶ τρέμω.

ΔΟΡΚΑΣ: Ἀλλὰ καὶ Φιλόστρατος προσέρχεται.

ΠΑΝΝΥΧΙΣ: Τίς γένωμαι; πῶς ἄν με ἡ γῆ καταπίοι;

ΦΙΛΟΣΤΡΑΤΟΣ: Τί οὐ πίνομεν, ὦ Παννυχί;

ΠΑΝΝΥΧΙΣ: Ἄνθρωπε, ἀπολώλεκάς με. σὺ δὲ χαῖρε, Πολέμων, χρόνιος φανείς.

ΠΟΛΕΜΩΝ: Οὗτος οὖν τίς ἐστιν ὁ προσιὼν ὑμῖν; σιωπᾷς; εὖ γε· οἴχου, ὦ Παννυχί. ἐγὼ δὲ πεμπταῖος ἐκ Πυλῶν διέπτην ἐπειγόμενος ἐπὶ τοιαύτην γυναῖκα. καὶ δίκαια μέντοι πέπονθα, καίτοι χάριν ἔχων· οὐκέτι γὰρ ἁρπασθήσομαι ὑπὸ σοῦ.

ἀπορία, ἡ: difficulty	πάσχω: to suffer
ἁρπάζω: to snatch away, plunder	πεμπταῖος, -α, -ον: on the fifth day
γῆ, ἡ: earth	πίνω: to drink
διαπέτομαι: to fly, hasten	προσέρχομαι: to approach
δίκαιος, -η, -ον: just	Πύλαι, αἱ: the Gates
ἐκλύω: to loose, undo	σιωπάω: to be silent
ἐπείγω: to press on, be eager for	τρέμω: to tremble with fear
εὖ: well	φαίνομαι: to appear
καταπίνω: to gulp or swallow down	χαίρω: to rejoice, be glad, be delighted
μέντοι: nevertheless	χάρις, -ιτος, ἡ: grace, thanks
οἴχομαι: to be gone, to have gone	χρόνιος, -α, -ον: after a long time, late
οὐκέτι: no more, no longer	

τίς γένωμαι: aor. subj. in deliberative questions, "what will I become"

καταπίοι: aor. opt. with πῶς ἄν indicating a wish, with a tragic overtone, "would that the earth would swallow me!"

ἀπολώλεκας: perf. of ἀπόλλυμι, "you have destroyed me"

φανείς: aor. part. pass., "you, *having appeared*"

οἴχου: pres. imper., "be gone!"

ἐκ Πυλῶν: "from the (hot) Gates" i.e. Thermopylae

διέπτην: aor. pass. of δια-πέτομαι, "I flew" i.e. I rushed

πέπονθα: perf. of πάσχω, "I have suffered"

χάριν ἔχων: pres. part. concessive, "yet giving thanks" i.e. being grateful

ἁρπασθήσομαι: fut. pass., "no longer *will I be plundered*"

ΦΙΛΟΣΤΡΑΤΟΣ: Σὺ δὲ τίς εἶ, ὦ βέλτιστε;

ΠΟΛΕΜΩΝ: Ὅτι Πολέμων ὁ Στειριεὺς Πανδιονίδος φυλῆς, ἀκούεις: χιλιαρχήσας τὸ πρῶτον, νῦν δὲ ἐξαναστήσας πεντακισχιλίαν ἀσπίδα, ἐραστὴς Παννυχίδος, ὅτε ᾤμην ἔτι ἀνθρώπινα φρονεῖν αὐτήν.

ΦΙΛΟΣΤΡΑΤΟΣ: Ἀλλὰ τὰ νῦν σοι, ὦ ξεναγέ, Παννυχὶς ἐμή ἐστι, καὶ τάλαντον εἴληφε, λήψεται δὲ ἤδη καὶ ἕτερον, ἐπειδὰν τὰ φορτία διαθώμεθα. καὶ νῦν ἀκολούθει μοι, ὦ Παννυχί, τοῦτον δὲ παρ' Ὀδρύσαις χιλιαρχεῖν ἔα.

ΠΟΛΕΜΩΝ: Ἐλευθέρα μέν ἐστι καὶ ἀκολουθήσει, ἢν ἐθέλῃ.

ΠΑΝΝΥΧΙΣ: Τί ποιῶ, Δορκάς;

ἀκολουθέω: to follow
ἀνθρώπινος, -η, -ον: human, mortal
ἀσπίς, -ίδος, ἡ: a round shield
βέλτιστος, -η, -ον: best
διατίθημι: to arrange, dispose of
ἐάω: to allow (+ inf.)
ἐθέλω: to will, wish, purpose
ἐλεύθερος, -α, -ον: free
ἐξανίστημι: to raise up: to make one
ἐπειδάν: whenever
ἐραστής, -οῦ, ὁ: a lover

λαμβάνω: to take
ξεναγός, ὁ: a commander of mercenary troops
Ὀδρύσαι, -ων, οἱ: the Odrysians, a Thracian tribe
πεντακισχιλίος, -α, -ον: five-thousand fold
πρῶτος, -η, -ον: first
φορτίον, τό: a load, burden
φρονέω: to be minded, think
φυλή, ἡ: a race or tribe
χιλιαρχέω: to be a leader of 1000 men

ὅτι (sc. εἰμι): "you hear that (I am) Polemon"

ὁ Στειριεὺς: "of the Stirian deme"

Πανδιονίδος φυλῆς: "of the tribe of Pandion"

ἐξαναστήσας: aor. part. transitive of ἐξ-ανα-ίστημι, "having raised up" i.e. recruited

πεντακισχιλίαν ἀσπίδα: acc. sing., "raised up 5000 men-at-arms"

ἀνθρώπινα: neut. pl. acc., "that she thought mortal (thoughts)" i.e. as opposed to divine ones

τὰ νῦν: acc. adverbial, "for the present"

εἴληφε: perf. of λαμβάνω, "she has received"

λήψεται: fut., "she will take another"

διαθώμεθα: aor. subj. of δια-τίθημι in general temporal clause, "whenever we dispose of"

ἐθέλῃ: pres. subj. in future more vivid protasis, "if she wishes"

ποιῶ: pres. subj. in deliberative question, "What should I do?"

ΔΟΡΚΑΣ: Εἰσιέναι ἄμεινον, ὀργιζομένῳ οὐχ οἷόν τε παρεῖναι Πολέμωνι, καὶ μᾶλλον ἐπιταθήσεται ζηλοτυπῶν.

ΠΑΝΝΥΧΙΣ: Εἰ θέλεις, εἰσίωμεν.

ἀμείνων, -ον: better	μᾶλλον: more
εἰσέρχομαι: to go into	οἷός τε εἰμι: to be possible
ἐπιτείνω: to stretch upon, to torture	ὀργίζω: to make angry, irritate
ζηλοτυπέω: to be jealous of	πάρειμι: to be present

εἰσιέναι: pres. inf. epexegetic of εἰς-έρχομαι after ἄμεινον, "it is better *to go inside*"

οὐχ οἷόν τε (sc. ἐστι): "it is not possible to" + inf.

ἐπιταθήσεται: fut. pass. of ἐπιτείνω, "*he will be tortured* more"

ζηλοτυπῶν: pres. part. instrumental, "tortured *by being jealous*"

εἰσίωμεν: pres. subj. hortatory of εἰς-έρχομαι, "let's go in"

Circumstantial Participles

Circumstantial participles are added to a noun or a pronoun to set forth some circumstance under which an action takes place. The circumstances can be of the following types: time, manner, means, cause, purpose, concession, condition or attendant circumstance. Although sometimes particles can specify the type of circumstance, often only the context can clarify its force. Here are some examples:

Time: χιλιαρχήσας τὸ πρῶτον, νῦν δὲ ἐξαναστήσας πεντακισχιλίαν: "at first *having become a leader of 1000 men*, and now *having raised up 5000*"

Means: ἐπιταθήσεται ζηλοτυπῶν: "he will by tortured *by being jealous*"

Purpose: ἡκόντων ἐμφράξαντες τὸν στενωπὸν: "may they come *in order to block up* the narrow part"

Concession: δίκαια μέντοι πέπονθα, καίτοι χάριν ἔχων; "indeed I have suffered just things, *yet giving thanks*"

Cause: ἠνέσχετο οὐ βουληθεὶς τὴν πλουσίαν ἐκείνην γῆμαι. "he was ashamed *because he did not wish* to marry that rich girl"

Condition: ἐλυπούμην γὰρ σὲ μὴ ἔχουσα. "for I was grieving *if not having* you"
* Note that μὴ is used instead of οὐ when the participle is conditional.

Attendant Circumstance: ἀνέχωμαι διὰ τοῦτο ὑβριζομένη ὑπ' αὐτοῦ: "should I endure this *while being abused* by him?"

The circumstantial participle can also stand in the genitive absolute construction:

καίτοι ἔναγχος ἀποθανόντος αὐτῷ τοῦ πατρὸς. "although his father *having died* just now"

ΠΟΛΕΜΩΝ: Ἀλλὰ προλέγω ὑμῖν ὅτι τὸ ὕστατον πίε-
σθε τήμερον, ἢ μάτην ἐγὼ τοσούτοις φόνοις ἐγγεγυμνασμένος πάρειμι. τοὺς Θρᾷκας, ὦ Παρμένων·
ὡπλισμένοι ἡκόντων ἐμφράξαντες τὸν στενωπὸν τῇ
φάλαγγι· ἐπὶ μετώπου μὲν τὸ ὁπλιτικόν, παρ' ἑκάτερα
δὲ οἱ σφενδονῆται καὶ τοξόται, οἱ δὲ ἄλλοι κατόπιν.

ΦΙΛΟΣΤΡΑΤΟΣ: Ὡς βρεφυλλίοις ταῦτα, ὦ μισθοφόρε,
ἡμῖν λέγεις καὶ μορμολύττῃ. σὺ γὰρ ἀλεκτρυόνα πώποτε
ἀπέκτεινας ἢ πόλεμον εἶδες; ἐρυμάτιον ἐφρούρεις τάχα
διμοιρίτης ὤν, ἵνα καὶ τοῦτο προσχαρίσωμαί σοι.

ἀλεκτρυών, -ονος, ὁ: a cock
ἀποκτείνω: to kill, slay
βρεφύλλιον, τό: a little baby
διμοιρίτης, ὁ: one who receives double pay
ἐγγυμνάζω: to train, exercise
ἑκάτερος, -α, -ον: each of two
ἐμφράττω: to block up
ἐρυμάτιον, τό: a little fence
Θρᾷξ, -κος, ὁ: a Thracian
κατόπιν: behind, after
μάτην: in vain
μέτωπον, -ἡ, τό: the forehead, front
μισθοφόρος, ὁ: a mercenary
μορμολύττομαι: to frighten, scare
ὁπλίζω: to make ready, arm

ὁπλιτικός, -ή, -όν: of a man-at-arms
πόλεμος, ὁ: battle, fight, war
προλέγω: to proclaim
προσχαρίζομαι: to stretch a point in one's favor
πώποτε: ever yet
στενωπός, -ὁ: a narrow place, strait
σφενδονήτης, -ου, ὁ: a slinger
τάχα: probably, perhaps
τήμερον: to-day
τοξότης, -ου, ὁ: a bowman, archer
τοσοῦτος, -αύτη, -οῦτο: so large, so tall
ὕστατος, -η, -ον: last
φάλαγξ, -αγγος, ἡ: a line of battle
φόνος, ὁ: murder, slaughter
φρουρέω: to keep watch or guard

τὸ ὕστατον: acc. adverbial, "you will drink *for the last time*"

φόνοις: dat. of means, "trained with such great *slaughters*"

ἐγγεγυμνασμένος: perf. part. used periphrastically with πάρειμι, "I have trained"

ὡπλισμένοι: perf. part. mid., "they (the Thracians) *having armed themselves*"

ἡκόντων: 3 pl. imper., "may they come!"

ἐμφράξαντες: aor. part. indicating purpose, "come *in order to block up*"

ἐπὶ μετώπου: "in the front line"

παρ' ἑκάτερα: "on each (of the two sides)" i.e. the flanks

ὡς βρεφυλλίοις: dat. agreeing with ἡμῖν, "as though we were babies"

ἀπέκτεινας: aor., "did you ever kill?"

εἶδες: aor., "did you see?"

καὶ τοῦτο: acc. of respect, "to stretch a point *even in this*"

προσχαρίσωμαι: aor. subj. in purpose clause, "in order to stretch a point in your favor " i.e. to give the benefit of the doubt

ΠΟΛΕΜΩΝ: Καὶ μὴν εἴσῃ μετ' ὀλίγον, ἐπειδὰν προσιόντας ἡμᾶς ἐπὶ δόρυ θεάσῃ στίλβοντας τοῖς ὅπλοις.

ΦΙΛΟΣΤΡΑΤΟΣ: Ἥκετε μόνον συσκευασάμενοι. ἐγὼ δὲ καὶ Τίβειος οὗτος — μόνος γὰρ οὗτος ἔπεταί μοι — βάλλοντες ὑμᾶς λίθοις τε καὶ ὀστράκοις οὕτω διασκεδάσομεν, ὡς μηδὲ ὅποι οἴχεσθε ἔχοιτε εἰδέναι.

βάλλω: to throw	οἴχομαι: to be gone, to have gone
διασκεδάζω: disperse	ὀλίγος, -η, -ον: few, little
δόρυ, τό: a spear	ὅπλον, τό: a weapon
ἐπειδάν: whenever (+ *subj.*)	ὄστρακον, τό: a potsherd
ἕπομαι: to follow (+ *dat.*)	προσέρχομαι: to approach, attack
θεάομαι: to view, behold	στίλβω: to glisten
λίθος, ὁ: a stone	συσκευάζω: to make ready by putting
μόνος, -η, -ον: alone, only	together

καὶ μὴν: "*and yet you will know*" responding to the previous statement

εἴσῃ: fut. of **οἶδα**, "you will know"

προσιόντας ... στίλβοντας: pres. part. circum. agreeing with ἡμᾶς, "see us *attacking ... glistening*"

θεάσῃ: aor., subj. in general temporal clause, "when (ever) *you see*"

ἐπὶ δόρυ: "against the spear side" i.e. against the right flank, the hand in which the spear was held

συσκευασάμενοι: perf. part. mid., "come *having prepared yourselves*"

βάλλοντες: pres. part. instrumental, "we will disperse you *by striking*"

οὕτω ... ὡς: correlatives, "we will disperse you *in such a way ... so that*"

ὡς μηδὲ ... ἔχοιτε: pres. opt. pot. in result clause, "so that you wouldn't be able" + inf.

ὅποι οἴχεσθε: pres. in vivid ind. quest., "know *whither you go*"

Purpose Clauses

Purpose clauses take the subjunctive with ἄν or the optative depending on the sequence of tenses:

> μὴ ἀποκρύψῃ με, ὡς ἂν καὶ τοῦτο ἀπολαύσω: "don't hide it from me, *so that I can enjoy it too*"

> προσέπαιζες ὡς λυποίης ἐμέ: you were flirting *in order to annoy* me.

The future participle is also regularly used to express purpose:

> νῦν δ' ἄπιθι λουσομένῃ: "now go away *in order to bathe*"

After verbs involving motion, the infinitive can express purpose:

> παρέδωκέ με φιλοσοφεῖν αὐτῷ: "he handed me over to him *in order to philosophize* me"

10. Chelidonium and Doris

The courtesan Doris finds that her lover Clinias has been put under the care of a philosopher, who refuses to allow him carnal pleasures. Doris' friend Cheldonium plans to help by charging the philosopher with corrupting the youth.

ΧΕΛΙΔΟΝΙΟΝ: Οὐκέτι φοιτᾷ παρὰ σέ, ὦ Δροσί, τὸ μειράκιον ὁ Κλεινίας; οὐ γὰρ ἑώρακα, πολὺς ἤδη χρόνος, αὐτὸν παρ᾽ ὑμῖν.

ΔΡΟΣΙΣ: Οὐκέτι, ὦ Χελιδόνιον· ὁ γὰρ διδάσκαλος αὐτὸν εἶρξε μηκέτι μοι προσιέναι.

ΧΕΛΙΔΟΝΙΟΝ: Τίς οὗτος; μή τι τὸν παιδοτρίβην Διότιμον λέγεις; ἐπεὶ ἐκεῖνός γε φίλος ἐστίν.

ΔΡΟΣΙΣ: Οὔκ, ἀλλ᾽ ὁ κάκιστα φιλοσόφων ἀπολούμενος Ἀρισταίνετος.

ἀπόλλυμι: to destroy utterly
Ἀρισταίνετος, ὁ: Aristainetos, a philosopher
διδάσκαλος, ὁ: a teacher, master
ἔργω: to shut out, prevent
κακός, -ή, -όν: bad
μειράκιον, τό: a boy, lad
μηκέτι: no more

ὁράω: to see
οὐκέτι: no more, no longer, no further
παιδοτρίβης, -ου, ὁ: a gymnastic master
φίλος, -η, -ον: loved, beloved, dear
φιλόσοφος, ὁ: a philosopher
φοιτάω: to go to and fro
χρόνος, ὁ: time

ἑώρακα: perf., "for I have not seen"
πολὺς χρόνος: a parenthesis instead of an acc. of time, "the time has been long"
εἶρξε: aor., "his teacher *prevented* him *from*" + inf.
προσιέναι: pres. inf. of προσ-έρχομαι after εἶρξε, "prevented him from *visiting anymore*" the negative μηκέτι is emphatic
μή τι ... λέγεις: expecting a negative answer, "surely you don't mean?"
ὁ κάκιστα: an adverb used attributively, "*that most cursed* of philosophers"
ἀπολούμενος: fut. part. of ἀπόλλυμι expressing purpose, "who intends to destroy"

70

ΧΕΛΙΔΟΝΙΟΝ: Τὸν σκυθρωπὸν λέγεις, τὸν δασύν, τὸν βαθυπώγωνα, ὃς εἴωθε μετὰ τῶν μειρακίων περιπατεῖν ἐν τῇ Ποικίλῃ;

ΔΡΟΣΙΣ: Ἐκεῖνόν φημι τὸν ἀλαζόνα, ὃν κάκιστα ἐπίδοιμι ἀπολούμενον, ἑλκόμενον τοῦ πώγωνος ὑπὸ δημίου.

ΧΕΛΙΔΟΝΙΟΝ: Τί παθὼν δὲ ἐκεῖνος τοιαῦτα ἔπεισε τὸν Κλεινίαν;

ΔΡΟΣΙΣ: Οὐκ οἶδα, ὦ Χελιδόνιον. ἀλλ’ ὁ μηδέποτε ἀπόκοιτός μου γενόμενος ἀφ’ οὗ γυναικὶ ὁμιλεῖν ἤρξατο — πρῶτον δὲ ὡμίλησέ μοι — τριῶν τούτων ἑξῆς ἡμερῶν οὐδὲ προσῆλθε τῷ στενωπῷ· ἐπεὶ δὲ ἠνιώμην — οὐκ οἶδα δὲ

ἀλαζών, -όνος, ὁ: a vagabond
ἀνιάω: to grieve, distress
ἀπόκοιτος, -ον: sleeping apart from
ἄρχομαι: to begin to (+ *inf.*)
βαθυπώγων, -ον: "with thick beard"
γυνή, γυναικός, ἡ: a woman
δασύς, -εῖα, -ύ: hairy, shaggy
δήμιος, ὁ: a public executioner
ἔθω: to be accustomed to (+ *inf.*)
ἕλκω: to draw, drag
ἑξῆς: one after another
ἐπεῖδον: to look upon, behold

ἡμέρα, ἡ: a day
κακός, -ή, -όν: bad
ὁμιλέω: to consort with (+ *dat.*)
πάσχω: to suffer
πείθω: to persuade
περιπατέω: to walk about
προσέρχομαι: to approach (+ *dat.*)
πώγων, -ωνος, ὁ: a beard
σκυθρωπός, -ή, -όν: sullen
στενωπός, ὁ: narrow street
τοιοῦτος, -αύτη, -οῦτο: such as this
τρεῖς, τρία: three

εἴωθε: perf. of ἔθω with present force, "who is accustomed to" + inf.

ἐν τῇ Ποικίλῃ (sc. στοᾷ): "in the Painted Stoa" of the agora, which gave its name to the philosophical school "Stoicism" by metonymy

ἐπίδοιμι: aor. opt. pot. of ἐπι-εῖδον, "I would like to behold"

ἀπολούμενον: fut. part. circum., "behold him *being destroyed*"

τοῦ πώγωνος: gen. after ἑλκόμενον, "being dragged *from the beard*" i.e. by the beard

παθὼν: aor. part. of πάσχω, "*having suffered* what?" i.e. why?

ὁ ... γενόμενος: aor. part. attributive, "the one who had been"

μου: gen. sep. after ἀπόκοιτός, "sleeping apart *from me*"

ἀφ’ οὗ (sc. χρόνου): "from the time"

τριῶν ... ἡμερῶν: gen. of time within which, "in the course of three days"

ἠνιώμην: impf., "because *I was upset*"

ὅπως τι ἔπαθον ἐπ' αὐτῷ—ἔπεμψα τὴν Νεβρίδα περισκεψομένην αὐτὸν ἢ ἐν ἀγορᾷ διατρίβοντα ἢ ἐν Ποικίλῃ:
ἡ δὲ περιπατοῦντα ἔφη ἰδοῦσα μετὰ τοῦ Ἀρισταινέτου
νεῦσαι πόρρω, ἐκεῖνον δὲ ἐρυθριάσαντα κάτω ὁρᾶν καὶ
μηκέτι παρενεγκεῖν τὸν ὀφθαλμόν. εἶτ' ἐβάδιζον ἅμα ἐς
τὴν Ἀκαδημίαν: ἡ δὲ ἄχρι τοῦ Διπύλου ἀκολουθήσασα, ἐπεὶ μηδ' ὅλως ἐπεστράφη, ἐπανῆκεν οὐδὲν σαφὲς

ἀγορά, -ᾶς, ἡ: the market
Ἀκαδήμεια: the Academy
ἀκολουθέω: to follow
ἄχρι: up to (+ gen.)
βαδίζω: to go slowly, to walk
διατρίβω: to spend time
δίπυλος, -ον: double-gated
ἐπανήκω: to have come back, to return
ἐπιστρέφω: to turn about, turn round
ἐρυθριάω: to blush

κάτω: down, downwards
Νεβρίς, -ίδος, ἡ: Nebris, a servant
νεύω: to nod or beckon
ὅλος, -η, -ον: whole, entire
ὀφθαλμός, ὁ: the eye
παραφέρω: to bring towards
πέμπω: to send, despatch
περισκοπέω: to examine, spy on
πόρρω: forwards, onwards, further
σαφής, -ές: clear, plain

οὐκ οἶδα δὲ ὅπως: parenthetical, "I don't know how" i.e. "somehow"

τι ἔπαθον: aor., "*I felt something* for him"

περισκεψομένην: fut. part. acc. expressing purpose, "I sent Nebris *in order to examine*"

διατρίβοντα: pres. part. circum. acc. agreeing with αὐτὸν, "to examine him *passing time*"

ἐν Ποικίλῃ (sc. στόᾳ): "in the Painted Stoa, at the edge of the *agora*"

ἰδοῦσα: aor. part. circum. nom., "she said that, she *having seen* him"

περιπατοῦντα: pres. part. circum., "having seen him *walking around*"

νεῦσαι: aor. inf. in ind. st. after ἔφη, "she said *that she nodded*" i.e. gestured to get his attention

ἐρυθριάσαντα: aor. part. circum. acc. agreeing with ἐκεῖνον, "but that that one, *having blushed*"

ὁρᾶν: pres. inf. also in ind. st. after ἔφη, "but *that he looked* down"

παρενεγκεῖν: aor. inf. of παρα-φέρω also in ind. st. after ἔφη, "*that he no longer brought* his eye *toward*"

Ἀκαδημίαν: an area, like the painted stoa, frequented by philosophers

ἡ δὲ: "but she" i.e. Nebris the servant

τοῦ Διπύλου: one of the city gates of Athens

ἀκολουθήσασα: aor. part. circum., "she, *having followed*"

ἐπεὶ ... ἐπεστράφη: aor. pass. of ἐπι-στρέφω, "when he didn't *turn back*"

ἐπανῆκεν: from ἐπι-ανα-ήκω, "she (Nebris) returned"

ἀπαγγεῖλαι ἔχουσα. πῶς με οἴει διάγειν τὸ μετὰ ταῦτα
οὐκ ἔχουσαν εἰκάσαι ὅ τι μοι πέπονθεν ὁ μειρακίσκος;
ἀλλὰ μὴ ἐλύπησά τι αὐτόν, ἔλεγον, ἤ τινος ἄλλης
ἠράσθη μισήσας ἐμέ; ἀλλ' ὁ πατὴρ διεκώλυσεν αὐτόν;
πολλὰ τοιαῦτα ἡ ἀθλία ἔστρεφον. ἤδη δὲ περὶ δείλην
ὀψίαν ἧκέ μοι Δρόμων τὸ γραμμάτιον τουτὶ παρ' αὐτοῦ
κομίζων. ἀνάγνωθι λαβοῦσα, ὦ Χελιδόνιον: οἶσθα γὰρ
δή που γράμματα.

ἄθλιος, -α, -ον: miserable	**ἔραμαι**: to be in love with
ἀναγιγνώσκω: to read	**ἥκω**: to have come, be present, be here
ἀπαγγέλλω: to report	**κομίζω**: to conduct, convey
γράμμα, -ατος, τό: that which is written or drawn	**λυπέω**: to grieve, annoy
γραμμάτιον, τό: a written epistle	**μειρακίσκος, ὁ**: a lad, stripling
δείλη, ἡ: afternoon	**μισέω**: to hate
διάγω: to carry on, to live	**οἴομαι**: to suppose, think
διακωλύω: to hinder, prevent	**ὄψιος, -α, -ον**: late
εἰκάζω: to liken, conjecture	**πῶς**: how? in what way or manner?
	στρέφω: to turn about or aside, turn

ἀπαγγεῖλαι: aor. inf. complementing **ἔχουσα**, "she, being able *to report*"

με ... διάγειν: pres. inf. in ind. st. after **οἴει**, "how do you suppose *that I carry on?*" i.e. continue living

τὸ μετὰ ταῦτα: an attributive phrase serving as the object of **διάγειν**, "the (time) after these things" i.e. since then

ἔχουσαν: pres. part. circum. agreeing with **με**, "me not *being able to*" + inf.

πέπονθεν: perf. of **πάσχω**, "to conjecture what *he has suffered*" i.e. what happened to him

ἐλύπησα: aor. in a doubtful assertion with **μὴ**, "but (perhaps) *I grieved* him?" i.e. "I didn't grieve him, did I?"

ἠράσθη: aor. pass., also doubtful assertion, "he (perhaps) had become enamoured with?" + gen.

μισήσας: aor. part. inceptive, "he *having begun to hate*"

ἡ ἀθλία: an attributive phrase, "I *the miserable one*"

ἔστρεφον: impf., "*I was turning over* (in my mind) such things"

ἀνάγνωθι: aor. imper., "read!"

λαβοῦσα: aor. part. of **λαμβάνω**, "you, having taken it" i.e. take and read

δή που: combining exactness and doubt, "for *presumably* you know"

ΧΕΛΙΔΟΝΙΟΝ: Φέρ' ἴδωμεν· τὰ γράμματα οὐ πάνυ σαφῆ, ἀλλὰ ἐπισεσυρμένα δηλοῦντα ἔπειξίν τινα τοῦ γεγραφότος. λέγει δέ «πῶς μὲν ἐφίλησά σε, ὦ Δροσί, τοὺς θεοὺς ποιοῦμαι μάρτυρας.»

ΔΡΟΣΙΣ: Αἰαῖ τάλαν, οὐδὲ τὸ χαίρειν προσέγραψε.

ΧΕΛΙΔΟΝΙΟΝ: «Καὶ νῦν δὲ οὐ κατὰ μῖσος, ἀλλὰ κατ' ἀνάγκην ἀφίσταμαί σου· ὁ πατὴρ γὰρ Ἀρισταινέτῳ παρέδωκέ με φιλοσοφεῖν αὐτῷ, κἀκεῖνος — ἔμαθε γὰρ

αἰαῖ: ah!
ἀνάγκη, ἡ: constraint, necessity
ἀφίστημι: to remove
γράφω: to write
δηλόω: to show, exhibit
ἔπειξις, -εως, ἡ: haste
ἐπισύρω: to drag after, to write carelessly
μανθάνω: to learn
μῖσος, -εος, τό: hate, hatred

πάνυ: altogether, entirely
παραδίδωμι: to hand over X (acc.) to Y (dat.)
προσγράφω: to add in writing
σαφής, -ές: clear, plain
τάλας, -αινα, -αν: suffering, wretched
φιλέω: to love
φιλοσοφέω: to philosophize
χαίρω: to rejoice, to be well

ἴδωμεν: aor. subj. hortatory, "come on, *let me see!*"

ἐπισεσυρμένα: perf. part. nom. pl. agreeing with **γράμματα**, "the letters are *written carelessly*"

δηλοῦντα: pres. part. also agreeing with **γράμματα**, "*indicating* haste"

τοῦ γεγραφότος: perf. part. gen., "haste *of the one who wrote*"

μάρτυρας: acc. pred. "I make the gods *witnesses*"

τὸ χαίρειν: articular inf., "he didn't write *the greeting*"

ἀφίσταμαι: pres. mid. of **ἀπο-ἵστημι**, "I remove myself from" + gen.

παρέδωκε: aor., "my father *has handed over to*" + dat.

φιλοσοφεῖν: inf. of purpose after **παρέδωκε**, "handed over *in order to philosophize*"

ἔμαθε: aor. of **μανθάνω**, "and that one (Aristaenetos) *learned* everything"

Subjunctive in Main Clauses

1. The **hortatory subjunctive** is used in sentences that urge a course of action.

    Φέρ' ἴδωμεν: "Come, let me see!"

    Εὖ γε, ὦ Μυρτάλη, λογισώμεθα: "Ok Myrtalis, let's calculate!"

2. The subjunctive is used in **deliberative questions**, where someone ponders a course of action.

    τί μὴ λέγω; "Why should I not speak?"

τὰ καθ' ἡμᾶς ἅπαντα — πάνυ πολλὰ ἐπετίμησέ μοι
ἀπρεπὲς εἶναι λέγων ἑταίρᾳ συνεῖναι Ἀρχιτέλους καὶ
Ἐρασικλείας υἱὸν ὄντα: πολὺ γὰρ ἄμεινον εἶναι τὴν
ἀρετὴν προτιμᾶν τῆς ἡδονῆς.»

ΔΡΟΣΙΣ: Μὴ ὥρασιν ἵκοιτο ὁ λῆρος ἐκεῖνος τοιαῦτα παι-
δεύων τὸ μειράκιον.

ΧΕΛΙΔΟΝΙΟΝ: «Ὥστε ἀνάγκη πείθεσθαι αὐτῷ: παρα-
κολουθεῖ γὰρ ἀκριβῶς παραφυλάσσων, καὶ ὅλως οὐδὲ
προσβλέπειν ἄλλῳ οὐδενὶ ἔξεστιν ὅτι μὴ ἐκείνῳ: εἰ δὲ
σωφρονοῖμι καὶ πάντα πεισθείην αὐτῷ, ὑπισχνεῖται

ἀκριβής, -ές: exact, careful
ἀμείνων, -ον: better
ἀνάγκη, ἡ: constraint, necessity
ἀπρεπής, -ές: unseemly, indecent
ἀρετή, ἡ: virtue, excellence
ἔξεστι: it is possible (+ *inf.*)
ἐπιτιμάω: to lay a value upon, censure (+ *dat.*)
ἑταίρα, ἡ: a courtesan
ἡδονή, ἡ: pleasure
ἱκνέομαι: to come

λῆρος, ὁ: silly talk, a silly talker
παιδεύω: to teach X (*acc.*) Y (*acc.*)
παρακολουθέω: to follow closely
παραφυλάσσω: to guard closely
πείθομαι: to obey (+ *dat.*)
προσβλέπω: to look at or upon (+ *dat.*)
προτιμάω: to esteem X (*acc.*) before Y (*gen.*)
σύνειμι: to be together with, consort with
σωφρονέω: to be sound of mind
ὑπισχνέομαι: to promise or engage
ὥρασι: (*adv.*) in good time

πάνυ πολλὰ: adverbial, "he censured me *very much*"

ἀπρεπὲς: nom. pred. "saying that it was *indecent*"

συνεῖναι: pres. inf. epexegetic after ἀπρεπὲς, "indecent *to consort with*" + dat.

ὄντα: pres. part. acc. causal agreeing with the acc. subject of συνεῖναι, "*since I am* the son"

εἶναι: continuing ind. st. after λέγων, "saying *that it is* better"

προτιμᾶν: pres. inf. epexegetic after ἄμεινον, "better *to esteem*"

μὴ ... ἵκοιτο: aor. opt. in wish for the future, "*may he not come* in good season!" i.e. bad luck to him!

πείθεσθαι: pres. inf. mid., after ἀνάγκη, "it is necessary *to obey*"

οὐδὲ ... ἄλλῳ οὐδενὶ: the double negative is emphatic, "nor to look on any other"

ὅτι μὴ ἐκείνῳ: "except on that one" i.e. Aristaenetos

σωφρονοῖμι: pres. opt. in present general protasis, "if I am sound of mind"

πάντα: acc. of respect, "obey *in all things*"

πεισθείην: aor. opt. pass. with middle sense in present general protasis, "if I obey"

πάνυ εὐδαίμονα ἔσεσθαί με καὶ ἐνάρετον καταστήσεσθαι
τοῖς πόνοις προγεγυμνασμένον. ταῦτά σοι μόλις ἔγραψα ὑποκλέψας ἐμαυτόν. σὺ δέ μοι εὐτύχει καὶ μέμνησο
Κλεινίου.»

ΔΡΟΣΙΣ: Τί σοι δοκεῖ ἡ ἐπιστολή, ὦ Χελιδόνιον;

ΧΕΛΙΔΟΝΙΟΝ: Τὰ μὲν ἄλλα ἡ ἀπὸ Σκυθῶν ῥῆσις, τὸ δὲ
«μέμνησο Κλεινίου» ἔχει τινὰ ὑπόλοιπον ἐλπίδα.

ΔΡΟΣΙΣ: Κἀμοὶ οὕτως ἔδοξεν: ἀπόλλυμαι δ' οὖν ὑπὸ
τοῦ ἔρωτος. ὁ μέντοι Δρόμων ἔφασκε παιδεραστὴν
τινα εἶναι τὸν Ἀρισταίνετον καὶ ἐπὶ προφάσει τῶν
μαθημάτων συνεῖναι τοῖς ὡραιοτάτοις τῶν νέων καὶ

ἀπόλλυμαι: to be destroyed
γράφω: to write
ἐλπίς, -ίδος, ἡ: hope
ἐνάρετος, -ον: virtuous
ἐπιστολή, ἡ: a message
εὐδαίμων, -ον: blessed, happy
εὐτυχέω: to be well off
καθίσταμαι: to be made, to become
μάθημα, -ατος, τό: a lesson, teaching
μιμνήσκομαι: to remember (+ gen.)
μόλις: scarcely

νέος, ὁ: youth
παιδεραστής, -οῦ, ὁ: a lover of boys
πόνος, ὁ: work
προγυμνάζω: to exercise beforehand
πρόφασις, -εως, ἡ: a pretext
ῥῆσις, -εως, ἡ: a saying, speaking,
Σκύθης, -ου: a Scythian
ὑποκλέπτω: to steal away
ὑπόλοιπος, -ον: left over
ὡραῖος, -α, -ον: produced at the right season, ripe

ἔσεσθαι: fut. inf. complementing ὑπισχνεῖται, "he promises *that I will be*"
καταστήσεσθαι: fut. mid. inf. also complementing ὑπισχνεῖται, "promises *that I will become*"
προγεγυμνασμένον: perf. part. instrumental, "become *by having been exercised*"
ὑποκλέψας: aor. part. circum., "having stolen myself away" i.e. in secret
εὐτύχει: imper., "be well!"
μέμνησο: perf. mid. imper., "remember!" + gen.
τὰ μὲν ἄλλα ... τὸ δὲ: "as for the rest ... but the (last phrase)"
ἀπὸ Σκυθῶν: "from Scythians" i.e. barbarous
κἀμοὶ (=καὶ ἐμοί): "*also to me* it seems"
ὑπὸ τοῦ ἔρωτος: the agency expression, "destroyed *by love*"
παιδεραστήν τινα: acc. pred. in ind. st., "claimed that Aristaineos is *a pederast*"
εἶναι ... συνεῖναι ... λογοποιεῖσθαι: pres. inf. in ind. st. after ἔφασκε, "claimed *that he is ... that he consorts with ... that he invents*"

ἰδίᾳ λογοποιεῖσθαι πρὸς τὸν Κλεινίαν ὑποσχέσεις τινὰς
ὑπισχνούμενον ὡς ἰσόθεον ἀποφανεῖ αὐτόν. ἀλλὰ καὶ
ἀναγιγνώσκει μετ' αὐτοῦ ἐρωτικούς τινας λόγους τῶν
παλαιῶν φιλοσόφων πρὸς τοὺς μαθητάς, καὶ ὅλος περὶ
τὸ μειράκιόν ἐστιν. ἠπείλει δὲ καὶ τῷ πατρὶ τοῦ Κλεινίου
κατερεῖν ταῦτα.

ΧΕΛΙΔΟΝΙΟΝ: Ἐχρῆν, ὦ Δροσί, γαστρίσαι τὸν Δρόμωνα.

ΔΡΟΣΙΣ: Ἐγάστρισα, καὶ ἄνευ δὲ τούτου ἐμός ἐστι: κέκνισται γὰρ κἀκεῖνος τῆς Νεβρίδος.

ΧΕΛΙΔΟΝΙΟΝ: Θάρρει, πάντα ἔσται καλῶς. ἐγὼ δὲ καὶ
ἐπιγράψειν μοι δοκῶ ἐπὶ τοῦ τοίχου ἐν Κεραμεικῷ, ἔνθα

ἄνευ: without (+ *gen.*)
ἀπειλέω: to threaten to (+ *inf.*)
ἀποφαίνω: to show forth, display, produce
γαστρίζω: to stuff
ἐμός, -ή, -όν: mine
ἔνθα: in the place where
ἐπιγράφω: to write
ἐρωτικός, -ή, -όν: amatory
θαρρέω: to be of good courage
ἰδίᾳ: "in private"
ἰσόθεος, -ον: equal to the gods, godlike
κατερέω: to speak against, accuse

κνίζω: to provoke, tickle
λογοποιέω: to invent stories
μαθητής, -οῦ, ὁ: a learner, pupil
μειράκιον, τό: a boy, lad, stripling
μέντοι: nevertheless, yet
παλαιός, -ά, -όν: old in years
πατήρ, πατρός, ὁ: a father
τοῖχος, ὁ: the wall
ὑπόσχεσις, -εως, ἡ: a promise
φιλόσοφος, ὁ: a lover of wisdom
χρή: it is necessary

ὑποσχέσεις: cognate acc. with ὑπισχνούμενον, "promising *promises*"

ὑπισχνούμενον: pres. part. circum. agreeing with Ἀρισταίνετον, "making promises"

ὡς ... ἀποφανεῖ: fut. in ind. st. after ὑπισχνούμενον, "promising *that he will make him*"

ὅλος: "he is *all* about the lad" i.e. he is totally into him

ἠπείλει δὲ: "but he (Dromon) was threatening"

γαστρίσαι: aor. inf. after ἐχρῆν, "we should *stuff* Dromon" i.e. reward him with food

ἐμός: nom. pred., "he is *mine*"

κέκνισται: perf., "he is tickled with" + gen.

ἐν Κεραμεικῷ: "in the Keramikos" the potter's quarter in Athens which was a public cemetery

ὁ Ἀρχιτέλης εἴωθε περιπατεῖν, «Ἀρισταίνετος διαφθείρει Κλεινίαν,» ὥστε καὶ ἐκ τούτου συνδραμεῖν τῇ παρὰ τοῦ Δρόμωνος διαβολῇ.

ΔΡΟΣΙΣ: Πῶς δ᾽ ἂν λάθοις ἐπιγράψασα;

ΧΕΛΙΔΟΝΙΟΝ: Τῆς νυκτός, Δροσί, ἄνθρακά ποθεν λαβοῦσα.

ΔΡΟΣΙΣ: Εὖ γε, συστράτευε μόνον, ὦ Χελιδόνιον, κατὰ τοῦ ἀλαζόνος Ἀρισταινέτου.

ἀλαζών, -όνος, ὁ: a vagabond	μόνος, -η, -ον: alone, left alone
ἄνθραξ, -ακος, ὁ: charcoal, coal	νύξ, νυκτός, ἡ: the night
διαβολή, ἡ: slander	περιπατέω: to walk about
διαφθείρω: to destroy utterly	πῶς: how? in what way or manner?
ἔθω: to be accustomed	συντρέχω: to encounter
ἐπιγράφω: to write on	συστρατεύω: to join or share in an
λανθάνω: to escape notice (+ *part.*)	expedition

ἐγώ ... μοι δοκῶ: "I seem to myself" i.e. I think that I will + inf.

εἴωθε: perf. with present sense, "where he is accustomed to" + inf.

συνδραμεῖν: aor. inf. of συν-τρέχω in result clause, "so that he encounters" + dat.

ἂν λάθοις: aor. opt. pot., "how *could you escape the notice* + part. i.e. *how could you* write *secretly*

τῆς νυκτός: gen. of time within which, "in the course of the night"

λαβοῦσα: aor. part. instrumental, "I will escape notice *by having taken*"

Verbal Aspect: Aorist vs. Imperfect

While the imperfect aspect considers an action as ongoing, the aorist considers an action as a simple event: "he was looking" vs. "he looked." For example, the imperfect inceptive indicates that an action begins and continues: "he started (and kept on) looking at her." The aorist inceptive occurs with so-called "stative" verbs and indicate when a certain state begins, "then he became king."

ἄλλης ἠράσθη μισήσας ἐμέ; "Did he, *having begun to hate me*, become enamoured with another?"

τηρήσας τὴν θύραν ἔκλαεν: "having stationed himself at the door, *he started crying*"

11. Tryphaina and Charmides

Charmides has hired Tryphaina for the night, but is actually in love with another. Tryphaina helps him get over his obsession.

ΤΡΥΦΑΙΝΑ: Ἑταίραν δέ τις παραλαβὼν πέντε δραχμὰς τὸ μίσθωμα δοὺς καθεύδει ἀποστραφεὶς δακρύων καὶ στένων; ἀλλ' οὔτε πέπωκας ἡδέως, οἶμαι, οὔτε δειπνῆσαι μόνος ἠθέλησας: ἔκλαες γὰρ καὶ παρὰ τὸ δεῖπνον, ἑώρων γάρ: καὶ νῦν δὲ οὐ διαλέλοιπας ἀναλύζων ὥσπερ βρέφος. ταῦτα οὖν, ὦ Χαρμίδη, τίνος ἕνεκα ποιεῖς; μὴ ἀποκρύψῃ με, ὡς ἂν καὶ τοῦτο ἀπολαύσω τῆς νυκτὸς ἀγρυπνήσασα μετὰ σοῦ.

ἀγρυπνέω: to lie awake, be wakeful	ἐθέλω: to will, wish, purpose
ἀναλύζω: to cry out loud	ἕνεκα: because of (+ *gen.*)
ἀποκρύπτω: to keep hidden from	ἡδέως: sweetly, pleasantly
ἀπολαύω: to enjoy	καθεύδω: to lie down to sleep, sleep
ἀποστρέφω: to turn	κλάω: to weep, lament, wail
βρέφος, -εος, τό: a baby	μίσθωμα, -ατος, τό: a fee
δακρύω: to weep, shed tears	οἶμαι: to suppose, think, deem, imagine
δειπνέω: to make a meal	παραλαμβάνω: to take X (*acc.*) for oneself, hire
δεῖπνον, τό: meal	
διαλείπω: to leave an interval between, cease from (+ *part.*)	πέντε: five
	πίνω: to drink
δίδωμι: to give, pay	ποιέω: to make
δραχμή, ἡ: a drachma	στένω: to moan, sigh, groan

παραλαβὼν: aor. part. temporal, "*after having hired* a courtesan"

δοὺς: aor. part. of δίδωμι, "*after having paid* the fee"

καθεύδει: the subject is τις, "does someone lie down?"

ἀποστραφεὶς: aor. pass. part. with middle sense, "having turned himself around"

πέπωκας: perf. of πίνω, "neither *have you drunk*"

δειπνῆσαι: aor. inf. complementing ἠθέλησας, "you didn't wish *to eat*"

ἑώρων: impf. of ὁράω, "for *I was watching*"

οὐ διαλέλοιπας: perf., "you have not ceased" + part.

μὴ ἀποκρύψῃ: aor. subj. in prohibition, "don't hide away!"

ὡς ἂν ... ἀπολαύσω: aor. subj. in purpose clause, "*so that I can enjoy* this too" ironic

τῆς νυκτὸς: gen. of time within which, "having been awake *during the night*"

ΧΑΡΜΙΔΗΣ: Ἔρως με ἀπόλλυσιν, ὦ Τρύφαινα, καὶ οὐκέτ᾿ ἀντέχω πρὸς τὸ δεινόν.

ΤΡΥΦΑΙΝΑ: Ἀλλ᾿ ὅτι μὲν οὐκ ἐμοῦ ἐρᾷς, δῆλον· οὐ γὰρ ἂν ἔχων με ἠμέλεις καὶ ἀπωθοῦ περιπλέκεσθαι θέλουσαν καὶ τέλος διετείχιζες τὸ μεταξὺ ἡμῶν τῷ ἱματίῳ δεδιὼς μὴ ψαύσαιμί σου. τίς δὲ ὅμως ἐκείνη ἐστίν, εἰπέ· τάχα γὰρ ἄν τι καὶ συντελέσαιμι πρὸς τὸν ἔρωτα, οἶδα γὰρ ὡς χρὴ τὰ τοιαῦτα διακονεῖσθαι.

ΧΑΡΜΙΔΗΣ: Καὶ μὴν οἶσθα καὶ πάνυ ἀκριβῶς αὐτὴν κἀκείνη σέ· οὐ γὰρ ἀφανὴς ἑταίρα ἐστίν.

ἀκριβής, -ές: exact, accurate
ἀμελέω: to have no care for, be neglectful of
ἀντέχω: to hold against
ἀπόλλυμι: to destroy
ἀπωθέω: to thrust away, push back
ἀφανής, -ές: unseen, invisible
δεινός, -ή, -όν: fearful, terrible
δῆλος, -η, -ον: visible, clear
διακονέω: to serve
διατειχίζω: to cut off and fortify by a wall
εἶπον: to speak, say (aor.)
ἐράω: to love

ἔρως, ἔροτος, ὁ: love
ἱμάτιον, τό: an outer garment, a cloak
μεταξύ: betwixt, between
οἶδα: to know (perf.)
οὐκέτι: no more, no longer, no further
πάνυ: altogether, entirely
περιπλέκω: to twine or enfold round
συντελέω: to accomplish
τάχα: quickly, presently
τέλος, -εος, τό: the fulfilment or completion
τοιοῦτος, -αύτη, -οῦτο: such as this
ψαύομαι: to touch

οὐ γὰρ ἂν ... ἠμέλεις: impf. in present contrafactual apodosis, "for (otherwise) *you wouldn't be neglecting* me"

ἔχων: pres. part. circum., "*when having* me" i.e. right next to you

ἀπωθοῦ: impf. also contrafactual, "you wouldn't be pushing me away"

θέλουσαν: pres. part. acc. agreeing with με, "pushing away me *wishing to*" + inf.

τέλος: acc. adverbial, "finally"

διετείχιζες: impf. also contrafactual, "you wouldn't be fortifying"

τῷ ἱματίῳ: dat. of means, "fortifying *with a cloak*"

δεδιὼς: perf. part. of δέδια with present sense, "being afraid"

μὴ ψαύσαιμι: aor. opt. in clause of fearing, "fearing *I will touch* you"

ἂν ... συντελέσαιμι: aor. opt. pot., "perhaps *I would like to accomplish* something"

ὡς χρή: ind. st., "I know *that it is necessary*" + inf.

καὶ μήν: "and indeed!"

κἀκείνη σέ (=καὶ ἐκείνη): "*and she* knows *you*"

ΤΡΥΦΑΙΝΑ: Εἰπὲ τοὔνομα, ὦ Χαρμίδη.

ΧΑΡΜΙΔΗΣ: Φιλημάτιον, ὦ Τρύφαινα.

ΤΡΥΦΑΙΝΑ: Ὁποτέραν λέγεις; δύο γάρ εἰσι: τὴν ἐκ Πειραιῶς, τὴν ἄρτι διακεκορευμένην, ἧς ἐρᾷ Δαμύλος ὁ τοῦ
νῦν στρατηγοῦντος υἱός, ἢ τὴν ἑτέραν, ἣν Παγίδα ἐπι-
καλοῦσιν;

ΧΑΡΜΙΔΗΣ: Ἐκείνην, καὶ ἑάλωκα ὁ κακοδαίμων καὶ
συνείλημμαι πρὸς αὐτῆς.

ΤΡΥΦΑΙΝΑ: Οὐκοῦν δι' ἐκείνην ἔκλαες;

ΧΑΡΜΙΔΗΣ: Καὶ μάλα.

ΤΡΥΦΑΙΝΑ: Πολὺς δὲ χρόνος ἔστι σοι ἐρῶντι ἢ νεοτελής
τις εἶ;

ΧΑΡΜΙΔΗΣ: Οὐ νεοτελής, ἀλλὰ μῆνες ἑπτὰ σχεδὸν ἀπὸ
Διονυσίων, ὅτε πρώτως εἶδον αὐτήν.

ἁλίσκομαι: to be taken, conquered	**νεοτελής, -ές**: newly initiated
ἄρτι: just, recently	**ὄνομα, τό**: name
Διονύσια, τά: the feast of Dionysus	**ὁπότερος, -α, -ον**: which of two
εἶδον: to see (*aor.*)	**οὐκοῦν**: therefore, then, accordingly
ἐπικαλέω: to call, name	**Πειραιεύς, ὁ**: Peiraeeus, Athens' port
ἑπτά: seven	**πρῶτος, -η, -ον**: first
κακοδαίμων, -ον: ill-fated, ill-starred	**στρατηγέω**: to be general
κλάω: to weep, lament, wail	**συλλαμβάνω**: to collect, capture
κορεύομαι: to be deflowered	**σχεδόν**: nearly
μάλα: very, very much	**υἱός, ὁ**: son
μείς, μῆνος, ἡ: a month	**χρόνος, ὁ**: time

διακεκορευμένην: perf. part., "*the one having been deflowered* recently"

τοῦ νῦν στρατηγοῦντος: pres. part. attributive, "son of *the one presently serving as a general*"

ἑάλωκα: perf. of **ἁλίσκομαι**, "I have been taken"

συνείλημμαι: perf. of **συν-λαμβάνω**, "I have been captured"

πρὸς αὐτῆς: expressing agency, "captured *at her hands*"

ἐρῶντι: pres. part. circum., "to you *loving* her?" i.e. since you are in love with her

ΤΡΥΦΑΙΝΑ: Εἶδες δὲ ὅλην ἀκριβῶς, ἢ τὸ πρόσωπον μόνον καὶ ὅσα τοῦ σώματος φανερὰ εἶδες Φιληματίου, καὶ ὡς χρῆν γυναῖκα πέντε καὶ τετταράκοντα ἔτη γεγονυῖαν ἤδη;

ΧΑΡΜΙΔΗΣ: Καὶ μὴν ἐπόμνυται δύο καὶ εἴκοσιν ἐς τὸν ἐσόμενον Ἐλαφηβολιῶνα τελέσειν.

ΤΡΥΦΑΙΝΑ: Σὺ δὲ ποτέροις πιστεύσειας ἄν, τοῖς ἐκείνης ὅρκοις ἢ τοῖς σεαυτοῦ ὀφθαλμοῖς; ἐπίσκεψαι γὰρ ἀκριβῶς ὑποβλέψας ποτὲ τοὺς κροτάφους αὐτῆς, ἔνθα μόνον τὰς αὑτῆς τρίχας ἔχει: τὰ δὲ ἄλλα φενάκη βαθεῖα. παρὰ δὲ τοὺς κροτάφους ὁπόταν ἀσθενήσῃ τὸ φάρμακον, ᾧ

ἀσθενέω: to be ill or weak
βαθύς, -εῖα, ύ: deep, thick
εἴκοσι: twenty
Ἐλαφηβολιών, -ῶνος, ὁ: the Elaphebolia, a winter festival to Artemis
ἔνθα: there
ἐπισκέπτομαι: to pass in review, inspect
ἐπόμνυμι: to swear
ἔτος, -εος, τό: a year
θρίξ, τρίχος, ἡ: a hair
κρόταφος, ὁ: the side of the forehead
ὅλος, -η, -ον: whole, entire
ὁπόταν: whensoever (+ subj.)

ὅρκος, ὁ: an oath
ὅσος, -η, -ον: as much as
ὀφθαλμός, ὁ: the eye
πιστεύω: to trust, believe in (+ dat.)
πότερος, -α, -ον: whether of the two?
πρόσωπον, τό: the face
σῶμα, σώματος, τό: a body
τελέω: to complete, fulfil, accomplish
τεσσαράκοντα: forty
ὑποβλέπω: to look suspiciously at
φανερός, -ά, -όν: visible
φάρμακον, τό: a drug, dye
φενάκη, ἡ: a wig

ὅσα ... φανερὰ: "did you see *as much* of the body *as is visible?*"
ὡς χρῆν: impf. (unaugmented) in ind. st. "did you see *as much as was necessary?*"
γεγονυῖαν: perf. part. circum. agreeing with γυναῖκα, "the woman already *having become*" i.e. already being 45 years old
τὸν ἐσόμενον: fut. part. attributive, "in *the about to be* festival" i.e. the next
τελέσειν: fut. inf. after ἐπόμνυται, "swears *that she will be*"
πιστεύσειας ἄν: aor. opt. pot., "which *would you believe?*"
ἐπίσκεψαι: aor. imper., "inspect carefully!"
ὑποβλέψας: aor. part. instrumental, "inspect *by having looked suspiciously*"
τὰς αὑτῆς τρίχας: "where she has *her own hair*"
ὁπόταν ἀσθενήσῃ: aor. subj. in general temporal clause, "*whenever* the dye *is weak*"

βάπτεται, ὑπολευκαίνεται τὰ πολλά. καίτοι τί τοῦτο; βίασαί ποτε καὶ γυμνὴν αὐτὴν ἰδεῖν.

ΧΑΡΜΙΔΗΣ: Οὐδεπώποτέ μοι πρὸς τοῦτο ἐνέδωκεν.

ΤΡΥΦΑΙΝΑ: Εἰκότως· ἠπίστατο γὰρ μυσαχθησόμενόν σε τὰς λεύκας. ὅλη δὲ ἀπὸ τοῦ αὐχένος ἐς τὰ γόνατα παρδάλει ἔοικεν. ἀλλὰ σὺ ἐδάκρυες τοιαύτῃ μὴ συνών; ἦ που τάχα καὶ ἐλύπει σε καὶ ὑπερεώρα;

ΧΑΡΜΙΔΗΣ: Ναί, ὦ Τρύφαινα, καίτοι τοσαῦτα παρ' ἐμοῦ λαμβάνουσα. καὶ νῦν ἐπειδὴ χιλίας αἰτούσῃ οὐκ εἶχον διδόναι ῥᾳδίως ἅτε ὑπὸ πατρὶ φειδομένῳ τρεφόμενος,

---

αἰτέω: to ask, beg
ἅτε: because (+ *part.*)
αὐχήν, -ένος, ὁ: the neck, throat
βάπτω: to dip in water, to dye
βιάζω: to constrain, insist (+ *inf.*)
γόνυ, -γόνατος, τό: the knee
γυμνός, -ή, -όν: naked, unclad
δίδωμι: to give
εἰκότως: reasonably, naturally
ἐνδίδωμι: to give in, allow
ἔοικα: to be like (+ *dat.*)
ἐπίσταμαι: to know
ἦ: in truth, truly, verily, of a surety
καίτοι: and yet
λαμβάνω: to take
λεύκη, ἡ: white spot

λυπέω: to pain, distress, grieve, vex
μυσάττομαι: to feel disgust at
οὐδεπώποτε: never yet at any time
πάρδαλις, -εως, ἡ: the leopard
πατήρ, πατρός ὁ: a father
ῥᾳδίως: easily
σύνειμι: to be with, consort with
τάχα: quickly, presently, forthwith
τοσοῦτος, -αύτη, -οῦτο: so large, so tall
τρέφω: to rear
ὑπεροράω: to look down upon, be haughty
ὑπολευκαίνομαι: to become white underneath
φείδομαι: to spare, be frugal
χίλιοι, -αι: a thousand

βίασαι: aor. imper., "*insist* to see her!"

ἐνέδωκεν: aor. of ἐν-δίδωμι, "never *did she allow*"

μυσαχθησόμενόν: fut. part. pass., with middle meaning in ind. st. after ἠπίστατο, "she knew *that you would feel disgust at*"

μὴ συνών: pres. part. concessive, "although not consorting with"

ἦ που τάχα: in a question which is really a statement, "*I suppose perhaps* she also..."

ὑπερεώρα: impf. of ὑπερ-όραω, "she was haughty?"

καίτοι ... λαμβάνουσα: pres. part. concessive, "*even though receiving* such things"

αἰτούσῃ: pres. part. dat. agreeing with the ind. obj. of διδόναι, "to give *to (her) seeking*"

διδόναι: pres. inf. complementing εἶχον, "I was not able *to give*"

ἅτε ... τρεφόμενος: pres. part. pass. causal, "because I am reared"

Μοσχίωνα ἐσδεξαμένη ἀπέκλεισέ με, ἀνθ᾽ ὧν λυπῆσαι καὶ αὐτὸς ἐθέλων αὐτὴν σὲ παρείληφα.

ΤΡΥΦΑΙΝΑ: Μὰ τὴν Ἀφροδίτην οὐκ ἂν ἧκον, εἴ μοι προεῖπέ τις ὡς ἐπὶ τούτοις παραλαμβανοίμην, λυπῆσαι ἄλλην, καὶ ταῦτα Φιλημάτιον τὴν σορόν. ἀλλ᾽ ἄπειμι, καὶ γὰρ ἤδη τρίτον τοῦτο ᾖσεν ἀλεκτρυών.

ἀείδω: to sing	λυπέω: to cause to grieve
ἀλεκτρυών, -ονος, ὁ: a cock	μά: in affirmation (+ acc.)
ἄπειμι: to go away (fut.)	Μοσχίων, -ωνα, ὁ: Moschion, another client
ἀποκλείω: to shut out of, debar	παραλαμβάνω: to receive, hire
ἐθέλω: to will, wish, purpose	προεῖπον: to tell or state before
εἰσδέχομαι: to take into, admit	σορός, ἡ: a coffin, urn
ἥκω: to have come, be present, be here	τρίτος, -η, -ον: the third

ἐσδεξαμένη: aor. part., "she *having admitted* Moschion"

ἀπέκλεισε: aor., "she locked me out"

ἀνθ᾽ ὧν: "in retaliation for which things"

παρείληφα: perf. of παρα-λαμβάνω, "*I received* you"

οὐκ ἂν ἧκον: impf. in present contrafactual apodosis, "I would not be here"

εἴ μοι προεῖπε: aor. in past contrafactual protasis, "if someone had told me"

ὡς ... παραλαμβανοίμην: aor. opt. in ind. st. in secondary sequence, "told me *that I was being hired*"

λυπῆσαι: aor. inf. in apposition to ἐπὶ τούτοις, "for this, namely, *in order to vex*"

τρίτον: adverbial acc., "the cock has sung *for the third time*" i.e. it's morning

ᾖσεν: aor. of ἀείδω, "he has sung"

Contrafactual Conditions

A present contrafactual condition has εἰ plus the imperfect indicative in the protasis, ἂν plus the imperfect indicative in the apodosis.

> Ἀλλ᾽ ὅτι μὲν οὐκ ἐμοῦ ἐρᾷς, δῆλον· οὐ γὰρ ἄν με ἠμέλεις: But it is clear you do not love me; (otherwise) you wouldn't be neglecting me .

A past contrafactual condition has εἰ plus the aorist indicative in the protasis, ἂν plus the aorist indicative in the apodosis.

> εἰ μὲν καὶ ξίφος ἔχων ἦλθον, οὐκ ἂν ὤκνησα: "if I had come with a sword, I would not have shrunk from (using it)"

The parts retain their contrafactual force when used separately or when mixed:

> οὐκ ἂν ἧκον, εἴ μοι προεῖπέ τις: "I would not (now) be here, if someone had told me"

ΧΑΡΜΙΔΗΣ: Μὴ σύ γε οὕτως ταχέως, ὦ Τρύφαινα: εἰ γὰρ
ἀληθῆ ἐστιν ἃ φῂς περὶ Φιληματίου, τὴν πηνήκην καὶ ὅτι
βάπτεται καὶ τὸ τῶν ἄλλων ἀλφῶν, οὐδὲ προσβλέπειν
ἂν ἔτι ἐδυνάμην αὐτῇ.

ΤΡΥΦΑΙΝΑ: Ἐροῦ τὴν μητέρα, εἴ ποτε λέλουται μετ' αὐτῆς:
περὶ γὰρ τῶν ἐτῶν κἂν ὁ πάππος διηγήσεταί σοι, εἴ γε
ζῇ ἔτι.

ΧΑΡΜΙΔΗΣ: Οὐκοῦν ἐπεὶ τοιαύτη ἐκείνη, ἀφῃρήσθω μὲν
ἤδη τὸ διατείχισμα, περιβάλλωμεν δὲ ἀλλήλους καὶ
φιλῶμεν καὶ ἀληθῶς συνῶμεν: Φιλημάτιον δὲ πολλὰ
χαιρέτω.

ἀληθής, -ές: unconcealed, true
ἀλλήλων: of one another
ἀλφός, ὁ: whiteness
ἀφαιρέω: to take from, remove
βάπτω: to dip in water, dye
διατείχισμα, -ατος, τό: a barrier
διηγέομαι: to set out in detail
δύναμαι: to be able (+ *inf.*)
ἐρωτάω: to ask, enquire
ζάω: to live

λούω: to wash
μήτηρ, μητέρος, ἡ: a mother
οὐκοῦν: therefore, then, accordingly
πάππος, ὁ: a grandfather
περιβάλλω: to throw round, embrace
πηνήκη, ἡ: false hair, wig
προσβλέπω: to look at or upon
ταχέως: swiftly
φιλέω: to kiss
χαίρω: to rejoice, be glad, be delighted

ἂν ἔτι ἐδυνάμην: impf. in pres. contrafactual apodosis, "I wouldn't be able to" + inf.

ἐροῦ: aor. imper. of ἐρωτάω, "*ask* your mother!"

εἴ ποτε λέλουται: perf. in ind. quest. after ἐροῦ, "ask *whether she has ever washed* with her"

κἂν ὁ πάππος διηγήσεται: a rare fut. with ἄν, "*he would definitely tell you* if he still lives"

ἀφῃρήσθω: perf. imper. 3 s., " let it be removed!"

περιβάλλωμεν: pres. subj. hortatory, "let's embrace!"

συνῶμεν: pres. subj. hortatory of σύν-ειμι, "let's consort!"

χαιρέτω: pres. imper. 3 s., "let's bid her fare well!" i.e. goodbye to her!

12. Ioessa, Pythias, and Lysias

A misunderstanding is cleared up and two lovers are reunited.

ΙΟΕΣΣΑ: Θρύπτῃ, ὦ Λυσία, πρὸς ἐμέ; καὶ καλῶς, ὅτι μήτε ἀργύριον πώποτε ᾔτησά σε μήτ᾽ ἀπέκλεισα ἐλθόντα, ἔνδον ἕτερος, εἰποῦσα, μήτε παραλογισάμενον τὸν πατέρα ἢ ὑφελόμενον τῆς μητρὸς ἠνάγκασα ἐμοί τι κομίσαι, ὁποῖα αἱ ἄλλαι ποιοῦσιν, ἀλλ᾽ εὐθὺς ἐξ ἀρχῆς ἄμισθον, ἀξύμβολον εἰσεδεξάμην, οἶσθα ὅσους ἐραστὰς παραπεμψαμένη, Θεοκλέα τὸν πρυτανεύοντα νῦν καὶ Πασίωνα τὸν ναύκληρον καὶ τὸν συνέφηβόν

αἰτέω: to ask X (*acc.*) from Y (*acc.*)
ἄμισθος, -ον: without hire or pay
ἀναγκάζω: to force, compel
ἀποκλείω: to shut out
ἀργύριον: a piece of silver, a silver coin
ἀρχή, ἡ: a beginning
ἀσύμβολος, -ον: not paying one's share
εἰσδέχομαι: to take into, admit
ἔνδον: in, in the house
ἐραστής, -οῦ, ὁ: a lover

θρύπτω: to break; to be haughty
κομίζω: to provide for, bring
ναύκληρος, ὁ: a shipowner, ship-master
ὁποῖος, -α, -ον: of what sort?
παραλογίζομαι: to cheat
παραπέμπω: to send past, dismiss
πρυτανεύω: to be, a council-member
πώποτε: ever yet
συνέφηβος, ὁ: a young comrade
ὑφαιρέω: to seize underneath or inwardly

θρύπτῃ: pres. 2 s. mid., "are you being haughty?"

καὶ καλῶς: "and well done!" ironic

ᾔτησα ... ἀπέκλεισα: aor., "I never *asked* for silver ... nor *closed you out*"

ἐλθόντα: aor. part. acc. "closed you out *when you came*"

ἔνδον ἕτερος: in vivid ind. st. after εἰποῦσα, "having said *'another is inside'*"

παραλογισάμενον ... ὑφελόμενον: aor. part. agreeing with σε instrumental, "nor did I compel you *by having cheated ... by having taken away from*"

τῆς μητρός: gen. of separation after ὑφελόμενον, "taken away something *from your mother*"

κομίσαι: aor. inf. after ἠνάγκασα, "nor did I compel you *to bring*"

εἰσεδεξάμην: aor. of εἰσ-δέχομαι, "*I admitted* you"

παραπεμψαμένη: aor. part. in ind. st. after οἶσθα, "you know how many lovers *I have dismissed*"

σου Μέλισσον, καίτοι ἔναγχος ἀποθανόντος αὐτῷ τοῦ
πατρὸς καὶ κύριον αὐτὸν ὄντα τῆς οὐσίας: ἐγὼ δὲ τὸν
Φάωνα μόνον εἶχον οὔτε τινὰ προσβλέπουσα ἕτερον
οὔτε προσιεμένη ὅτι μὴ σέ: ᾤμην γὰρ ἡ ἀνόητος ἀληθῆ
εἶναι ἃ ὤμνυες, καὶ διὰ τοῦτό σοι προσέχουσα ὥσπερ

ἀνόητος, -ον: mindless, unreasonable
ἀποθνήσκω: to die off, die
ἔναγχος: (*adv.*) just now
κύριος, ὁ: a lord, master
μόνος, -η, -ον: alone
οἴομαι: to suppose, think, deem, imagine

ὄμνυμι: to swear
οὐσία, ἡ: one's property
προσβλέπω: to look at
προσέχω: to devote oneself to (+ *dat.*)
προσίημι: to let come to

καίτοι ἀποθανόντος τοῦ πατρὸς: aor. part. in gen. abs. concessive, "although his father having died"

ὄντα: pres. part. agreeing with **Μέλισσον**, "and Melissos *being* the master"

τὸν Φάωνα: pred. acc., "I considered you *my Phaon*" Phaon was turned young by Aphrodite in return for a favor and became the beloved of Sappho. Ovid tells their story in the *Heroides*

προσιεμένη: pres. part. of **προσίημι**, "I, neither *admitting*"

ὅτι μὴ σέ: "admitting another *besides you*"

ἡ ἀνόητος: an attributive phrase, " I, *the mindless one*"

εἶναι: pres. inf. in ind. st. after **ᾤμην**, "I thought what you swore *to be* true"

ὤμνυες: aor. of **ὄμνυμι**, "what *you swore*"

Genitive Absolutes

Genitive absolutes combine a participle with a noun or pronoun that is not the subject or object of the main clause in order to set forth some circumstance under which an action takes place. Like other circumstantial participles, they can indicate time, manner, means, cause, purpose, concession, condition or attendant circumstance. Sometimes the noun or pronoun is suppressed and must be supplied by the context:

ἐσωφρόνουν ἐπιβοωμένης τῆς μητρός: "I was being chaste *with my mother all the while shouting*"

ἄρτι μὲν Λυκαίνη προσέπαιζες ἐμοῦ ὁρώσης: "you were flirting with Lykaina *with me watching*""

μετ᾽ ὀλίγον ἐπέστητε ἤδη φευγόντων: "after a while, you all arrived, *with (the enemy) fleeing* already"

ἡ Πηνελόπη ἐσωφρόνουν, ἐπιβοωμένης τῆς μητρὸς καὶ πρὸς τὰς φίλας ἐγκαλούσης. σὺ δὲ ἐπείπερ ἔμαθες ὑποχείριον ἔχων με τετηκυῖαν ἐπὶ σοί, ἄρτι μὲν Λυκαίνῃ προσέπαιζες ἐμοῦ ὁρώσης, ὡς λυποίης ἐμέ, ἄρτι δὲ σὺν ἐμοὶ κατακείμενος ἐπῄνεις Μαγίδιον τὴν ψάλτριαν· ἐγὼ δ' ἐπὶ τούτοις δακρύω καὶ συνίημι ὑβριζομένη. πρῴην δὲ ὁπότε συνεπίνετε Θράσων καὶ σὺ καὶ Δίφιλος, παρῆσαν καὶ ἡ αὐλητρὶς Κυμβάλιον καὶ Πυραλλὶς ἐχθρὰ οὖσα ἐμοί. σὺ δὲ τοῦτ' εἰδὼς τὴν Κυμβάλιον μὲν οὔ μοι πάνυ ἐμέλησεν ὅτι πεντάκις ἐφίλησας· σεαυτὸν γὰρ ὕβριζες

ἄρτι: just, now
αὐλητρίς, -ίδος, ἡ: a flute-girl
δακρύω: to weep, shed tears
ἐγκαλέω: to quarrel
ἐπαινέω: to approve, applaud
ἐπείπερ: seeing that
ἐπιβοάω: to cry out to
ἐχθρός, -ά, -όν: hated, hateful
κατάκειμαι: to lie down (to eat)
Λυκαίνη, ἡ: Lykaene, a courtesan
Μαγίδιον, ἡ: Magigion, a harpist
μανθάνω: to learn
μέλω: to be an object of care to
ὁράω: to see

πάρειμι: to be present
πεντάκις: five times
Πηνελόπη, ἡ: Penelope, faithful wife of Odysseus
προσπαίζω: to play or sport with
πρῴην: earlier
συμπίνω: to join in a drinking bout
συνίημι: to perceive
σωφρονέω: to be chaste
τήκω: to melt
ὑβρίζω: to insult
ὑποχείριος, -ον: in hand
φίλος, -η, -ον: loved, beloved, dear
ψάλτρια, ἡ: a harpist

ἐπιβοωμένης ... ἐγκαλούσης: pres. part. in gen. abs., "with my mother *shouting and quarelling*"

ἔμαθες: aor. of μανθάνω, "after *you learned*"

ἔχων: pres. part. in ind. st. after ἔμαθες, "learned *that you had* me"

τετηκυῖαν: perf. part. agreeing with με, "had me *having melted*" i.e. from love

ἐμοῦ ὁρώσης: gen. abs., "with me watching"

ὡς λυποίης: aor. opt. in purpose clause in secondary sequence after προσέπαιζες, "you were playing *in order to annoy* me"

ἐπῄνεις: impf., "you kept praising"

ὑβριζομένη: pres. part. in ind. st. after συνίημι, "I perceive *that I am insulted*"

παρῆσαν: impf. of παρά-ειμι, "they *were present*"

εἰδὼς: perf. part. of οἶδα with present force, "you *knowing* this" namely, that Pyrallis was her enemy

τὴν Κυμβάλιον μὲν ... Πυραλλίδα δὲ, "as for Kymbalion ... but Pyrallis"

τοιαύτην φιλῶν· Πυραλλίδα δὲ ὅσον ἐνένευες, καὶ πιὼν
ἂν ἐκείνῃ μὲν ἀπέδειξας τὸ ποτήριον, ἀποδιδοὺς δὲ τῷ
παιδὶ πρὸς τὸ οὖς ἐκέλευες, εἰ μὴ Πυραλλὶς αἰτήσειε,
μὴ ἂν ἄλλῳ ἐγχέαι· τέλος δὲ τοῦ μήλου ἀποδακών,
ὁπότε τὸν Δίφιλον εἶδες ἀσχολούμενον — ἐλάλει γὰρ
Θράσωνι — προκύψας πως εὐστόχως προσηκόντισας
ἐς τὸν κόλπον αὐτῆς, οὐδὲ λαθεῖν γε πειρώμενος ἐμέ·

ἀποδάκνω: to bite off a piece of	μῆλον, τό: apple
ἀποδείκνυμι: to present X (*acc.*) to Y (*dat.*)	ὅσος, -η, -ον: how much?
ἀποδίδωμι: to give back, return	οὖς, τό: the ear
ἀσχολέω: to engage, occupy	παῖς, -δός, ὁ: a child
ἐγχέω: to pour in, fill (a cup)	πειράω: to attempt, endeavour, try
ἐννεύω: to make signs to	πίνω: to drink
εὔστοχος, -ον: well-aimed	ποτήριον, τό: a drinking-cup
κελεύω: to command, order	προκύπτω: to stoop and bend forward
κόλπος, ὁ: the bosom	προσακοντίζω: to shoot like a javelin
λαλέω: to talk, chat	πως: in some way
λανθάνω: to escape notice	τέλος: finally

φιλῶν: pres. part. instrumental, "you insult yourself *by kissing*"

πιὼν: aor. part. temporal, "when you drank"

ἀπέδειξας: aor. with ἂν indicating repeated action, "*you always presented* the cup"

ἀποδιδοὺς: pres. part. indicating repeated action, "you, *returning* it to the slave"

πρὸς τὸ οὖς: "you would order *in the ear*" i.e. you would whisper

αἰτήσειε: aor. opt. in future less vivid protasis, "unless Pyrallis *would ask for* it"

μὴ ἂν ἄλλῳ ἐγχέαι: aor. opt. in future less vivid apodosis which is also an ind. com.
  after ἐκέλευες, "you would order *that he not pour it* for another"

ἀποδακών: aor. part. of ἀπο-δάκνω, "you, *having bitten from*" + gen.

ἀσχολούμενον: pres. part. in ind. st. after εἶδες, "saw *that he was occupied*"

προσηκόντισας: aor. part., "having shot (the piece of apple) like a javelin

λαθεῖν: aor. inf. complementing πειρώμενος, "not even trying *to escape the notice*"

Indirect Command

Indirect command in Greek follows the same rules as indirect statement. It can occur with an infinitive or with a finite verb, in the latter case changing to the optative in secondary sequence.

  με παραγγείλας τῷ θυρωρῷ μὴ ἀνοίγειν: "having instructed me *not to open* the door"

  ἐκέλευες ... μὴ ἂν ἄλλῳ ἐγχέαι: "you would order *not to pour* it for another (ἂν here is potential)"

ἡ δὲ φιλήσασα μεταξὺ τῶν μαστῶν ὑπὸ τῷ ἀποδέσμῳ
παρεβύσατο. ταῦτα οὖν τίνος ἕνεκα ποιεῖς; τί σε ἢ μέγα
ἢ μικρὸν ἐγὼ ἠδίκησα ἢ λελύπηκα; τίνα ἕτερον εἶδον;
οὐ πρὸς μόνον σὲ ζῶ; οὐ μέγα, ὦ Λυσία, τοῦτο ποιεῖς
γύναιον ἄθλιον λυπῶν μεμηνὸς ἐπὶ σοί; ἔστι τις θεὸς
ἡ Ἀδράστεια καὶ τὰ τοιαῦτα ὁρᾷ· σὺ δέ ποτε λυπήσῃ
τάχα, ἂν ἀκούσῃς τι περὶ ἐμοῦ, κειμένην με ἤτοι βρόχῳ
ἐμαυτὴν ἀποπνίξασαν ἢ ἐς τὸ φρέαρ ἐπὶ κεφαλὴν
ἐμπεσοῦσαν, ἢ ἕνα γέ τινα τρόπον εὑρήσω θανάτου, ὡς

ἀδικέω: to do wrong
ἄθλιος, -α, -ον: miserable
ἀκούω: to hear
ἀπόδεσμος, ὁ: a breastband, girdle
ἀποπνίγω: to choke
βρόχος, ὁ: a noose
γύναιον, τό: a weak woman
ἐμπίπτω: fall upon
ἕνεκα: on account of (+ gen.)
εὑρίσκω: to find
ζάω: to live
ἤτοι: now surely, truly, verily
θάνατος, ὁ: death

κεῖμαι: to be laid
κεφαλή, ἡ: the head
λυπέω: to grieve, annoy
μαίνομαι: to rage, be furious
μαστός, ὁ: the breast
μεταξύ: between
μικρός, -ά, -όν: small, little
παραβύω: to stuff in, insert
ποιέω: to do
τάχα: quickly, presently, forthwith
τοιοῦτος, -αύτη, -οῦτο: such as this
τρόπος, ὁ: a course, manner
φρέαρ, τό: a well

ἡ δὲ: "but she" i.e. Pyrallis
φιλήσασα: aor. part., "she *having kissed* it"
τίνος ἕνεκα: "on account of what?" i.e. why?
λελύπηκα: perf., "by what *have I grieved you?*"
οὐ μέγα: pred. "*not great* is this thing you do"
μεμηνὸς: perf. part. act. neut. of μαίνομαι agreeing with γύναιον, "a weak woman
    who is driven mad"
ἡ Ἀδράστεια: "the inevitable," an epithet of Nemesis, goddess of revenge
ἂν ἀκούσῃς: aor. subj. in future more vivid protasis, "if you hear"
κειμένην: pres. part. in ind. st. after ἀκούσῃς, "if you hear something, namely *that I
    am laid out*" i.e. that I am dead
ἀποπνίξασαν ... ἐμπεσοῦσαν: aor. part. acc. s. agreeing with με and instrumental,
    "that I am dead *by having choked ... or by having fallen into*"
εὑρήσω: fut., "or *I will find* some single way"

μηκέτ᾽ ἐνοχλοίην βλεπομένη. πομπεύσεις τότε ὡς μέγα
καὶ λαμπρὸν ἔργον ἐργασάμενος. τί με ὑποβλέπεις καὶ
πρίεις τοὺς ὀδόντας; εἰ γάρ τι ἐγκαλεῖς, εἰπέ, Πυθιὰς
ἡμῖν αὕτη δικασάτω. τί τοῦτο; οὐδὲ ἀποκρινάμενος
ἀπέρχῃ καταλιπών με; ὁρᾷς, ὦ Πυθιάς, οἷα πάσχω ὑπὸ
Λυσίου;

ΠΥΘΙΑΣ: Ὦ τῆς ἀγριότητος, τὸ μηδὲ ἐπικλασθῆναι δακρυούσης: λίθος, οὐκ ἄνθρωπός ἐστι. πλὴν ἀλλ᾽ εἴ γε χρὴ
τἀληθὲς εἰπεῖν, σύ, ὦ Ἰόεσσα, διέφθειρας αὐτὸν ὑπεραγαπῶσα καὶ τοῦτο ἐμφαίνουσα. ἐχρῆν δὲ μὴ πάνυ

ἀγριότης, -ητος, ἡ: wildness, savageness
ἀληθής, -ές: unconcealed,
ἀπέρχομαι: to go away, depart from
ἀποκρίνομαι: to answer, respond
βλέπω: to see
δακρύω: to weep, shed tears
διαφθείρω: to destroy, spoil
δικάζω: to judge, to give judgment on
ἐγκαλέω: to call in, make an accusation
ἐμφαίνω: to exhibit, display
ἐνοχλέω: to trouble, annoy
ἐπικλάω: to bend to
ἐργάζομαι: to work, accomplish
καταλείπω: to leave behind

λαμπρός, -ά, -όν: brilliant, radiant
λίθος, ὁ: a stone
μηκέτι: no longer
ὀδούς, -όντος, ὁ: tooth
οἷος, -α, -ον: what sort of?
πάνυ: altogether, entirely
πάσχω: to suffer
πομπεύω: to strut, swagger
πρίω: to saw, grind
τότε: at that time, then
ὑπεραγαπάω: to love exceedingly
ὑποβλέπω: to look up from under
χρή: it is fated, necessary

ὡς μηκέτ᾽ ἐνοχλοίην: pres. opt. pot. in result clause, "so that I could no longer annoy" ironic

βλεπομένη: pres. part. pass. instrumental, "annoy you *by being seen*"

ὡς ... ἐργασάμενος: aor. part. giving an alleged motive, "you will boast *as though having accomplished*"

δικασάτω: aor. 3 sing. imper., "let her judge!"

ἀποκρινάμενος ... καταλιπών: aor. part. circumstantial, "will you depart *not having responded ... having left me behind*?"

τὸ μηδὲ ἐπικλασθῆναι: aor. inf. pass. articular, "the not to have been bent"

δακρυούσης: pres. part. gen. after ἐπικλασθῆναι, "bent to *the one weeping*" i.e. to be moved by the plea

πλὴν ἀλλ᾽ εἴ γε: "but really if..." indicating a change of view

ὑπεραγαπῶσα ... ἐμφαίνουσα: pres. part. instrumental, "you spoiled him *by loving excessively ... by displaying* this fact"

ἐχρῆν: the impf. indicates what should have been done, but wasn't

αὐτὸν ζηλοῦν· ὑπερόπται γὰρ αἰσθανόμενοι γίγνονται.
παῦ᾽, ὦ τάλαινα, δακρύουσα, καὶ ἤν μοι πείθῃ, ἅπαξ ἢ
δὶς ἀπόκλεισον ἐλθόντα· ὄψει γὰρ ἀνακαιόμενον αὐτὸν
πάνυ καὶ ἀντιμεμηνότα ἀληθῶς.

ΙΟΕΣΣΑ: Ἀλλὰ μηδ᾽ εἴπῃς, ἄπαγε. ἀποκλείσω Λυσίαν; εἴθε
μὴ αὐτὸς ἀποσταίη φθάσας.

ΠΥΘΙΑΣ: Ἀλλ᾽ ἐπανέρχεται αὖθις.

ΙΟΕΣΣΑ: Ἀπολώλεκας ἡμᾶς, ὦ Πυθιάς· ἠκρόαταί σου ἴσως
«ἀπόκλεισον» λεγούσης.

αἰσθάνομαι: to perceive
ἀκροάομαι: to hearken to, listen to
ἀληθῶς: truly, really
ἀνακαίω: to light up
ἀντιμαίνομαι: to rage or bluster against
ἄπαγε: away! begone! hands off!
ἅπαξ: once
ἀποκλείω: to shut out of
ἀπόλλυμι: to destroy utterly
αὖθις: back, back again
ἀφίστημι: to put away, remove

δακρύω: to cry
δίς: twice, doubly
ἐπανέρχομαι: to go back, return
ζηλόω: to desire emulously
ἦλθον: to come or go (aor.)
παύω: to make to cease
πείθομαι: to obey, be persuaded
τάλας, -αινα, -αν: suffering, wretched
ὑπερόπτης, -ου, ὁ: a disdainer (of)
φθάνω: to come or do first

ζηλοῦν: pres. inf. after ἐχρῆν, "it was necessary not *to desire* strongly"

ὑπερόπται: nom. pred. "(men) become *disdainers*"

ἤν μοι πείθῃ: pres. subj. of πείθομαι in future more vivid protasis, "if you obey me"

ἀπόκλεισον: aor. imper., "shut him out!"

ὄψει: fut. of ὁράω, "*you will see* him"

ἀντιμεμηνότα: perf. part. acc. circumstantial, "see him *having become angry*"

μηδ᾽ εἴπῃς: aor. subj. in prohibition, "don't say!"

ἀποκλείσω: fut. in rhetorical question, "Shall I shut him out?"

εἴθε μὴ ... ἀποσταίη: aor. opt. intransitive of ἀπο-ίστημι in wish for the future,
    "would that he would not stay away!"

φθάσας: aor. part., "he, *having done it first*" i.e. having done it spontaneously

ἀπολώλεκας: perf. of ἀπο-όλλυμι, "*you have destroyed* us"

ἠκρόαταί: perf. of ἀκροάομαι, "perhaps *he has heard*"

«ἀπόκλεισον»: imperative, the word itself is the object of λεγούσης

σου λεγούσης: pres. part. gen. of source., "he heard *you saying*"

ΛΥΣΙΑΣ: Οὐχὶ ταύτης ἕνεκεν, ὦ Πυθιάς, ἐπανελήλυθα, ἣν
οὐδὲ προσβλέψαιμι ἔτι τοιαύτην οὖσαν, ἀλλὰ διὰ σέ, ὡς
μὴ καταγιγνώσκῃς ἐμοῦ καὶ λέγῃς, «Ἄτεγκτος ὁ Λυσίας
ἐστίν.»

ΠΥΘΙΑΣ: Ἀμέλει καὶ ἔλεγον, ὦ Λυσία.

ΛΥΣΙΑΣ: Φέρειν οὖν ἐθέλεις, ὦ Πυθιάς, Ἰόεσσαν ταύτην
τὴν νῦν δακρύουσαν αὐτὸν ἐπιστάντα αὐτῇ ποτε μετὰ
νεανίου καθευδούσῃ ἐμοῦ ἀποστάσῃ;

ΠΥΘΙΑΣ: Λυσία, τὸ μὲν ὅλον ἑταίρα ἐστί. πῶς δ' οὖν
κατέλαβες αὐτοὺς συγκαθεύδοντας;

ἀμελέω: to not mind or care	καταγιγνώσκω: to condemn (+ gen.)
ἄτεγκτος, -ον: hard-hearted	καταλαμβάνω: to seize upon, lay hold of
ἀφίστημι: to put away, remove	νεανίας, -ου, ὁ: a youth
ἐθέλω: to will, wish, purpose	ὅλος, -η, -ον: whole, entire
ἕνεκα: on account of (+ gen.)	προσβλέπω: to look at or upon
ἑταίρα, ἡ: a courtesan	πῶς: how? in what way or manner?
ἐφίστημι: to set or place upon	συνκαθεύδω: to sleep with
καθεύδω: to lie down to sleep	φέρω: to bear

ἐπανελήλυθα: perf. of ἐπι-ανα-έρχομαι, "I have come back"

ταύτης ... ἣν: "on account of *this one* (Joessa) *whom*"

οὐδὲ προσβλέψαιμι: aor. opt. pot. (without ἄν), "whom *I would not like to look at*"

οὖσαν: pres. part. causal, "*since she is such a one*"

ὡς μὴ καταγιγνώσκῃς ἐμοῦ καὶ λέγῃς: pres. subj. in purpose clause, "lest you
  condemn me and say"

ἀμέλει: imper., "never mind!" i.e. *indeed*, I was just saying

δακρύουσαν: pres. part. circumstantial, "to endure this Joessa *weeping*"

αὐτὸν ἐπιστάντα: aor. part. acc. sing. in apposition to the subject of φέρειν, "do you
  wish (me) *the very one who came upon* her"

καθευδούσῃ: pres. part. fem., agreeing with αὐτῇ, "came upon her *sleeping with*"

ἀποστάσῃ: aor. part. intransitive of ἀπο-ἵστημι, also agreeing with αὐτῇ, "her, *having
  removed* herself from me"

κατέλαβες: aor., "how *did you catch* them"

93

ΛΥΣΙΑΣ: Ἕκτην σχεδὸν ταύτην ἡμέραν, νὴ Δί, ἕκτην γε, δευτέρᾳ ἱσταμένου· τὸ τήμερον δὲ ἑβδόμη ἐστίν. ὁ πατὴρ εἰδὼς ὡς πάλαι ἐρῴην ταυτησὶ τῆς χρηστῆς, ἐνέκλεισέ με παραγγείλας τῷ θυρωρῷ μὴ ἀνοίγειν· ἐγὼ δέ, οὐ γὰρ ἔφερον μὴ οὐχὶ συνεῖναι αὐτῇ, τὸν Δρόμωνα ἐκέλευσα παρακύψαντα παρὰ τὸν θριγκὸν τῆς αὐλῆς, ᾗ ταπεινότατον ἦν, ἀναδέξασθαί με ἐπὶ τὸν νῶτον· ῥᾷον γὰρ οὕτως ἀναβήσεσθαι ἔμελλον. τί ἂν μακρὰ λέγοιμι;

ἀναβαίνω: to go up, mount
ἀναδέχομαι: to take up, receive
ἀνοίγω: to open
αὐλή, ἡ: a court
δεύτερος, -α, -ον: second
ἕβδομος, -η, -ον: seventh
ἐγκλείω: to shut in, close
ἕκτος, -η, -ον: sixth
ἐράω: to love
ἡμέρα, ἡ: day
θριγκός, ὁ: the topmost course of stones in a wall
θυρωρός, ὁ: a door-keeper, porter
ἵστημι: to make to stand
κελεύω: to command, order

μακρός, -ά, -ον: long
μέλλω: to intend to do, to be about to do
νῶτον, τό: the back
πάλαι: long ago
παραγγέλλω: to transmit as a message to (+ dat.)
παρακύπτω: to stoop sideways
ῥᾷος, -α, -ον: more easy
σύνειμι: to be with, consort with (+ dat.)
σχεδόν: nearly
ταπεινός, -ή, -όν: low
τήμερον, τό: today
φέρω: to bear
χρηστός, -ή, -όν: useful

ἕκτην σχεδὸν ... ἕκτην γε: "about the sixth day ... by Zeus, exactly the sixth"

δευτέρᾳ (sc. ἡμέρᾳ): "on the second day"

ἱσταμένου (sc. μηνός): "from (the month) beginning"

ὡς πάλαι ἐρῴην: pres. opt. of ἐράω in ind. st. in secondary sequence after εἰδὼς, "knowing that I was long in love with" + gen.

χρηστῆς: "in love with this useful woman" ironic

παραγγείλας: aor. part., "he (the father) locked me in having instructed" + dat.

μὴ ἀνοίγειν: pres. inf. in ind. com. after παραγγείλας, "instructed not to open"

οὐ γὰρ ἔφερον: impf., "for I was not bearing" i.e. I couldn't stand"

μὴ οὐχὶ: the double negative is redundant after a negated verb, "I couldn't bear not to be with her"

παρακύψαντα: aor. part. instrumental, "I ordered Dromon by having stooped down"

ἀναδέξασθαι: aor. inf. mid. after ἐκέλευσα, "I ordered him to receive me on his back"

ἀναβήσεσθαι: fut. inf. mid. complementing ἔμελλον, "I intended to mount"

λέγοιμι: pres. opt. pot., "why should I speak at length?"

ὑπερέβην, ἧκον, τὴν αὔλειον εὗρον ἀποκεκλεισμένην
ἐπιμελῶς· μέσαι γὰρ νύκτες ἦσαν. οὐκ ἔκοψα δ' οὖν, ἀλλ'
ἐπάρας ἠρέμα τὴν θύραν, ἤδη δὲ καὶ ἄλλοτ' ἐπεποιήκειν
αὐτό, παραγαγὼν τὸν στροφέα παρεισῆλθον ἀψοφητί.
ἐκάθευδον δὲ πάντες, εἶτα ἐπαφώμενος τοῦ τοίχου
ἐφίσταμαι τῇ κλίνῃ.

ΙΟΕΣΣΑ: Τί ἐρεῖς, ὦ Δάματερ; ἀγωνιῶ γάρ.

ΛΥΣΙΑΣ: Ἐπειδὴ δὲ οὐχ ἑώρων τὸ ᾆσθμα ἕν, τὸ μὲν
πρῶτον ᾤμην τὴν Λυδὴν αὐτῇ συγκαθεύδειν· τὸ δ' οὐκ
ἦν, ὦ Πυθιάς, ἀλλ' ἐφαψάμενος εὗρον ἀγένειόν τινα
πάνυ ἁπαλόν, ἐν χρῷ κεκαρμένον, μύρων καὶ αὐτὸν

ἀγένειος, -ον: beardless
ἀγωνιάω: to contend eagerly, struggle
ἄλλοτε: at another time
ἁπαλός, -ή, -όν: tender
ᾆσθμα, τό: breathing
αὔλειος, ἡ: a courtyard
ἀψοφητί: noiselessly
εἷς, μία, ἕν: one
ἐπαίρω: to lift up
ἐπαφάω: to touch lightly (+ *gen.*)
ἐπιμελής, -ές: careful
ἐρῶ: I will say or speak
ἐφάπτομαι: to lay a hand on
ἐφίσταμαι: to stand near (+ *dat.*)
ἥκω: to have come
ἠρέμα: (*adv.*) gently

θύρα, ἡ: a door
καθεύδω: to lie down, sleep
κείρω: to cut
κλίνη, ἡ: a couch or bed
κόπτω: to strike, knock
μέσος, -η, -ον: middle
μύρον, τό: unguent, balsam
νύξ, νυκτός, ἡ: the night
οἴομαι: to suppose, think
ὁράω: το see
παράγω: to lead by or past
παρεισέρχομαι: to go in secretly
στροφεύς, -έως, ὁ: the socket
τοῖχος, ὁ: a wall
ὑπερβαίνω: to step over, mount, scale
χρώς, ὁ: the surface of the body, the skin

ἀποκεκλεισμένην: perf. part. circum. after εὗρον, "I found the courtyard *closed*"
ἐπάρας: aor. part. of ἐπι-αἴρω, "I, *having lifted*"
ἐπεποιήκειν: plupf., "*I had done* this other times"
παραγαγὼν: aor. part. of παρα-ἄγω, "I, *having lead* the socket *past*" i.e. unlocked
παρεισῆλθον: aor. of παρα-εἰς-έρχομαι, "I entered secretly"
ἕν: pred., "saw the breathing was not *one*"
τὸ μὲν πρῶτον: adverbial acc., "while at first"
συγκαθεύδειν: pres. inf. in ind. st. after ᾤμην, "I thought that Lyde *was sleeping with*"
τὸ δ' οὐκ ἦν: "but this was not so"
ἐν χρῷ: "on the skin," i.e. close-shaved
κεκαρμένον: perf. part. pass. of κείρω, "him *having been shaved*"

ἀποπνέοντα. τοῦτο ἰδὼν εἰ μὲν καὶ ξίφος ἔχων ἦλθον, οὐκ ἂν ὤκνησα, εὖ ἴστε. τί γελᾶτε, ὦ Πυθιάς; γέλωτος ἄξια δοκῶ σοι διηγεῖσθαι;

ΙΟΕΣΣΑ: Τοῦτό σε, ὦ Λυσία, λελύπηκεν; ἡ Πυθιὰς αὕτη μοι συνεκάθευδε.

ΠΥΘΙΑΣ: Μὴ λέγε, ὦ Ἰόεσσα, πρὸς αὐτόν.

ΙΟΕΣΣΑ: Τί μὴ λέγω; Πυθιὰς ἦν, φίλτατε, μετακληθεῖσα ὑπ' ἐμοῦ, ὡς ἅμα καθεύδοιμεν· ἐλυπούμην γὰρ σὲ μὴ ἔχουσα.

ΛΥΣΙΑΣ: Πυθιὰς ὁ ἐν χρῷ κεκαρμένος; εἶτα δι' ἕκτης ἡμέρας ἀνεκόμησε τοσαύτην κόμην;

ἀνακομάω: to grow new hair
ἄξιος, -ία, -ον: worthy of (+ gen.)
ἀποπνέω: to breathe forth, to smell of (+ gen.)
γελάω: to laugh
γέλως, -τος, ὁ: laughter
διηγέομαι: to describe in full
εἶτα: then, next
ἡμέρα, ἡ: a day

κείρω: to cut
κόμη, ἡ: the hair
λυπέω: to grieve
μετακαλέω: to summon
ξίφος, -εος, τό: a sword
ὀκνέω: to shrink
τοσοῦτος, -αύτη, -οῦτο: so large, so tall
φίλτατος, -η, -ον: most dear
χρώς, ὁ: the skin

ἰδών: aor. part. of εἶδον, "I, *having seen* this"

εἰ ... ἦλθον: aor. in past contrafactual apodosis, "*if I had come* having a sword"

οὐκ ἂν ὤκνησα: aor. in contrafactual apodosis, "I would not have shrunk" i.e. from using the sword

ἄξια: acc. neut. pl. obj. of διηγεῖσθαι, "to say *things worthy of*" (+ gen.)

λελύπηκεν: perf., "this *has grieved* you?"

τί μὴ λέγω: pres. subj. in deliberative question, "Why should I not speak?"

μετακληθεῖσα: aor. part. pass., "she *having been summoned*"

ὡς ... καθεύδοιμεν: pres. opt. in purpose clause in secondary sequence, "so that we would sleep together"

ἔχουσα: pres. part. with μὴ indicating conditional sense, "if not *having* you"

κόμην: acc. cognate, "she grew so much *hair*"

ΙΟΕΣΣΑ: Ἀπὸ τῆς νόσου ἐξυρήσατο, ὦ Λυσία: ὑπέρρεον γὰρ αὐτῇ αἱ τρίχες. νῦν δὲ καὶ τὴν πηνήκην ἐπέθετο. δεῖξον, ὦ Πυθιάς, δεῖξον οὕτως ὄν, πεῖσον αὐτόν. ἰδοὺ τὸ μειράκιον ὁ μοιχὸς ὄν ἐζηλοτύπεις.

ΛΥΣΙΑΣ: Οὐκ ἐχρῆν οὖν, ὦ Ἰόεσσα, καὶ ταῦτα ἐρῶντα ἐφαψάμενον αὐτόν;

ΙΟΕΣΣΑ: Οὐκοῦν σὺ μὲν ἤδη πέπεισαι: βούλει δὲ ἀντι-λυπήσω σε καὶ αὐτή; ὀργίζομαι δικαίως ἐν τῷ μέρει.

ΛΥΣΙΑΣ: Μηδαμῶς, ἀλλὰ πίνωμεν ἤδη, καὶ Πυθιὰς μεθ' ἡμῶν: ἄξιον γὰρ αὐτὴν παρεῖναι ταῖς σπονδαῖς.

ἀντιλυπέω: to vex in return
βούλομαι: to will, wish
δείκνυμι: to display, exhibit
δίκαιος, -α, -ον: just
ἐπιτίθημι: to lay, place upon
ἐράω: to love
ἐφάπτομαι: to lay a hand on
ζηλοτυπέω: to be jealous of X (*acc.*)
ἤδη: now
θρίξ, τρίχος, ἡ: the hair of the head
μειράκιον, τό: a boy, lad
μέρος, -εος, τό: a part, share

μηδαμῶς: in no way
μοιχός, ὁ: an adulterer
νόσος, ἡ: sickness, disease
ξυρέω: to shave
ὀργίζομαι: to be angry
πάρειμι: to be present (+ *dat.*)
πείθω: to persuade
πηνήκη, ἡ: false hair, wig
πίνω: to drink
σπονδή, ἡ: a drink-offering
ὑπορρέω: to flow from under
χρή: it is necessary

ὑπέρρεον: impf. of ὑπο-ρέω, "they were flowing out" i.e. falling out

ἐπέθετο: aor. of ἐπι-τίθημι, "*she has placed* a wig *on* (her head)"

δεῖξον: aor. imper., "show!"

ὄν: pres. part. in ind. st. after δεῖξον, "show *that it is* so"

πεῖσον: aor. imper., "persuade!"

τὸ μειράκιον ὁ μοιχὸς: nom. pred., "(here is) the lad, the adulterer"

οὐκ ἐχρῆν: impf. indicating what should have been, "was it not necessary (to be jealous)?"

ἐρῶντα ἐφαψάμενον: circumstantial part. agreeing with με understood after ἐχρῆν, "necessary for me, *since I was in love and had touched* him"

πέπεισαι: perf. pass. of πείθω, "and so *you have been persuaded*"

ἀντιλυπήσω: aor. subj. hortatory after βούλει, "you wish *that I should be angry in return*?"

πίνωμεν: aor. subj. of πίνω, "let us drink!"

παρεῖναι: pres. inf. epexegetic after ἄξιον, "it is worthy *that she be present*"

ΙΟΕΣΣΑ: Παρέσται. οἷα πέπονθα διὰ σέ, ὦ γενναιότατε νεανίσκων Πυθίας.

ΠΥΘΙΑΣ: Ἀλλὰ καὶ διήλλαξα ὑμᾶς ὁ αὐτός, ὥστε μή μοι χαλέπαινε. πλὴν τὸ δεῖνα, ὅρα, ὦ Λυσία, μή τινι εἴπῃς τὸ περὶ τῆς κόμης.

Reclining courtesan playing kottabos. *(From Attic Red-Figure Kylix by Onesimos, c. 500 BC. J. Paul Getty Museum.)*

γενναῖος, -α, -ον: noble
δεῖνα, τό: indecl.: such a one
διαλλάττω: to interchange
εἶπον: to speak (*aor.*)
κόμη, ἡ: the hair

νεάνισκος, ὁ: a young man
οἷος, -α, -ον: what sort of
ὁράω: to see
πλήν: besides, in addition
χαλεπαίνω: to be sore at (+ *dat.*)

παρέσται: fut., "she will be present"

πέπονθα: perf. of πάσχω, "what things *I have suffered*"

διήλλαξα: aor. of διαλλάττω, "but *I changed back*"

ὁ αὐτός: nom. pred., "I was *the same one*" joking about the confusion by using the masculine gender

τὸ δεῖνα: an interjection to indicate a sudden realization, "by the way!"

μή ... εἴπῃς: aor. subj. in noun clause after ὅρα, "see to it *that you do not speak!*"

τὸ περὶ: "*the (matter) concerning* the hair"

13. Leontichus, Chenidas, and Hymnis

A boastful warrior imagines that tales of his fierce exploits will make him desirable. But when it has the opposite effect on the delicate young Hymnis, he decides to change his story.

ΛΕΟΝΤΙΧΟΣ: Ἐν δὲ τῇ πρὸς τοὺς Γαλάτας μάχῃ εἰπέ, ὦ
Χηνίδα, ὅπως μὲν προεξήλασα τῶν ἄλλων ἱππέων ἐπὶ
τοῦ ἵππου τοῦ λευκοῦ, ὅπως δὲ οἱ Γαλάται καίτοι ἄλκι-
μοι ὄντες ἔτρεσάν εὐθὺς ὡς εἶδον καὶ οὐδεὶς ἔτι ὑπέστη.
τότε τοίνυν ἐγὼ τὴν μὲν λόγχην ἀκοντίσας διέπειρα τὸν
ἵππαρχον αὐτὸν καὶ τὸν ἵππον, ἐπὶ δὲ τὸ συνεστηκὸς ἔτι
αὐτῶν—ἦσαν γάρ τινες οἳ ἔμενον διαλύσαντες μὲν τὴν
φάλαγγα, ἐς πλαίσιον δὲ συναγαγόντες αὑτούς—ἐπὶ
τούτους ἐγὼ σπασάμενος τὴν σπάθην ἅπαντι τῷ θυμῷ

ἀκοντίζω: to hurl a javelin
ἄλκιμος, -ον: strong, stout
Γαλάται, οἱ: the Galatians, a Celtic people in Anatolia
διαλύω: to loose, undo
διαπείρω: to drive through
θυμός, ὁ: the soul, emotion, fury
ἵππαρχος, ὁ: a general of cavalry
ἱππεύς, -ῆος, ὁ: a horseman
ἵππος, ὁ: a horse, mare
λευκός, -ή, -όν: white, bright
λόγχη, ἡ: a spear-head, javelin-head
μάχη, ἡ: battle, fight, combat

μένω: to stay where one is
πλαίσιον, τό: an oblong figure
προεξελαύνω: to ride out before (+ *gen.*)
σπάθη, ἡ: a flat blade
σπάω: to draw
συνάγω: to collect
συνίστημι: to unite, band together
τοίνυν: therefore, accordingly
τότε: at that time, then
τρέω: to flee away
ὑφίσταμαι: to stand under as a support
φάλαγξ, -αγγος, ἡ: a line of battle

προεξήλασα: aor. of προ-εξ-ελαύνω, "say how I *rode out ahead of*" (+ *gen.*)

ὄντες: pres. part. concessive, "saw how the Galatians, *although being* strong"

εὐθὺς ὡς εἶδον: "as soon as they saw"

ὑπέστη: aor. intransitive after εἶδον, "saw how no one *stood*"

διέπειρα: aor. of δια-πείρω, "I pierced through"

τὸ συνεστηκὸς: perf. part. of συν-ίστημι, "the having united" i.e. the group that was still (ἔτι) standing their ground

συναγαγόντες: aor. part., "they, *having collected* themselves"

ἅπαντι τῷ θυμῷ: dat. of manner, "driven upon them *with all my fury*"

ἐπελάσας ἀνατρέπω μὲν ὅσον ἑπτὰ τοὺς προεστῶτας
αὐτῶν τῇ ἐμβολῇ τοῦ ἵππου: τῷ ξίφει δὲ κατενεγκὼν
διέτεμον τῶν λοχαγῶν ἑνὸς ἐς δύο τὴν κεφαλὴν αὐτῷ
κράνει. ὑμεῖς δέ, ὦ Χηνίδα, μετ' ὀλίγον ἐπέστητε ἤδη
φευγόντων.

ΧΗΝΙΔΑΣ: Ὅτε γάρ, ὦ Λεόντιχε, περὶ Παφλαγονίαν ἐμο-
νομάχησας τῷ σατράπῃ, οὐ μεγάλα ἐπεδείξω καὶ τότε;

ΛΕΟΝΤΙΧΟΣ: Καλῶς ὑπέμνησας οὐκ ἀγεννοῦς οὐδ' ἐκείνης
τῆς πράξεως: ὁ γὰρ σατράπης μέγιστος ὤν, ὁπλομάχων

ἀγεννής, -ές: low-born, ignoble
ἀνατρέπω: to overturn, upset
διατέμνω: to cut through, divide
ἐμβολή, ἡ: a charge
ἐπεδείκνυμι: to show
ἐπελαύνω: to drive upon
ἑπτά: seven
ἐφίσταμαι: to stand near, arrive
καταφέρω: to bring down
κεφαλή, ἡ: the head
κράνος, ὁ: a helmet

λοχαγός: the leader of an armed band
μονομαχέω: to fight in single combat
ξίφος, -εος, τό: a sword
ὀλίγος, -η, -ον: little, small
ὁπλομάχος, -ον: fighting in heavy arms
ὅσος, -η, -ον: how many
πρᾶξις, -εως, ἡ: a doing, deal
προΐστημι: to set before
σατράπης, -ου, ὁ: a satrap, viceroy
ὑπομιμνήσκω: to remind
φεύγω: to flee, take flight, run away

ἐπελάσας: aor. part. circum. of ἐπι-ελαύνω, "I, *having driven upon* them"

τοὺς προεστῶτας: perf. part. attributive of προ-ἵστημι and acc. obj. of ἀνατρέπω, "I turn against *those standing forward*"

τῇ ἐμβολῇ: dat. of means, "I upset them *with the charge*"

κατενεγκὼν: aor. part. of κατα-φέρω, "*having brought down* with my sword" i.e. having struck

διέτεμον: aor., "*I divided* the head"

ἐς δύο: "divided *into two*"

αὐτῷ κράνει: dat., "even with the helmet" i.e. helmet and all

μετ' ὀλίγον (sc. χρόνον): "after a short time"

ἐπέστητε: aor. intransitive of ἐπι-ἵστημι, "you all arrived"

φευγόντων: pres. part. in gen. abs., "while (the enemy) already *were fleeing*"

ἐπεδείξω: aor. 2. sing. mid., "didn't you display?"

ὑπέμνησας: aor., "you reminded me of" + *gen.*

οὐκ ... οὐδ': redundant negative, "*of that not* ignoble *at all*"

ἄριστος δοκῶν εἶναι, καταφρονήσας τοῦ Ἑλληνικοῦ,
προπηδήσας ἐς τὸ μέσον προὐκαλεῖτο εἴ τις ἐθέλοι
αὐτῷ μονομαχῆσαι. οἱ μὲν οὖν ἄλλοι κατεπεπλήγεσαν οἱ
λοχαγοὶ καὶ οἱ ταξίαρχοι καὶ ὁ ἡγεμὼν αὐτὸς καίτοι οὐκ
ἀγεννὴς ἄνθρωπος ὤν· Ἀρίσταιχμος γὰρ ἡμῶν ἡγεῖτο
Αἰτωλὸς ἀκοντιστὴς ἄριστος, ἐγὼ δὲ ἐχιλιάρχουν ἔτι.
τολμήσας δ᾽ ὅμως καὶ τοὺς ἑταίρους ἐπιλαμβανομένους
ἀποσεισάμενος, ἐδεδοίκεσαν γὰρ ὑπὲρ ἐμοῦ ὁρῶντες
ἀποστίλβοντα μὲν τὸν βάρβαρον ἐπιχρύσοις τοῖς ὅπλοις,
μέγαν δὲ καὶ φοβερὸν ὄντα τὸν λόφον, κραδαίνοντα τὴν
λόγχην —

ἀγεννής, -ές: low-born
ἀκοντιστής, -οῦ, ὁ: a javelin thrower
ἀποσείω: to shake off
ἀποστίλβω: to be bright from
ἄριστος, -η, -ον: best
βάρβαρος, ὁ: a barbarian
δέδια: to fear (*perf.*)
ἐθέλω: to will, wish, purpose
Ἑλληνικός, -ή, -όν: Greek
ἐπιλαμβάνω: to hold back
ἐπίχρυσος, -ον: overlaid with gold
ἑταῖρος, ὁ: a comrade, companion, mate
ἡγεμών, -όνος, ἡ: a leader
ἡγέομαι: to go before, lead the way
καταπλήττω: to strike down

καταφρονέω: to think down upon, despise (+ *gen.*)
κραδαίνω: to brandish
λόγχη, ἡ: a spear-head, javelin-head
λόφος, ὁ: a crest (of a helmet)
λοχαγός, ὁ: the leader of an armed band
μονομαχέω: to fight in single combat
ὅπλον, τό: armor
προκαλέω: to call forth, challenge
προπηδάω: to spring before
ταξίαρχος, ὁ: the commander of a squadron
τολμάω: to undertake, dare
φοβερός, -ά, -όν: fearful
χιλιαρχέω: to be a commander of 1000 men

ἄριστος: nom. pred., "seeming to be *the best*"

προὐκαλεῖτο: impf. of προ-καλέω, "he kept challenging"

εἴ τις ἐθέλοι: pres. opt. in ind. question in secondary sequence, "kept challenging *whether anyone wished*" + inf.

κατεπεπλήγεσαν: plupf. pass. of κατα-πλήττω, "the others *had been struck* with fear"

καίτοι ... ὤν: pres. part. concessive, "he, *although being* not low born"

ἐπιλαμβανομένους: pres. part. acc. circumstantial, "the companions *who were holding me back*"

ἐδεδοίκεσαν: plupf. of δέδια with impf. meaning, "for they were fearing"

ὑπὲρ ἐμοῦ: "fearing *on my behalf*"

ὅπλοις: dat. of description, "gleaming *with gold armor*"

τὸν λόφον: acc. respect, "him being fearful *with respect to his crest*"

ΧΗΝΙΔΑΣ: Κἀγὼ ἔδεισα τότε, ὦ Λεόντιχε, καὶ οἶσθα ὡς εἰχόμην σου δεόμενος μὴ προκινδυνεύειν· ἀβίωτα γὰρ ἦν μοι σοῦ ἀποθανόντος.

ΛΕΟΝΤΙΧΟΣ: Ἀλλ' ἐγὼ τολμήσας παρῆλθον ἐς τὸ μέσον οὐ χεῖρον τοῦ Παφλαγόνος ὡπλισμένος, ἀλλὰ πάγχρυσος καὶ αὐτός, ὥστε βοὴ εὐθὺς ἐγένετο καὶ παρ' ἡμῶν καὶ παρὰ τῶν βαρβάρων· ἐγνώρισαν γάρ με κἀκεῖνοι ἰδόντες ἀπὸ τῆς πέλτης μάλιστα καὶ τῶν φαλάρων καὶ τοῦ λόφου. εἰπέ, ὦ Χηνίδα, τίνι με τότε πάντες εἴκαζον;

ἀβίωτος, -ον: not to be lived
ἀποθνήσκω: to die off, die
βοή, ἡ: a loud cry, shout
γνωρίζω: to make known
δέομαι: to beg
εἰκάζω: to liken, compare
λόφος, ὁ; a crest (of a helmet)
μέσος, -η, -ον: middle, in the middle
οἶδα: to know (*perf.*)

ὁπλίζω: to make or get ready
πάγχρυσεος, -ον: all-golden, of solid gold
παρέρχομαι: to go by
Παφλαγών, -όνος, ὁ: a Paphlagonian
πέλτη, ἡ: a small light shield
προκινδυνεύω: to run risk before
τολμάω: to undertake, take heart
φάλαρον, τό: boss (of a shield)
χείρων, -ον: worse, meaner, inferior

κἀγὼ (= καί ἐγώ): "*I too* was afraid"

ὡς εἰχόμην: impf. in ind. quest. after οἶσθα, "you know *how I was holding you back*"

μὴ προκινδυνεύειν: pres. inf. in ind. quest. after δεόμενος, "begging you *not to run the risk*"

ἀβίωτα: nom. pred. "life is *not worth living*"

ἀποθανόντος: aor. part. in gen. abs. "with you *havning died*"

τοῦ Παφλαγόνος: gen. of comp. after χεῖρον, "armed no worse *than the Paphlagopnian*"

ὡπλισμένος: perf. part. "I *having been armed*"

ἐγένετο: aor. of γίγνομαι, "a shout immediately *happened*"

τίνι: dat. ind. obj. of εἴκαζον, "*to whom* were they comparing?"

ΧΗΝΙΔΑΣ: Τίνι δὲ ἄλλῳ ἢ Ἀχιλλεῖ νὴ Δία τῷ Θέτιδος καὶ Πηλέως; οὕτως ἔπρεπε μέν σοι ἡ κόρυς, ἡ φοινικὶς δὲ ἐπήνθει καὶ ἡ πέλτη ἐμάρμαιρεν.

ΛΕΟΝΤΙΧΟΣ: Ἐπεὶ δὲ συνέστημεν, ὁ βάρβαρος πρότερος τιτρώσκει με ὀλίγον ὅσον ἐπιψαύσας τῷ δόρατι μικρὸν ὑπὲρ τὸ γόνυ, ἐγὼ δὲ διελάσας τὴν ἀσπίδα τῇ σαρίσῃ παίω διαμπὰξ ἐς τὸ στέρνον, εἶτ' ἐπιδραμὼν ἀπεδειροτόμησα τῇ σπάθῃ ῥᾳδίως καὶ τὰ ὅπλα ἔχων ἐπανῆλθον ἅμα καὶ τὴν κεφαλὴν ἐπὶ τῆς σαρίσης πεπηγυῖαν κομίζων λελουμένος τῷ φόνῳ.

ἀποδειροτομέω: to slaughter by cutting off the head
ἀσπίς, -ίδος, ἡ: a round shield
Ἀχιλλεύς, -έως, ὁ: Achilles, hero of the *Iliad*
γόνυ, τό: the knee
διαμπάξ: right through
διελαύνω: to drive through
δόρυ, -ατος, τό: a spear
ἐπανέρχομαι: to go back, return
ἐπανθέω: to bloom, be in flower
ἐπιτρέχω: to run upon or at
ἐπιψαύω: to touch lightly
Θέτις, -ιδος, ἡ: Thetis, Achilleus' mother
κομίζω: to take care of
κόρυς, -υθος, ἡ: a helmet
λούω: to wash

μαρμαίρω: to flash, sparkle
μικρός, -ά, -όν: small, little
ὀλίγος, -η, -ον: little, small
παίω: strike, smite
πέλτη, ἡ: a small light shield
πήγνυμι: to make fast
Πηλεύς, -έως, ὁ: Peleus, Achilleus' father
πρέπω: to be clearly seen
ῥᾳδίως: easily
σάρισα, ἡ: the sarissa, a lance
σπάθη, ἡ: a flat blade
στέρνον, τό: the breast, chest
συνίστημι: to combine, associate, unite
τιτρώσκω: to wound
φοινικίς, -ίδος, ἡ: a red or purple cloth
φόνος, ὁ: murder, homicide, slaughter

τίνι ἄλλῳ ἢ: "to whom other than?"

τῷ Θέτιδος (sc. υἱῷ): "than *to the (son) of Thetis*"

ἐπήνθει: impf. of ἐπι-ανθέω, "your red (mantle) *was blooming*"

συνέστημεν: aor. intransitive, "when *we met*"

διελάσας: aor. part. of διελαύνω, "I *having pierced*"

τῇ σαρίσῃ: dat. means, "pierced *with my sarissa*" a long lance

ἐπιδραμών: aor. part. of ἐπιτρέχω, "I *having charged*"

ἐπανῆλθον: aor. of ἐπι-ανα-έρχομαι: "I *returned*"

πεπηγυῖαν: perf. part. with passive meaning, agreeing with κεφαλήν, "bringing the head *having been fixed*"

λελουμένος: perf. part. mid, "I *having washed myself*"

ΥΜΝΙΣ: Ἄπαγε, ὦ Λεόντιχε, μιαρὰ ταῦτα καὶ φοβερὰ περὶ σαυτοῦ διηγῇ, καὶ οὐκ ἂν ἔτι σε οὐδὲ προσβλέψειέ τις οὕτω χαίροντα τῷ λύθρῳ, οὐχ ὅπως συμπίοι ἢ συγκοιμηθείη. ἔγωγ' οὖν ἄπειμι.

ΛΕΟΝΤΙΧΟΣ: Διπλάσιον ἀπόλαβε τὸ μίσθωμα.

ΥΜΝΙΣ: Οὐκ ἂν ὑπομείναιμι ἀνδροφόνῳ συγκαθεύδειν.

ΛΕΟΝΤΙΧΟΣ: Μὴ δέδιθι, ὦ Ὑμνί: ἐν Παφλαγόσιν ἐκεῖνα πέπρακται, νῦν δὲ εἰρήνην ἄγω.

ΥΜΝΙΣ: Ἀλλ' ἐναγὴς ἄνθρωπος εἶ, καὶ τὸ αἷμα κατέσταζέ σου ἀπὸ τῆς κεφαλῆς τοῦ βαρβάρου, ἣν ἔφερες ἐπὶ τῇ σαρίσῃ. εἶτ' ἐγὼ τοιοῦτον ἄνδρα περιβάλω καὶ φιλήσω;

ἄγω: to lead, do
αἷμα, -ατος, τό: blood
ἀνδροφόνος, -ον: man-slaying
ἄπαγε: away! begone!
ἄπειμι: to go away (*fut.*)
ἀπολαμβάνω: to take or receive from
βάρβαρος, ὁ: a barbarian
δέδια: to fear (*perf.*)
διηγέομαι: to describe in full
διπλάσιος, -α, -ον: twofold, double
εἰρήνη, ἡ: peace
ἐναγής, -ές: under a curse
καταστάζω: to drip over (+ *gen.*)
λύθρον, τό: gore

μιαρός, -ά, -όν: stained
μίσθωμα, -ατος, τό: the price
περιβάλλω: to throw round, embrace
πράττω: to do
προσβλέπω: to look at or upon
συγκαθεύδω: to lie down with
συγκοιμάομαι: to lie with
συμπίνω: to drink together
τοιοῦτος, -αύτη, -οῦτο: such as this
ὑπομένω: to stay behind, endure
φέρω: to bear
φιλέω: to love, kiss
φοβερός, -ά, -όν: fearful
χαίρω: to rejoice, be glad

διηγῇ: pres. 2 s. mid., "you are narrating"
προσβλέψειε: aor. opt. pot., "no one *would look upon*"
χαίροντα: pres. part. agreeing with σε, "you *rejoicing in*" + dat.
συμπίοι: aor. opt. pot. of συμπίνω, "nor *would* anyone *drink with*"
συγκοιμηθείη: aor. pass. opt. pot., "nor *would they lie with*"
ὑπομείναιμι: aor. opt. pot., "I would not endure" + inf.
μὴ δέδιθι: perf. imper., "don't fear"
πέπρακται: perf. of πράττω, "these things *have been done*"
ἣν ἔφερες: impf. in relative clause, "the head *which you were carrying*"
περιβάλω: aor. subj. in deliberative question, "should I embrace?"
φιλήσω: aor. subj. in deliberative question, "should I kiss?"

μή, ὦ Χάριτες, γένοιτο· οὐδὲν γὰρ οὗτος ἀμείνων τοῦ
δημίου.

ΛΕΟΝΤΙΧΟΣ: Καὶ μὴν εἴ με εἶδες ἐν τοῖς ὅπλοις, εὖ οἶδα,
ἠράσθης ἄν.

ΥΜΝΙΣ: Ἀκούουσα μόνον, ὦ Λεόντιχε, ναυτιῶ καὶ φρίττω
καὶ τὰς σκιάς μοι δοκῶ ὁρᾶν καὶ τὰ εἴδωλα τῶν πεφονευμένων καὶ μάλιστα τοῦ ἀθλίου λοχαγοῦ ἐς δύο τὴν
κεφαλὴν διῃρημένου. τί οἴει, τὸ ἔργον αὐτὸ καὶ τὸ αἷμα
εἰ ἐθεασάμην καὶ κειμένους τοὺς νεκρούς; ἐκθανεῖν δή
μοι δοκῶ· οὐδ' ἀλεκτρυόνα πώποτε φονευόμενον εἶδον.

ἄθλιος, -α, -ον: miserable	θεάομαι: to behold
αἷμα, -ατος, τό: blood	κεῖμαι: to be laid
ἀκούω: to hear	λοχαγός, ὁ: a leader
ἀλεκτρυών, -ονος, ὁ: a cock	μόνος, -η, -ον: alone, only
ἀμείνων, -ον: better than (+ gen.)	ναυτιάω: to suffer from nausea
δήμιος, ὁ: a public executioner	νεκρός, ὁ: a corpse
διαιρέω: to cleave in two	οἴομαι: to suppose, think
δοκέω; to seem to (+ inf.)	ὅπλον, τό: armor
δύο: two	ὁράω: to see
εἶδον: to see (aor.)	πώποτε: ever yet
εἴδωλον, τό: an image	σκιά, -ᾶς, ἡ: a shadow
ἐκθνῄσκω: to die away	φονεύω: to murder, kill
ἔραμαι: to be in love with	φρίττω: to bristle
ἔργον, τό: deed, work	Χάριτες, αἱ: the Graces

μή ... γένοιτο: aor. opt. in wish for the future, "may these things never happen!"
οὐδὲν: acc. of respect, "better *in no way*"
εἴ με εἶδες: aor. in past contrafactual protasis, "if you had seen me"
ἠράσθης: aor. pass. in past contrafactual apodosis, "you would have fallen in love"
ἀκούουσα: pres. part. instrumental, "I am nauseated only *by hearing*"
μοι δοκῶ: "I seem to myself to" + inf.
πεφονευμένων: perf. part. gen. pl. part., "images *of those who have been killed*"
διῃρημένου: perf. part. of διαιρέω, "of the leader *who was split* in two"
εἰ ἐθεασάμην: aor. in past contrafactual apodosis, "*if I had seen* the act itself"

ΛΕΟΝΤΙΧΟΣ: Οὕτως ἀγεννής, ὦ Ὑμνί, καὶ μικρόψυχος εἶ;
ἐγὼ δὲ ᾤμην ἡσθήσεσθαί σε ἀκούουσαν.

ΥΜΝΙΣ: Ἀλλὰ τέρπε τοῖς διηγήμασι τούτοις εἴ τινας
Λημνιάδας ἢ Δαναΐδας εὕροις· ἐγὼ δ' ἀποτρέχω παρὰ
τὴν μητέρα, ἕως ἔτι ἡμέρα ἐστίν. ἕπου καὶ σύ, ὦ Γραμμί·
σὺ δὲ ἔρρωσο, χιλιάρχων ἄριστε καὶ φονεῦ ὁπόσων ἂν
ἐθέλῃς.

ΛΕΟΝΤΙΧΟΣ: Μεῖνον, ὦ Ὑμνί, μεῖνον — ἀπελήλυθε.

ΧΗΝΙΔΑΣ: Σὺ γάρ, ὦ Λεόντιχε, ἀφελῆ παιδίσκην κατεφόβη-
σας ἐπισείων λόφους καὶ ἀπιθάνους ἀριστείας διεξιών·

ἀγεννής, -ές: of no family, ignoble
ἀπέρχομαι: to go away, depart from
ἀπίθανος, -ον: incredible, unlikely
ἀποτρέχω: to run off or away
ἀριστεία, ἡ: excellence, prowess
ἄριστος, -η, -ον: best
ἀφελής, -ές: simple
Δαναΐς, -δος, ἡ: a daughter of Danaus
διήγημα, -ατος, τό:
ἐπισείω: to shake at or against
ἕπομαι: to follow
εὑρίσκω: to find
ἕως: until, till
ἥδομαι: to enjoy oneself

ἡμέρα, ἡ: a day
καταφοβέω: to strike with fear
Λημνιάς, -αδος, ἡ: a Lemnian woman
λόφος, ὁ: the back of the neck
μένω: to stay where one is
μήτηρ, μητέρος, ἡ: a mother
μικρόψυχος, -ον: mean-spirited
ὁπόσος, -η, -ον: as many as
παιδίσκη, ἡ: a young girl, maiden
ῥώννυμι: to make strong
τέρπω: to delight, gladden
φονεύς, -έως, ὁ: a murderer
χιλίαρχος, ὁ: the commander of a thousand men

ἡσθήσεσθαί: fut. inf. pass. in ind. st. after ᾤμην, "I supposed *that you would enjoy*"

ἀκούουσαν: pres. part. supplementing ἡσθήσεσθαί, "would enjoy *hearing*"

διηγήμασι: dat. of means, "(you) gladden *with these stories!*"

εἰ ... εὕροις: aor. opt. in present general protasis, "if ever you find any"

Λημνιάδας ἢ Δαναΐδας: the women of Lemnos murdered their husbands, as did the 50 daughters of Danaus

ἕπου: aor. imper. of ἕπομαι, "you follow too!"

ἔρρωσο: perf. imper. of ῥώννυμι, "you be strong!"

ἄριστε καὶ φονεῦ: vocatives, "*Oh best of* Chiliarchs *and slayer!*"

ὁπόσων ἂν ἐθέλῃς: aor. subj. in general relative clause, "slayer of *whomsoever you wish*"

μεῖνον: aor. imper., "stay!"

ἀπελήλυθε: perf. of ἀπο-έρχομαι, "she has gone"

ἐπισείων: pres. part. instrumental, "you terrified *by shaking*"

διεξιών: pres. part. instrumental of δια-εξ-έρχομαι, "by narrating thoroughly"

ἐγὼ δὲ ἑώρων εὐθὺς ὅπως χλωρὰ ἐγένετο ἔτι σου τὰ κατὰ τὸν λοχαγὸν ἐκεῖνα διηγουμένου καὶ συνέστειλε τὸ πρόσωπον καὶ ὑπέφριξεν, ἐπεὶ διακόψαι τὴν κεφαλὴν ἔφης.

ΛΕΟΝΤΙΧΟΣ: ὤμην ἐρασμιώτερος αὐτῇ φανεῖσθαι. ἀλλὰ καὶ σύ με προσαπολώλεκας, ὦ Χηνίδα, τὸ μονομάχιον ὑποβαλών.

ΧΗΝΙΔΑΣ: Οὐκ ἔδει γὰρ συνεπιψεύδεσθαί σοι ὁρῶντα τὴν αἰτίαν τῆς ἀλαζονείας; σὺ δὲ πολὺ φοβερώτερον αὐτὸ ἐποίησας. ἔστω γάρ, ἀπέτεμες τοῦ κακοδαίμονος

αἰτία, ἡ: a cause, reason
ἀλαζονεία, ἡ: false pretension
ἀποτέμνω: to cut off, sever
δεῖ: it is necessary
διακόπτω: to cut in two
διηγέομαι: to describe in full
ἐράσμιος, -η, -ον: lovely
κακοδαίμων, -ον: cursed, miserable
κεφαλή, ἡ: the head
λοχαγός: a commander

μονομάχιον, τό: single combat
προσαπόλλυμι: to destroy besides or
πρόσωπον, τό: the face
συνεπιψεύδομαι: to join in lying
συστέλλω: to draw together
ὑποβάλλω: to throw in
ὑποφρίττω: to shudder slightly
φαίνομαι: to appear
φοβερός, -ά, -όν: fearful
χλωρός, -ά, -όν: greenish-yellow, pale

ἑώρων: impf. of ὁράω, "I was noticing"
διηγουμένου: pres. part. in gen. abs. with σου, "while you were narrating"
συνέστειλε: aor. of συν-στέλλω, "her face *drew together*" i.e. in a frown
διακόψαι: aor. inf. in ind. st. after ἔφης, "you said *that you cut in two*"
φανεῖσθαι: fut. inf. of φαίνομαι in ind. st. after ὤμην, I thought *that I would appear*"
προσαπολώλεκας: perf. of προσ-απόλλυμι, "you have destroyed me in addition"
ὑποβαλών: aor. part. instrumental, "destroyed *by having thrown in*"
οὐκ ἔδει: "wasn't it necessary?" + inf., expecting an affirmative answer
ὁρῶντα: pres. part. acc. agreeing with ἐμέ understood, the subject of συνεπιψεύδεσθαι, "necessary for me, *when seeing* to join in lying"
φοβερώτερον: acc. pred. after ἐποίησας, "you made it *more fearful*"
ἔστω: pres. imper. 3 s., "let it be!" i.e. it should have been enough
ἀπέτεμες: aor. of ἀπο-τέμνω in a noun clause which is the subject of ἔστω, "*that you cut off* should have been enough"

Παφλαγόνος τὴν κεφαλήν, τί καὶ κατέπηξας αὐτὴν ἐπὶ τῆς σαρίσης, ὥστε σου καταρρεῖν τὸ αἷμα;

ΛΕΟΝΤΙΧΟΣ: Τοῦτο μιαρὸν ὡς ἀληθῶς, ὦ Χηνίδα, ἐπεὶ τά γε ἄλλα οὐ κακῶς συνεπέπλαστο. ἄπιθι δ᾽ οὖν καὶ πεῖσον αὐτὴν συγκαθευδήσουσαν.

ΧΗΝΙΔΑΣ: Λέγω οὖν ὡς ἐψεύσω ἅπαντα γενναῖος αὐτῇ δόξαι βουλόμενος;

ΛΕΟΝΤΙΧΟΣ: Αἰσχρόν, ὦ Χηνίδα.

αἰσχρός, -ά, -όν: shameful	καταρρέω: to flow down
βούλομαι: to will, wish	μιαρός, -ά, -όν: foul
γενναῖος, -α, -ον: noble	πείθω: to persuade
κακός, -ή, -όν: bad	συμπλάττω: to mould or fashion together
καταπήγνυμι: to fix firmly	ψεύδομαι: to lie, beguile

κατέπηξας: aor. of καταπήγνυμι, "why *did you fix it firmly?*" i.e. why did you narrate that additional detail

ὥστε ... καταρρεῖν: pres. inf. in result clause, "so that it dripped on" + gen.

ὡς ἀληθῶς: "truly"

συνεπέπλαστο: plupf. of συν-πλάττω, "after the rest *had been moulded*"

ἄπιθι: pres. imper. of ἀπο-έρχομαι, "go away!"

πεῖσον: aor. imper. of πείθω, "persuade!"

συγκαθευδήσουσαν: fut part. agreeing with αὐτὴν and expressing purpose, "persuade her *in order that she lie down with*"

λέγω: pres. subj. in deliberative question, "should I say?"

ὡς ἐψεύσω: aor. 2 s. mid. in ind. st. after λέγω, "should I say *that you lied*"

γενναῖος: nom. pred., "to seem *noble*"

δόξαι: aor. inf. complementing βουλόμενος, "wishing *to seem*"

ΧΗΝΙΔΑΣ: Καὶ μὴν οὐκ ἄλλως ἀφίκοιτο. ἑλοῦ τοίνυν θάτερον ἢ μισεῖσθαι ἀριστεὺς εἶναι δοκῶν ἢ καθεύδειν μετὰ
Ὑμνίδος ἐψεῦσθαι ὁμολογῶν.

ΛΕΟΝΤΙΧΟΣ: Χαλεπὰ μὲν ἄμφω· αἱροῦμαι δ' ὅμως τὴν
Ὑμνίδα. ἄπιθι οὖν καὶ λέγε, ὦ Χηνίδα, ἐψεῦσθαι μέν, μὴ
πάντα δέ.

*Hetaira with lyre before an old man. (Tondo from an Attic red-figure kylix
by Onesimos, c. 500 BC. From Vulci, Italy. British Museum, London.)*

αἱρέομαι: to choose	**μισέω**: to hate
ἀριστεύς, -έως, ὁ: the best man	**ὁμολογέω**: to agree, admit
ἀφικνέομαι: to come to	**τοίνυν**: therefore, accordingly
καθεύδω: to lie down to sleep,	**χαλεπός, -ή, -όν**: hard to bear

---

ἀφίκοιτο: aor. opt. pot. (without **ἄν**), "otherwise *she would not come*"

ἑλοῦ: aor. imper. of **αἱρέομαι**, "choose!"

θάτερον (=**τό ἔτερον**): "choose *one of two*"

ἢ μισεῖσθαι ... ἢ καθεύδειν: pres. inf. in apposition to **θάτερον**, "one of two, namely *either to be hated ... or to sleep with*"

δοκῶν ... ὁμολογῶν: pres. part. instrumental, "*by seeming* to be the best man ... *by admitting* to have lied"

ἐψεῦσθαι μέν, μὴ πάντα δέ: "say *that I lied, but that not all* (were lies)"

14. Dorion and Myrtale

Dorion complains that Myrtale does not appreciate his humble gifts, leading to a crass reckoning of value.

ΔΩΡΙΩΝ: Νῦν με ἀποκλείεις, ὦ Μυρτάλη, νῦν, ὅτε πένης ἐγενόμην διὰ σέ, ὅτε δέ σοι τοσαῦτα ἐκόμιζον, ἐρώμενος, ἀνήρ, δεσπότης, πάντ' ἦν ἐγώ. ἐπεὶ δ' ἐγὼ μὲν αὖος ἤδη ἀκριβῶς, σὺ δὲ τὸν Βιθυνὸν ἔμπορον εὕρηκας ἐραστήν, ἀποκλείομαι μὲν ἐγὼ καὶ πρὸ τῶν θυρῶν ἔστηκα δακρύων, ὁ δὲ τῶν νυκτῶν φιλεῖται καὶ μόνος ἔνδον ἐστὶ καὶ παννυχίζεται, καὶ κυεῖν φῂς ἀπ' αὐτοῦ.

Erotic scene with youth and a courtesan. (Detail from an Attic red-figure oinochoe, c. 430 BC. From Locri, Italy.)

ἀκριβής, -ές: exact	ἐράω: to love
ἀνήρ, ἀνδρὸς, ὁ: man	θύρα, ἡ: a door
ἀποκλείω: to shut out	ἵστημι: to make to stand
αὖος, -η, -ον: drained dry	κομίζω: to provide
Βιθυνός, -η, -ον: Bithynian	κυέω: to be pregnant
δακρύω: to weep, shed tears	νύξ, νυκτός, ἡ: the night
δεσπότης, -ου: a master	παννυχίζω: to celebrate a night festival
ἔμπορος, ὁ: a merchant	πένης, -ητος, ὁ: a poor man
ἔνδον: inside	πρό: before (+ gen.)
ἐραστής, -οῦ, ὁ: a lover	φιλέω: to love, kiss

ἐγενόμην: aor. of γίγνομαι, "when *I became* poor"

ἐρώμενος: pres. part. pass., "I was your *beloved*" as opposed to an ἐραστής, a lover

εὕρηκας: perf. of εὑρίσκω, unreduplicated, "*you have found* for a lover"

ἔστηκα: perf. of ἵστημι with present sense, "*I stand* weeping" the typical pose of the *exclusus amator*

τῶν νυκτῶν: gen. of time within which, "he is kissed *during the nights*"

κυεῖν: pres. inf. in ind. st., "you claim *to be pregnant*"

ΜΥΡΤΑΛΗ: Ταῦτά με ἀποπνίγει, Δωρίων, μάλιστα ὁπόταν λέγῃς ὡς πολλὰ ἔδωκας καὶ πένης γεγένησαι δι' ἐμέ. λόγισαι γοῦν ἅπαντα ἐξ ἀρχῆς ὁπόσα μοι ἐκόμισας.

ΔΩΡΙΩΝ: Εὖ γε, ὦ Μυρτάλη, λογισώμεθα. ὑποδήματα ἐκ Σικυῶνος τὸ πρῶτον δύο δραχμῶν· τίθει δύο δραχμάς.

ΜΥΡΤΑΛΗ: Ἀλλ' ἐκοιμήθης νύκτας δύο.

ΔΩΡΙΩΝ: Καὶ ὁπότε ἧκον ἐκ Συρίας, ἀλάβαστρον μύρου ἐκ Φοινίκης, δύο καὶ τοῦτο δραχμῶν νὴ τὸν Ποσειδῶ.

ΜΥΡΤΑΛΗ: Ἐγὼ δέ σοι ἐκπλέοντι τὸ μικρὸν ἐκεῖνο χιτώνιον τὸ μέχρι τῶν μηρῶν, ὡς ἔχοις ἐρέττων, Ἐπιούρου τοῦ πρωρέως ἐκλαθομένου αὐτὸ παρ' ἡμῖν, ὁπότε ἐκάθευδε παρ' ἐμοί.

ἀλάβαστρον, τό: a box
ἀποπνίγω: to choke
ἀρχή, ἡ: a beginning
δίδωμι: to give
δραχμή, ἡ: a drachma
δύο: two
ἐκλανθάνομαι: to forget
ἐκπλέω: to sail out
ἐρέττω: to row
ἥκω: to have come, be present, be here
καθεύδω: to sleep
κοιμάομαι: to sleep with
λογίζομαι: to calculate, compute

μέχρι: up to (+ *gen.*)
μηρός, ὁ: the thigh
μικρός, -ά, -όν: small, little
μύρον, τό: balsam, myrrh
ὁπόσος, -η, -ον: how much
ὁπόταν: whensoever
πένης, -ητος, ὁ: a poor man
πρωρεύς, -εως, ὁ: the officer in command at the bow
Συρία, -ας, ἡ: Syria
τίθημι: to set, put, place
ὑπόδημα, -ατος, τό: a sandal
χιτώνιον, τό: a frock or shift

ὁπόταν λέγῃς: pres. subj. in present general clause, "whenever you say"

γεγένησαι: perf. mid., "say *that you have become*"

γοῦν λόγισαι: aor. imper., "and so calculate!"

λογισώμεθα: aor. subj., hortatory., "let's calculate!"

ἐκοιμήθης: aor. pass. with middle meaning, "*you slept with* me"

νύκτας δύο: acc. of duration, "for two nights"

δύο ... δραχμῶν: gen. of value, "a box *worth two drachmae*"

ὡς ἔχοις: pres. opt. in purpose clause in secondary sequence, "*so that you could have it* while rowing"

ἐκλαθομένου: aor. part. in gen. abs., "the officer Epiouros *having forgotten* it"

111

ΔΩΡΙΩΝ: Ἀπέλαβεν αὐτὸ γνωρίσας ὁ Ἐπίουρος πρῴην
ἐν Σάμῳ μετὰ πολλῆς γε, ὦ θεοί, τῆς μάχης. κρόμμυα
δὲ ἐκ Κύπρου καὶ σαπέρδας πέντε καὶ πέρκας τέτταρας, ὁπότε κατεπλεύσαμεν ἐκ Βοσπόρου, ἐκόμισά σοι.
τί οὖν; καὶ ἄρτους ὀκτὼ ναυτικοὺς ἐν γυργάθῳ ξηροὺς
καὶ ἰσχάδων βῖκον ἐκ Καρίας καὶ ὕστερον ἐκ Πατάρων
σανδάλια ἐπίχρυσα, ὦ ἀχάριστε· καὶ τυρόν ποτε μέμνημαι τὸν μέγαν ἐκ Γυθίου.

ΜΥΡΤΑΛΗ: Πέντε ἴσως δραχμῶν, ὦ Δωρίων, πάντα ταῦτα.

ἀπολαμβάνω: to take away
ἄρτος, ὁ: a loaf of wheat-bread
ἀχάριστος, -ον: ungracious, ungrateful
βῖκος, ὁ: a wine-jar
Βόσπορος, ὁ: the Bosporus, the strait that separates Asia and Europe at the site of modern Istanbul
γνωρίζω: to make known, discover
Γύθιον, τό: Gythion, a city on the southern tip of mainland Greece
γυργάθος, ὁ: a basket
ἐπίχρυσος, -ον: overlaid with gold
ἰσχάς, -άδος, ἡ: a dried fig
ἴσως: perhaps
Κάρια, -ας, ἡ: Caria, a region in Southwest modern Turkey
καταπλέω: to sail down
κομίζω: to provide to (+ dat.)
κρόμμυον, τό: onion

Κύπρος, ἡ: Cyprus, an island off the southern coast of modern Turkey
μάχη, ἡ: battle, fight
μιμνήσκομαι: to remember
ναυτικός, -ή, -όν: naval
ξηρός, -ά, -όν: dry
ὀκτώ: eight
Πατάραι, -ων, αἱ: Patara, a city in Lycia, in southwest modern Turkey
πέντε: five
πέρκη, ἡ: the perch
Σάμος, ὁ: Samos, an island off the coast of modern Turkey
σανδάλιον, τό: sandals
σαπέρδης, -ου, ὁ: the fish
τέσσαρες, -ων, οἱ: four
τυρός, ὁ: cheese
ὕστερον: later

ἀπέλαβεν: aor., "Epiouros *took it away*"

γνωρίσας: aor. part., "took it *once he recognized* it"

Σάμῳ, etc.: note the list of nautical destinations, the islands Samos, Cyprus, and ports in other parts of the Aegean

κρόμμυα, etc.: there now follows a long list of modest gifts that a poor sailor could afford

μέμνημαι: perf. with present sense, "*I remember* the cheese"

ΔΩΡΙΩΝ: Ὦ Μυρτάλη, ὅσα ναύτης ἄνθρωπος ἐδυνάμην μισθοῦ ἐπιπλέων. νῦν γὰρ ἤδη τοίχου ἄρχω τοῦ δεξιοῦ καὶ σὺ ἡμῶν ὑπερορᾷς, πρῴην δὲ ὁπότε τὰ Ἀφροδίσια ἦν, οὐχὶ δραχμὴν ἔθηκα πρὸ τοῖν ποδοῖν τῆς Ἀφροδίτης σοῦ ἕνεκεν ἀργυρᾶν; καὶ πάλιν τῇ μητρὶ εἰς ὑποδήματα δύο δραχμὰς καὶ Λυδῇ ταύτῃ πολλάκις εἰς τὴν χεῖρα νῦν μὲν δύο, νῦν δὲ τέτταρας ὀβολούς. ταῦτα πάντα συντεθέντα οὐσία ναύτου ἀνδρὸς ἦν.

ΜΥΡΤΑΛΗ: Τὰ κρόμμυα καὶ οἱ σαπέρδαι, ὦ Δωρίων;

ΔΩΡΙΩΝ: Ναί· οὐ γὰρ εἶχον πλείω κομίζειν· οὐ γὰρ ἂν ἤρεττον, εἴ γε πλουτῶν ἐτύγχανον. τῇ μητρὶ δὲ οὐδὲ

ἀργύρεος, -ᾶ, -οῦν: silver
ἄρχω: to be in charge of (+ *gen.*)
Ἀφροδίσια, τά: the festival of Aphrodite
δεξιός, -ά, -όν: on the right, the starboard
δύναμαι: to be able
ἕνεκα: for the sake of (+ *gen.*)
ἐπιπλέω: to sail
ἐρέττω: to row
μήτηρ, μητρός, ἡ: a mother
μισθός, ὁ: wages, pay, hire
ναύτης, -ου, ὁ: a sailor
ὀβολός, ὁ: an obol
ὁπότε: when
ὅσος, -η, -ον: how much?
οὐσία, ἡ: one's property

πάλιν: again
πλείων, -ον: more
πλουτέω: to be wealthy
πολλάκις: many times
πούς, ποδός, ὁ: a foot
πρῴην: earlier
σαπέρδης, -ου, ὁ: the fish
συντίθημι: to put together
τίθημι: to set, put, place
τοῖχος, ὁ: a wall, the side (of a ship)
τυγχάνω: to happen to (+ *part.*)
ὑπεροράω: to look down upon (+ *gen.*)
ὑπόδημα, -ατος, τό: a sandal
χείρ, χειρός, ἡ: the hand

ὅσα ... ἐδυνάμην: impf., "I gave *what I was able*"

μισθοῦ: gen. of purpose, "sailing *for a wage*"

οὐχὶ ... ἔθηκα: aor. of τίθημι in question expecting a positive answer, "did I not deposit?"

πρὸ τοῖν ποδοῖν: dual dat., "*before the feet* of Aphrodite"

συντεθέντα: aor. part. pass. neut. pl. of συν-τίθημι, "all these *combined* are the property"

οὐσία: nom. pred., "are *the property*"

εἶχον: impf. " I was not able" + inf.

πλείω (=πλείο(ν)α): acc. pl. neut., "provide *more things*"

οὐ ... ἂν ἤρεττον: impf. in past contrafactual apodosis, "I would not have rowed"

πλουτῶν: pres. part. supplementing ἐτύγχανον, "if I happened *to be wealthy*"

κεφαλίδα μίαν σκορόδου ἐκόμισα πώποτε. ἡδέως δ' ἂν
ἔμαθον ἅτινά σοι παρὰ Βιθυνοῦ τὰ δῶρα.

ΜΥΡΤΑΛΗ: Τουτὶ πρῶτον ὁρᾷς τὸ χιτώνιον; ἐκεῖνος ἐπρία-
το, καὶ τὸν ὅρμον τὸν παχύτερον.

ΔΩΡΙΩΝ: Ἐκεῖνος; ᾔδειν γάρ σε πάλαι ἔχουσαν.

ΜΥΡΤΑΛΗ: Ἀλλ' ὃν ᾔδεις, πολὺ λεπτότερος ἦν καὶ
σμαράγδους οὐκ εἶχε. καὶ ἐλλόβια ταυτὶ καὶ δάπιδα,
καὶ πρῴην δύο μνᾶς, καὶ τὸ ἐνοίκιον κατέβαλεν ὑπὲρ
ἡμῶν, οὐ σάνδαλα Παταρικὰ καὶ τυρὸν Γυθιακὸν καὶ
φλήναφους.

ΔΩΡΙΩΝ: Ἀλλὰ ἐκεῖνο οὐ λέγεις, οἵῳ ὄντι συγκαθεύδεις
αὐτῷ; ἔτη μὲν ὑπὲρ τὰ πεντήκοντα πάντως, ἀναφα-
λαντίας καὶ τὴν χρόαν οἷος κάραβος. οὐδὲ τοὺς ὀδόντας

ἀναφαλαντίας, -ον: bald in front	μνᾶ, ἡ: a mna (= 100 drachma)
Γυθιακός, -η, -ον: from Gythia	ὀδούς, -όντος, ὁ: tooth
δάπις, -ιδος, ἡ: a carpet	οἷος, -α, -ον: such as, what sort of?
δῶρον, τό: a gift, present	ὅρμος, ὁ: a chain
εἷς, μία, ἕν: one	πάλαι: long ago
ἐλλόβιον, τό: an earring	πάντως: altogether;
ἐνοίκιον, τό: a house rent	Παταρικός, -η, -ον: from Patara
ἐπριάμην: to buy (aor.)	παχύς, -εῖα, ύ: thick, stout
ἔτος, -εος, τό: a year	πεντήκοντα: fifty
ἡδέως: sweetly	σάνδαλον, τό: a sandal
κάραβος, -ο: a crayfish	σκόροδον, τό: garlic
καταβάλλω: to pay down	σμάραγδος, ὁ: emerald
κεφαλίς, -ίδος, ἡ: part of a shoe	φλήναφος, ὁ: idle talk, nonsense
λεπτός, -ή, -όν: thin	χιτώνιον, τό: a woman's frock
μανθάνω: to learn	χρόα, ἡ: the color of the skin

ἂν ἔμαθον: aor. in past contrafactual, "I would have liked to know"

τὸν παχύτερον: attributive, "*the thicker* chain"

ᾔδειν: plupf. of οἶδα, "I knew"

ἔχουσαν: pres. part. in ind. st. after ᾔδειν, "I knew *that you had* it"

ᾔδεις: plupf. of οἶδα, "(the one) whom *you knew*"

οἵῳ ὄντι: dat. with συγκαθεύδεις in an indirect question, "say with *being what sort*
you sleep" i.e. tell me what your lover is like

ἔτη ... τὴν χρόαν: acc. of respect, "fifty *in years* ... *in skin color* like a crayfish"

αὐτοῦ ὁρᾷς; αἱ μὲν γὰρ χάριτες, ὦ Διοσκόρω, πολλαί, καὶ μάλιστα ὁπόταν ᾄδῃ καὶ ἁβρὸς εἶναι θέλῃ, ὄνος αὐτολυρίζων, φασίν. ἀλλὰ ὄναιο αὐτοῦ ἀξία γε οὖσα καὶ γένοιτο ὑμῖν παιδίον ὅμοιον τῷ πατρί, ἐγὼ δὲ καὶ αὐτὸς εὑρήσω Δελφίδα ἢ Κυμβάλιόν τινα τῶν κατ᾽ ἐμὲ ἢ τὴν γείτονα ὑμῶν τὴν αὐλητρίδα ἢ πάντως τινά. δάπιδας δὲ καὶ ὅρμους καὶ διμναῖα μισθώματα οὐ πάντες ἔχομεν.

ΜΥΡΤΑΛΗ: Ὦ μακαρία ἐκείνη, ἥτις ἐραστὴν σέ, ὦ Δωρίων, ἕξει· κρόμμυα γὰρ αὐτῇ οἴσεις ἐκ Κύπρου καὶ τυρόν, ὅταν ἐκ Γυθίου καταπλέῃς.

ἁβρός, -ά, -όν: delicate, graceful
ᾄδω: to sing
ἄξιος, -ία, -ον: worthy of (+ *gen.*)
αὐλητρίς, -ίδος, ἡ: a flute-girl
αὐτολυρίζω: to play the lyre solo
γείτων, -ονος, ὁ: a neighbor
δάπις, -ιδος, ἡ: a carpet
διμναῖος, -α, -ον: worth two minae
ἐραστής, -οῦ, ὁ: a lover
θέλω: to will, wish, purpose
καταπλέω: to sail down
κρόμμυον, τό: onion

μακάριος, -α, -ον: blessed, happy
μίσθωμα, -ατος, τό: the price
ὅμοιος, -α, -ον: like
ὀνίνημι: to profit, benefit
ὄνος, ὁ: an ass
ὅρμος, ὁ: a chain, necklace
ὅστις, ἥτις, ὅτι: any one who
παιδίον, τό: a little child
πάντως: altogether;
τύρος, ὁ: cheese
χάρις, -ιτος, ἡ: a grace, charm

Διοσκόρω: dual vocative, "the Dioscoroi," Castor and Pollux, were patrons of sailors
ᾄδῃ … θέλῃ: pres. subj. in present general clause, "whenever he sings … wishes"
φασίν: "as they say" indicating a proverbial expression, i.e. an ass playing a solo on the lyre
ὄναιο: aor. opt. in wish for the future, "may you profit!"
οὖσα: pres. part. causal, "*since you are* worthy"
γένοιτο: aor. opt. of γίγνομαι in wish for the future, "*may* your child *become!*"
τῶν κατ᾽ ἐμέ: "one *of those like me*"
τὴν αὐλητρίδα: attributive, "your neighbor, *the flute-girl*"
ἕξει: fut. of ἔχω, "that one who *will have* you"
οἴσεις: fut. of φέρω, "you will bring"
καταπλέῃς: pres. subj. in general temporal clause, "whenever you sail out"

115

15. Cochlis and Parthenis

Parthenis tells Cochlis of a brawl involving soldiers, whom they agree make troublesome lovers.

ΚΟΧΛΙΣ: Τί δακρύεις, ὦ Παρθενί, ἢ πόθεν κατεαγότας τοὺς αὐλοὺς φέρεις;

ΠΑΡΘΕΝΙΣ: Ὁ στρατιώτης ὁ Αἰτωλὸς ὁ μέγας ὁ Κροκάλης ἐρῶν ἐρράπισέ με αὐλοῦσαν εὑρὼν παρὰ τῇ Κροκάλῃ ὑπὸ τοῦ ἀντεραστοῦ αὐτοῦ Γόργου μεμισθωμένην καὶ τούς τε αὐλούς μου συνέτριψε καὶ τὴν τράπεζαν μεταξὺ δειπνούντων ἀνέτρεψε καὶ τὸν κρατῆρα ἐξέχεεν ἐπεισπαίσας· τὸν μὲν γὰρ ἀγροῖκον ἐκεῖνον τὸν Γόργον ἀπὸ τοῦ συμποσίου κατασπάσας τῶν τριχῶν ἔπαιον

ἀγροῖκος, -η, -ον: rustic	κρατήρ, -ῆρος, ὁ: a mixing vessel
Αἰτωλός, -ον: from Aetolia	μέγας, μέγαλη, μέγαν: large
ἀνατρέπω: to overturn, upset	μεταξύ: between
ἀντεραστής, -οῦ, ὁ: a rival in love	μισθόμαι: to hire for a fee
αὐλέω: to play on the flute	παίω: strike, smite
αὐλός, ὁ: a flute	πόθεν: whence?
δειπνέω: to dine	ῥαπίζω: to strike with a stick
ἐκχέω: to pour out	στρατιώτης, -ου, ὁ: a soldier
ἐπεισπαίω: to burst in	συμπόσιον, τό: a symposium
θρίξ, τριχός, ἡ: the hair of the head	συντρίβω: to rub together, crush
κατάγνυμι: to shatter	τράπεζα, -ης, ἡ: a table
κατασπάω: to drag down	φέρω: to bear

κατεαγότας: perf. part. agreeing with αὐλοὺς, "those flutes *that are shattered*?"

ἐρράπισε: aor. of ῥαπίζω, "*he struck* me"

με αὐλοῦσαν: pres. part. circumstantial after εὑρὼν, "having discovered *me playing the flute*"

ὑπὸ ... Γόργου: gen. of agent, "me hired *by Gorgos*"

μεμισθωμένην: perf. part. circumstantial also agreeing with με, "me *having been hired*"

συνέτριψε ... ἀνέτρεψε ... ἐξέχεεν: aor., "he crushed ... overturned ... poured out"

ἐπεισπαίσας: aor. part. of ἐπι-εἰς-παίω, "he *having burst in*"

τῶν τριχῶν: gen. after κατασπάσας, "he having dragged *by the hairs*"

ἔπαιον: impf. inceptive, "*they began striking* him"

116

περιστάντες αὐτός τε ὁ στρατιώτης—Δεινόμαχος,
οἶμαι, καλεῖται—καὶ ὁ συστρατιώτης αὐτοῦ· ὥστε
οὐκ οἶδα εἰ βιώσεται ὁ ἄνθρωπος, ὦ Κοχλί· αἷμά τε
γὰρ ἐρρύη πολὺ ἀπὸ τῶν ῥινῶν καὶ τὸ πρόσωπον ὅλον
ἐξῴδηκεν αὐτοῦ καὶ πελιδνόν ἐστιν.

ΚΟΧΛΙΣ: Ἐμάνη ὁ ἄνθρωπος ἢ μέθη τις ἦν καὶ παροινία
τὸ πρᾶγμα;

ΠΑΡΘΕΝΙΣ: Ζηλοτυπία τις, ὦ Κοχλί, καὶ ἔρως ἔκτοπος· ἡ
Κροκάλη δὲ, οἶμαι, δύο τάλαντα αἰτήσασα, εἰ βούλεται
μόνος ἔχειν αὐτήν, ἐπεὶ μὴ ἐδίδου ὁ Δεινόμαχος, ἐκεῖνον
μὲν ἀπέκλεισεν ἥκοντα προσαράξασά γε αὐτῷ τὰς
θύρας, ὡς ἐλέγετο, τὸν Γόργον δὲ Οἰνοέα τινὰ γεωργὸν

αἷμα, -ατος, τό: blood	μόνος, -η, -ον: alone
αἰτέω: to ask	οἶδα: to know (*perf.*)
ἀποκλείω: to shut out	Οἰνοέης, -ες: from Oenoë
βιόω: to live	οἴομαι: to suppose, think
βούλομαι: to will, wish	ὅλος, -η, -ον: whole, all
γεωργός, ὁ: a farmer	παροινία, ἡ: drunken behavior
δίδωμι: to give	πελιδνός, -ή, -όν: black and blue
δύο: two	περιίστημι: to place round
ἔκτοπος, -ον: extraordinary	πρᾶγμα, -ατος, τό: the matter, business
ἐξοιδέω: to swell or be swollen up	προσαράσσω: to dash X (*acc.*) against Y
ἔρως, ὁ: love	(*dat.*)
ζηλοτυπία, ἡ: jealousy	πρόσωπον, τό: the face
ἥκω: to have come	ῥέω: to flow, run, stream, gush
θύρα, ἡ: a door	ῥίς, ῥινός, ἡ: the nose
μαίνομαι: to be mad	συστρατιώτης, -ου, ὁ: a fellow-soldier
μέθη, ἡ: drunkenness	τάλαντον, τό: a talant

περιστάντες: aor. part. intransitive of περι-ίστημι, "they *standing around*"

εἰ βιώσεται: fut. in ind. question after οἶδα, "I don't know know *whether he will live*"

ἐρρύη: aor. pass. of ῥέω with active meaning, "blood *flowed*"

ἐξῴδηκεν: perf. of ἐξ-οιδέω, "face *became swollen*"

ἐμάνη: aor. pass. of μαίνομαι with middle meaning, "*was he mad?*"

μέθη καὶ παροινία: nom. pred., "was the matter *drunkenness?*"

ἥκοντα: pres. part. temporal, "closed out that one *arriving*"

προσαράξασα: aor. part. of προσ-αράσσω, "she *having slammed* the doors on him"

εὔπορον ἐκ πολλοῦ ἐρῶντα καὶ χρηστὸν ἄνθρωπον
προσιεμένη ἔπινε μετ᾽ αὐτοῦ κἀμὲ παρέλαβεν αὐλήσουσαν αὐτοῖς. ἤδη δὲ προχωροῦντος τοῦ πότου ἐγὼ μὲν
ὑπέκρεκόν τι τῶν Λυδίων, ὁ γεωργὸς δὲ ἤδη ἀνίστατο
ὡς ὀρχησόμενος, ἡ Κροκάλη δὲ ἐκρότει, καὶ πάντα ἦν
ἡδέα· ἐν τοσούτῳ δὲ κτύπος ἠκούετο καὶ βοὴ καὶ ἡ αὔλειος ἠράσσετο, καὶ μετὰ μικρὸν ἐπεισέπεσον ὅσον ὀκτὼ
νεανίσκοι μάλα καρτεροὶ καὶ ὁ Μεγαρεὺς ἐν αὐτοῖς.

ἀκούω: to hear
ἀνίστημι: to make to stand up
ἀράσσω: to strike hard
αὔλειος, -ον: belonging to the court
αὐλέω: to play on the flute
βοή, ἡ: a loud cry, shout
ἐπεισπίπτω: to fall in upon
ἐράω: to love
εὔπορος, -ον: wealthy
ἡδύς, εῖα, ύ: sweet
καρτερός, -ά, -όν: strong, stout
κροτέω: to make to rattle
κτύπος, ὁ: a crash

Λύδιος, -α, -ον: Lydian
Μεγαρεύς, -έως, ὁ: a citizen of Megara
μικρός, -ά, -όν: small, little
νεανίσκος, ὁ: a youth
ὀκτώ: eight
ὀρχέομαι: to dance
παραλαμβάνω: to hire
πίνω: to drink
πότος, ὁ: a drinking-bout
προσίημι: to let come to
προχωρέω: to advance
ὑποκρέκω: to play an accompaniment
χρηστός, -ή, -όν: useful

ἐκ πολλοῦ (sc. χρόνου): "him, loving *from long ago*"
προσιεμένη: pres. part., "she *admitting* him"
ἔπινε: impf. inceptive, "*she began drinking* with him"
αὐλήσουσαν: fut. part. indicating purpose, "she hired me *to play the flute*"
προχωροῦντος: pres. part. in gen. abs., "the drinking already *progressing*"
ὑπέκρεκόν: impf. inceptive, "*I began playing* something Lydian"
ἀνίστατο: impf. intransitive, "he was just standing up"
ὡς ὀρχησόμενος: fut. part. of purpose, "in order to dance"
ἐν τοσούτῳ (sc. χρόνῳ): "at this moment"
ἡ αὔλειος (sc. θύρα): "the courtyard door"
ἠράσσετο: impf. pass., "was being struck"
ἐπεισέπεσον: aor. of ἐπι-εις-πίπτω, "they fell in upon"
ὅσον ὀκτὼ: "*eight or so* young men"
ὁ Μεγαρεὺς: "the Megarean" but the soldier was said to be Aetolian above, so this
expression must be some kind of insult

εὐθὺς οὖν ἀνετέτραπτο πάντα καὶ ὁ Γόργος, ὥσπερ
ἔφην, ἐπαίετο καὶ ἐπατεῖτο χαμαὶ κείμενος: ἡ Κροκάλη
δὲ οὐκ οἶδ' ὅπως ἔφθη ὑπεκφυγοῦσα παρὰ τὴν γείτονα
Θεσπιάδα: ἐμὲ δὲ ῥαπίσας ὁ Δεινόμαχος, «Ἐκφθείρου»
φησί, κατεαγότας μοι τοὺς αὐλοὺς προσρίψας. καὶ νῦν
ἀποτρέχω φράσουσα ταῦτα τῷ δεσπότῃ: ἀπέρχεται δὲ
καὶ ὁ γεωργὸς ὀψόμενός τινας φίλους τῶν ἀστικῶν, οἳ
παραδώσουσι τοῖς πρυτανεῦσι τὸν Μεγαρέα.

ΚΟΧΛΙΣ: Ταῦτ' ἐστὶν ἀπολαῦσαι τῶν στρατιωτικῶν τούτων
ἐραστῶν, πληγὰς καὶ δίκας: τὰ δὲ ἄλλα ἡγεμόνες εἶναι

ἀνατρέπω: to overturn, upset	παραδίδωμι: to hand over X (*acc.*) to Y (*dat.*)
ἀπέρχομαι: to go away, depart from	πατέω: to tread, walk
ἀπολαύω: to have enjoyment of	πληγή, ἡ: a blow, stroke
ἀποτρέχω: to run away	προσρίπτω: to throw X (*acc.*) at Y (*dat.*)
ἀστικός, -ή, -όν: of a city or town	πρυτανεύς, -έως, ὁ: a magistrate
δεσπότης, -ου: a master, lord	στρατιωτικός, -ή, -όν: of or for soldiers
δίκη, ἡ: a lawsuit	ὑπεκφεύγω: to escape
ἐκφθείρω: to destroy utterly	φημί: to declare, make known
ἡγεμών, -όνος, ἡ: a leader	φθάνω: to come or do first or before
Θεσπιάς, -άδας, ἡ: Thespias, a courtesan	φίλος, ὁ: a friend
κατάγνυμι: to break in pieces, shatter	φράζω: to point out to (+ *dat.*)
κεῖμαι: to be laid	χαμαί: on the earth, on the ground
παίω: strike, smite	

ἀνετέτραπτο: plupf. pass. of ἀνα-τρέπω, "everything *had been overturned*"
ἐπαίετο καὶ ἐπατεῖτο: impf. pass.,, "he was being beaten and trampled"
οὐκ οἶδ' ὅπως: parenthetical, "I don't know how"
ἔφθη: aor. of φθάνω, "she anticipated" + part.
ὑπεκφυγοῦσα: pres. part. supplementing ἔφθη, "anticipated *in fleeing*" i.e. she escaped
παρὰ τὴν γείτονα: "escaped *to the neighbor's* (house)"
ἐκφθείρου: pres. imper. pass., "be destroyed!" i.e. go to the devil!
κατεαγότας: perf. part. acc., "the flutes *that were broken*"
φράσουσα: fut. part. expressing purpose, "I am running off *to point out*"
ὀψόμενός: fut. part. of ὁράω, "the farmer is going *in order to see*"
τῶν ἀστικῶν: gen. partitive, "friends *from the townsmen*"
ἀπολαῦσαι: aor. inf. used as a pred., "these things are *to have enjoyment of*" + gen.
τὰ δὲ ἄλλα: acc. adverbial, "as for the rest"

καὶ χιλίαρχοι λέγοντες, ἤν τι δοῦναι δέῃ, «Περίμεινον»
φασί, «τὴν σύνταξιν, ὁπόταν ἀπολάβω τὴν μισθοφοράν,
καὶ ποιήσω πάντα.» ἐπιτριβεῖεν δ' οὖν ἀλαζόνες ὄντες·
ἔγωγ' οὖν εὖ ποιῶ μὴ προσιεμένη αὐτοὺς τὸ παράπαν.
ἁλιεύς τις ἐμοὶ γένοιτο ἢ ναύτης ἢ γεωργὸς ἰσότιμος
κολακεύειν εἰδὼς μικρὰ καὶ κομίζων πολλά, οἱ δὲ τοὺς
λόφους ἐπισείοντες οὗτοι καὶ τὰς μάχας διηγούμενοι,
ψόφοι, ὦ Παρθενί.

ἀλαζών, -όνος, ὁ: a vagabond
ἁλιεύς, ὁ: a fisherman
ἀπολαμβάνω: to receive from
διηγέομαι: to describe in full
ἐπισείω: to shake at or against
ἐπιτρίβω: to crush, perish
ἰσότιμος, -ον: held in equal honour
κολακεύω: to flatter
κομίζω: to provide for
λόφος, ὁ: the crest of a helmet
μάχη, ἡ: battle, fight, combat

μικρός, -α, -ον: small
μισθοφορά, ἡ: receipt of wages
ναύτης, -ου, ὁ: a mate or companion by sea
οἶδα: to know (perf.)
παράπαν: (adv.) altogether, absolutely
περιμένω: to wait for, await
προσίημι: to let come to
σύνταξις, -εως, ἡ: pay of soldiers
χιλίαρχος, ὁ: the commander of a thousand men
ψόφος, ὁ: a, noise

λέγοντες: pres. part. concessive, "*although claiming* to be"

ἤν ... δέῃ: pres. subj. of δεῖ in pres. gen. protasis, "if ever it is necessary to" + inf.

περίμεινον: aor. imper., "wait for!"

ὁπόταν ἀπολάβω: aor. subj. in general temporal clause, "*whenever I receive* it"

ἐπιτριβεῖεν: pres. opt. in wish for the future, "would that they would perish!"

ὄντες: causal, "since they are"

μὴ προσιεμένη: pres. part. conditional, "I do well *if not entertaining them*"

γένοιτο: aor. opt. in wish for the future, "*would that there would be* to me!"

εἰδὼς: perf. part., "he *knowing how*" + inf.

μικρὰ ... πολλά: "knowing how to flatter *little* ... providing *large*"

οἱ δὲ: "but they" i.e. the soldiers

ψόφοι: nom. pred., "they are *noises*"

Proper Names

Names in the *Dialogues of the Courtesans*

The information below about the provenance of proper names in inscriptions and literary sources is based on K. Mras (1916). We have suggested likely roots for the meanings of the names, which can play a role in their choice for a particular character.

Courtesans	Dialogue	Meaning	New Comedy	Other Sources
Ἀβρότονον	1	Balsam	•	•
Ἀμπελίς	8	Grape Vine	•	
Βακχίς	4	Bacchante	•	•
Γλυκέρα	1	Sweetie	•	•
Γοργόνα	1	The Grim One		•
Δελφίς	14	Dolphin	•	•
Δροσίς	10	Dew		•
Θαῖς	1, 3	Seeing	•	•
Ἰόεσσα	12	Violet		
Κλωνάριον	5	Twig		
Κόριννα	6	Doll Or Pupil		
Κολχίς	15	Seashell		
Κροκάλε	15	Pebble		
Κυμβάλιον	12, 14	Drummer		
Λέαινα	5	Lioness		•
Λυκαίνη	12	She Wolf		•
Λύρα	6	Lyre		
Μαγίδιον	12	Bread		
Μέλιττα	4	Honey		•
Μουσάριον	7	Musical		•

125

Courtesans *(Cont.)*	Dialogue	Meaning	New Comedy	Other Sources
Μυρτάλη	14	Myrtle		•
Μύρτιον	2	Myrtle		
Παγίς	11	Trap		
Παννυχίς	9	All-Night		•
Παρθενίς	15	Maiden		•
Πυραλλίς	12	Dove		
Σιμίχη	4	Flat-Nosed		•
Τρύφαινα	11	Dainty		•
Ὑμνίς	13	Hymn	•	•
Φιλαινίς	6	Fond Of Praise	•	•
Φιλημάτιον	11	Kiss	•	•
Φίλιννα	3	Kiss	•	•
Φοιβίς	4	Radiant	•	
Χελιδόνιον	10	Young Swallow		•
Χρυσίς	8	Goldy	•	•

Male Clients	Dialogue	Meaning	New Comedy	Other Sources
Ἀντιφῶν	7	Response	•	•
Γοργίας	8	Grim	•	•
Γόργος	15	Grim		•
Δαμύλος	11	Tame	•	•
Δημόφαντος	8	Notorious		•
Δίφιλος	3, 12	Double Lover		•
Δωρίων	14	Gift	•	•
Ἐρότιμος	4	Very Honored		•
Εὔκριτος	6	Well-Chosen		•
Θεοκλῆς	12	God's Glory		•

Male Clients *(Cont.)*	Dialogue	Meaning	New Comedy	Other Sources
Θράσων	12	Brave		•
Καλλίδης	8	Good-Looking		•
Κλεινίας	10	Renowned	•	•
Λαμπρίας	3	Radiance	•	•
Λεόντιχος	13	Ferocious		•
Λυσίας	12	Loose		•
Μέλισσος	12	Bee		•
Μοσχίων	11	Calf	•	•
Παμμένης	4	All Abiding		•
Πάμφιλος	2	All-Loving	•	•
Πασίων	12	Sprinkling		•
Πολέμον	9	Warlike	•	•
Φανίας	4	Clean	•	•
Φιλόστρατος	9	Army-Lover		•
Χαιρέας	7	Rejoice	•	•
Χαρίνος	4	Graceful	•	•
Χαρμίδης	2	Joyful	•	•

Other Men	Dialogue	Meaning	New Comedy	Other Sources
Ἀρίσταιχμος	13	Best Spear		•
Ἀρισταίνετος	2, 10	Best Praise		•
Ἀρχιτέλες	10	Chief Goal		•
Δεινόμαχος	15	Fearsome Battle		•
Δημέας	2	Public	•	•
Διότιμος	10	Honored By Zeus		•
Ἐπίσυρος	14	Overseer		
Κάλαμις	3	Pen-Case		•

Other Men *(Cont.)*	Dialogue	Meaning	New Comedy	Other Sources
Λάχης	7	Portion	•	•
Μενεράτης	7	Abiding Strength		•
Πραξίας	7	Working Man		•
Τιριδάτας	9	*(non-Greek)*		•
Φείδων	2	Sparing	•	•
Φιλῖνος	6	Kiss	•	•

Other Women	Dialogue	Meaning	New Comedy	Other Sources
Θεσπιάς	15	Oracular		•
Λεσβία	2	From Lesbos	•	•
Δαφνίς	6	Laurel		
Χρυσάριον	1	Gold		
Κρωβύλη	6	Hair Net	•	
Δεινομάχη	7	Fearsome Battle		•
Ἐρασίκλεια	10	Delighting in Glory		
Δημώνασσα	5	People's Princess		
Ἰσμηνοδώρα	5	Gift of the (Boeotian) River Ismenos		•
Μέγιλλα/-ος	5	Squinting Great One		•

Male Slaves	Dialogue	Meaning	New Comedy	Other Sources
Δρόμων	10, 12	At a Run	•	•
Παρμένων	9	Abiding	•	•
Τίβειος	9	Phrygian	•	•
Χηνίδας	13	Goose		

Female Slaves	Dialogue	Meaning	New Comedy	Other Sources
Ἀκίς	4	Needle		•
Γραμμίς	13	Writing	•	
Δορκάς	9	Roe		
Δωρίς	2	Gift	•	•
Λύδη	12, 14	Lydian		•
Νεβρίς	10	Fawn		
Πυθιάς	12	Priestess	•	•

List of Verbs

List of Verbs

The following is a list of verbs that have some irregularity in their conjugation. Contract verbs and other verbs that are completely predictable (-*ίζω*, -*εύω*, etc.) are generally not included. The principal parts of the Greek verb in order are 1. Present 2. Future 3. Aorist 4. Perfect Active 5. Perfect Middle 6. Aorist Passive, 7. Future Passive. We have not included the future passive below, since it is very rare. For many verbs not all forms are attested or are only poetic. Verbs are alphabetized under their main stem, followed by various compounds that occur in the *Dialogues of the Courtesans*, with a brief definition. A dash (-) before a form means that it occurs only or chiefly with a prefix. The list is based on the list of verbs in H. Smyth, *A Greek Grammar*.

ἄγνυμι: to break: -*άξω*, -*έαξα*, 2 perf. -*έαγα*, 2 aor. pass. -*εαγην*
  κατάγνυμι: to break in pieces, shatter
  περιρρήγνυμι: to rend, tear

ἀγγέλλω: to bear a message *ἀγγελῶ*, *ἤγγειλα*, *ἤγγελκα*, *ἤγγελμαι*, *ἠγγέλθην*
  ἀπαγγέλλω: to report
  ἐξαγγέλλω: to proclaim
  παραγγέλλω: to transmit as a message to
  προσαγγέλλω: to announce

ἄγω: to lead *ἄξω*, 2 aor. *ἤγαγον*, *ἦχα*, *ἦγμαι*, *ἤχθην*
  ἀπάγω: to lead away
  διάγω: to carry across, live
  κατάγω: to lead down
  παράγω: to lead by or past
  συνάγω: to collect
  ὑπάγω: to lead or bring under

ᾄδω: to sing *ᾄσομαι*, *ᾖσα*, *ᾖσμαι*, *ᾔσθην*
  ἐπᾴδω: to sing to or in accompaniment

αἰνέω: to praise -*αινέσω*, -*ήνεσα*, -*ήνεκα*, -*ήνημαι*, -*ηνέθην*.
  ἐπαινέω: to approve, applaud
  ὑπερεπαινέω: to praise above measure

αἱρέω: to take αἱρήσω, 2 aor. εἷλον, ᾕρηκα, ᾕρημαι, ᾑρέθην
    ἀφαιρέω: to take from, remove
    διαιρέω: to cleave in two
    ὑφαιρέω: to draw off, diminish

αἴρω: to lift ἀρῶ, ἦρα, ἦρκα, ἦρμαι, ἤρθην
    ἐπαίρω: to lift up

αἰσθάνομαι: to perceive αἰσθήσομαι, 2 aor. ᾐσθόμην, ᾔσθημαι

ἀκούω: to hear ἀκούσομαι, ἤκουσα, 2 perf. ἀκήκοα, ἠκούσθην
    παρακούω: to listen carelessly to

ἁλίσκομαι: to be captured ἁλώσομαι, 2 aor. ἑάλων, ἑάλωκα

ἀλλάττω: to change ἀλλάξω, ἤλλαξα, -ήλλαχα, ἤλλαγμαι, ἠλλάχθην or
  ἠλλάγην
    διαλλάττω: to change back

ἅπτω: to fasten, (mid.) to touch ἅψω, ἧψα, ἧμμαι, ἥφθην
    ἐφάπτω: to take hold of
    προσάπτω: to fasten on, touch

ἀράσσω: to strike ἀράξω, -ήραξα, -ηράχθην
    προσαράσσω: to dash against

ἄρχω: to be first, begin ἄρξω, ἦρξα, ἦργμαι, ἤρχθην

ἀφικνέομαι: to arrive at ἀφίξομαι, 2 aor. ἀφικόμην, ἀφῖγμαι

βαίνω: to step βήσομαι, 2 aor. ἔβην, βέβηκα
    ἀναβαίνω: to go up, mount
    διαβαίνω: to ford
    ἐπιβαίνω: to go upon
    μεταβαίνω: to pass over from one place to another
    ὑπερβαίνω: to step over, mount, scale

βάλλω: to throw βαλῶ, 2 aor. ἔβαλον, βέβληκα, βέβλημαι, ἐβλήθην
    ἐμβάλλω: to throw in, put in
    καταβάλλω: to throw down
    περιβάλλω: to embrace
    ὑπερβάλλω: to throw beyond, outdo
    ὑποβάλλω: to throw in

βλέπω: to look at βλέψομαι, ἔβλεψα
    ἀναβλέπω: to look up
    προσβλέπω: to look at
    ὑποβλέπω: to look up from under

βοάω: to shout βοήσομαι, ἐβόησα βέβωμαι, ἐβώσθην
    ἐπιβοάω: to call upon or to, cry out to

βούλομαι: to wish **βουλήσομαι, βεβούλημαι, ἐβουλήθην**

γαμέω: to marry **γαμῶ, ἔγημα, γεγάμηκα**

γελάω: to laugh **γελάσομαι, ἐγέλασα, ἐγελάσθην**

γί(γ)νομαι: to become **γενήσομαι, ἐγενόμην, γέγονα, γεγένημαι, ἐγενήθην**
    παραγίγνομαι: to be near, attend upon

γι(γ)νώσκω: to know **γνώσομαι, ἔγνων, ἔγνωκα, ἔγνωσμαι, ἐγνώσθην**
    ἀναγιγνώσκω: to read
    ἀπογιγνώσκω: give up, despair
    καταγιγνώσκω: to condemn

γράφω: to write **γράψω, ἔγραψα, γέγραφα, γέγραμμαι, ἐγράφην**
    ἐπιγράφω: to inscribe
    καταγράφω: to inscribe
    προσγράφω: to add in writing

δάκνω: to bite **δήξομαι,** 2 aor. **ἔδακον, δέδηγμαι, ἐδήχθην, δαχθήσομαι.**

δείκνυμι: to show **δείξω, ἔδειξα, δέδειχα, δέδειγμαι, ἐδείχθην**
    ἀποδείκνυμι: to present to
    ἐνδείκνυμι: to mark, point out
    ἐπεδείκνυμι: to show

δέομαι: to want, ask **δεήσομαι, δεδέημαι, ἐδεήθην** (from **δέω** 2)

δέχομαι: to receive **δέξομαι, ἐδεξάμην, δέδεγμαι, -εδέχθην**
    ἀναδέχομαι: to take up, receive
    εἰσδέχομαι: to take into, admit
    παραδέχομαι: to receive from

δέω (1): to bind **δήσω, ἔδησα, δέδεκα, δέδεμαι, ἐδέθην**
    ὑποδέω: to fasten under

δέω (2): to need, lack **δεήσω, ἐδήεσα δεδέηκα, δέδέημαι, ἐδεήθην**
    ἐνδέω: to lack, fall short

διδάσκω: to teach, (mid.) learn **διδάξω, ἐδίδαξα, δεδίδαχα, δεδίδαγμαι, ἐδιδάχθην**

δίδωμι: to give **δώσω,** 1 aor. **ἔδωκα** in s., 2 aor. **ἔδομεν** in pl. **δέδωκα, δέδομαι, ἐδόθην**
    ἀποδίδωμι: to give back, return
    ἐνδίδωμι: to give in, allow
    παραδίδωμι: to hand over

δοκέω: to think, seem **δόξω, ἔδοξα, δέδογμαι**

ἔδραμον: to run (used as aorist of **τρέχω**)

ἐγείρω: to wake up ἐγερῶ, ἤγειρα, 2 perf. ἐγρήγορα, ἐγήγερμαι, ἠγέρθην
    ἀνεγείρω: to wake up, rouse

ἐθέλω: to wish ἐθελήσω, ἠθέλησα, ἠθέληκα

εἶδον: to see (used as aor. of ὁράω), perf. οἶδα, to know
    ἐπεῖδον: to look upon, behold

εἰκάζω: to make like εἰκάσω, ἤκασα, ἤκασμαι, ἠκάσθην

εἰμί: to be, fut. ἔσομαι, impf. ἦν
    πάρειμι: to be present
    πρόσειμι: to be present
    σύνειμι: to be together with, consort with

εἶμι: to go, used as fut. of ἔρχομαι, pres. part. ἰών, imper. ἴτε, ἴθι

εἶπον: to say, used as 2 aor. of λέγω
    προεῖπον: to tell before

εἴργω: to shut in or out εἴρξω, εἶρξα, εἴργμαι, εἴρχθην

ἐλαύνω: to drive -ελῶ, -ήλασα, -ελήλακα, ἐλήλαμαι, ἠλάθην
    διελαύνω: to drive through
    ἐπελαύνω: to drive upon
    προεξελαύνω: to ride out before

ἕλκω: to draw -έλξω, εἵλκυσα, -είλκυκα, -είλκυσμαι, -ειλκύσθην

ἐπίσταμαι: to understand ἐπιστήσομαι, impf. ἠπιστάμην, ἠπιστήθην

ἕπομαι: to follow ἕψομαι, 2 aor. ἑσπόμην

ἐράω: to love, impf. ἤρων aor. ἠράσθην

ἐργάζομαι: to work ἐργάσομαι, ἠργασάμην, εἴργασμαι, ἠργάσθην

ἔρχομαι: to come or go to, fut. εἶμι, 2 aor. ἦλθον, 2 perf. ἐλήλυθα
    ἀνέρχομαι: to go up
    ἀπέρχομαι: to go away
    διέρχομαι: to pass through
    εἰσέρχομαι: to go into
    ἐπανέρχομαι: to go back, return
    κατέρχομαι: to go down from
    παρεισέρχομαι: to go in secretly
    παρέρχομαι: to go by
    προέρχομαι: to go forward
    ὑπέρχομαι: to go under, fawn on

ἐρωτάω: to ask ἐρήσομαι, 2 aor. ἠρόμην

εὑρίσκω: to find εὑρήσω, 2 aor. ηὗρον or εὗρον, ηὕρηκα or εὕρηκα, εὕρημαι, εὑρέθην
    ἐξευρίσκω: to discover

εὔχομαι: to offer prayers or vows εὔξομαι, ηὐξάμην, ηὗγμαι

ἔχω: to have ἕξω, 2 aor. ἔσχον, ἔσχηκα, imperf. εἶχον.
    ἀνέχω: to check
    ἀντέχω: to hold against
    παρέχω: to furnish, provide, supply
    προέχω: to surpass
    προσέχω: to hold to

ζάω: to live ζήσω, ἔζησα, ἔζηκα
    ἀποζάω: to live off

ἡγέομαι: to lead the way, consider ἡγήσομαι, ἡγησάμην, ἥγημαι
    διηγέομαι: to set out in detail, describe in full

ἥδομαι: to be happy, ἡσθήσομαι, ἥσθην
    ὑπερήδομαι: to be very happy

ἦλθον: to go, used as aorist of ἔρχομαι, perf. ἐλήλουθα

ἤνεγκα: to bear, used as aorist of φέρω, ἐνήνοχα, ἐνήνεγμαι, ἠνέχθην

θαυμάζω: to wonder, admire, fut. θαυμάσομαι

θλίβω: to squeeze ἔθλιψα, τέθλιφα, ἐθλίφθην

θνήσκω: to die θανοῦμαι, 2 aor. -έθανον, τέθνηκα
    ἀποθνήσκω: to die off
    ἐκθνήσκω: to die away

ἵημι: to let go, relax, to send forth ἥσω, ἧκα, εἷκα, εἷμαι, εἵθην
    ἀφίημι: to send forth, discharge
    καθίημι: to send down
    προίημι: to forgo, give up
    προσίημι: to let come to
    συνίημι: to perceive

ἵστημι: to make to stand, set στήσω, ἔστησα, 2 aor. ἔστην stood, ἕστηκα stand, ἐστάθην
    ἀνίστημι: to make to stand up
    ἀφίστημι: to put away, remove
    διίστημι: to separate
    ἐξανίστημι: to raise up: to make one
    ἐφίστημι: to set or place upon
    περιίστημι: to place round
    προίστημι: to set before
    συνίστημι: to combine, associate, unite

καίω: to burn καύσω, ἔκαυσα, -κέκαυκα, κέκαυμαι, ἐκαύθην
    ἀνακαίω: to light up

καλέω: to call καλῶ, ἐκάλεσα, κέκληκα, κέκλημαι, ἐκλήθην
    ἐγκαλέω: to call in, make an accusation
    ἐπικαλέω: to call, name
    μετακαλέω: to summon
    προκαλέω: to call forth, challenge

κάμνω: to labor, am weary: καμοῦμαι, ἔκαμον, κέκμηκα

κεῖμαι: to lie down: κείσομαι (used as passive of τίθημι)
    ἐπίκειμαι: to be laid upon
    κατάκειμαι: to lie down, lie outstretched

κεράννυμι: to mix ἐκέρασα, κέκραμαι, ἐκραάθην

κλάω(1): to weep κλαήσω, ἔκλαυσα

κλάω (2): to break, bend ἔκλασα, -κέκλασμαι, -εκλάσθην
    ἀνακλάω: to bend back
    ἐπικλάω: to bend to

κλείω: to shut κλείσω, ἔκλεισα, κέκλειμαι, ἐκλείσθην
    ἀποκλείω: to shut out
    ἐγκλείω: to shut in, close

κλέπτω: to steal: κλέψω, ἔκλεψα, κέκλοφα, κέκλεμμαι, ἐκλέφθην
    ὑποκλέπτω: to steal away

κλίνω: to bend κλινῶ, ἔκλινα, κέκλικα, κέκλιμαι, -εκλίνην
    κατακλίνω: to lay down

κόπτω: to strike κόψω, ἔκοψα, -κέκοφα, κέκομμαι, -εκόπην
    διακόπτω: to cut in two

κορέννυμι: to satiate κορέσω, ἐκόρεσα, κεκόρεσμαι, ἐκορέσθην

κρεμάννυμι: to hang κρεμῶ, ἐκρέμασα, ἐκρεμάσθην

κρίνω: to decide κρινῶ, ἔκρινα, κέκρικα, κέκριμαι, ἐκρίθην
    ἀνακρίνω: to examine closely
    ἀποκρίνομαι: to answer

κρύπτω: to hide from κρύψω, ἔκρυψα, κέκρυμμαι, ἐκρύφθην
    ἀποκρύπτω: to hide

κτάομαι: to acquire κτήσομαι, ἐκτησάμην, κέκτημαι το possess

κτείνω: to kill κτενῶ, ἔκτεινα, 2 perf. -έκτονα
    ἀποκτείνω: to kill, slay

κυέω: to be pregnant κυήσω, ἐκύησα conceived, κεκύηκα, -εκυήθην

λαμβάνω: to take λήψομαι, ἔλαβον, εἴληφα, εἴλημμαι, ἐλήφθην
    ἀπολαμβάνω: to receive
    ἐπιλαμβάνω: to hold back
    καταλαμβάνω: to lay hold of
    παραλαμβάνω: to hire
    περιλαμβάνω: to seize around, embrace
    συλλαμβάνω: to collect, capture

λανθάνω: to escape notice λήσω, ἔλαθον, λέληθα
    ἐπιλανθάνω: to forget

λέγω: to speak ἐρέω, εἶπον, εἴρηκα, λέλεγμαι, ἐλέχθην
    διαλέγω: to relate
    ἐπιλέγω: to say upon
    προλέγω: to proclaim

λείπω: to leave λείψω, ἔλιπον, λέλοιπα, λέλειμμαι, ἐλείφθην
    ἀπολείπω: to leave behind
    διαλείπω: to leave an interval between, cease from
    καταλείπω: to leave behind

μαίνω: to cause to be mad, be furious (mid.) μανοῦμαι, 2 aor. pass. ἐμάνην
    ἀντιμαίνομαι: to rage or bluster against
    ἐκμαίνω: to drive out of his mind

μανθάνω: to learn μαθήσομαι, ἔμαθον, μεμάθηκα
    ἐκμανθάνω: to learn thoroughly

μαραίνω: to quench ἐμάρανα, ἐμαράνθην
    ἀπομαραίνω: to lessen

μεθύσκω: to make drunk ἐμέθυσα, ἐμεθύσθην

μέλω: to be an object of care (used impersonally: μέλει it is a care) μελήσει,
    ἐμέλησε

μέλλω: to intend μελλήσω, ἐμέλλησα

μέμφομαι blame: μέμψομαι, ἐμεμψάμην, ἐμέμφθην

μένω: to stay μενῶ, ἔμεινα, μεμένηκα
    περιμένω: to await
    ὑπομένω: to stay behind, endure

μιμνήσκω: to remind, mid. to remember -μνήσω, -έμνησα, μέμνημαι, ἐμνήσθην
    ἀναμιμνήσκω: to remind
    ὑπομιμνήσκω: to remind

ὄζω: to smell ὀζήσω, ὤζησα
    ἀπόζω: to smell of

οἴγνυμι and οἴγω: to open -οίξω, -έῳξα, -έῳχα, ἀν-έῳγμαι, -εῴχθην
 ἀποιγέω: to open up
 ὑπανοίγω: to open slightly

οἶδα: to know, perf. of εἶδον with present sense, εἴσομαι, plup. ᾔδειν

οἴομαι: to suppose impf. ᾤμην, ᾠήθην

ὄλλυμι: to destroy -ολῶ, -ώλεσα, -ολώλεκα, -όλωλα
 ἀπόλλυμι: to destroy utterly
 προσαπόλλυμι: to destroy besides

ὄμνυμι: to swear ὀμοῦμαι, ὤμοσα, ὀμώμοκα, ὀμώμομαι, ὠμόθην
 διόμνυμι: to swear solemnly
 ἐπόμνυμι: to swear upon

ὁράω: to see ὄψομαι, 2 aor. εἶδον, ἑόρακα and ἑώρακα, ὤφθην, impf. ἑώρων
 ὑπεροράω: to look down upon

παίω: strike: παίσω, ἔπαισα, -πέπαικα, ἐπαίσθην.
 ἐπεισπαίω: to burst in

πάσχω: to experience πείσομαι, 2 aor. ἔπαθον, 2 perf. πέπονθα

πείθω: to persuade πείσω, ἔπεισα, 2 perf. πέποιθα, πέπεισμαι, ἐπείσθην
 συμπείθω: to assist in persuading

πείρω: to pierce ἔπειρα, πέπαρμαι, 2 aor. pass. -επάρην
 διαπείρω: to drive through

πέμπω: to convey πέμψω, ἔπεμψα, 2 perf. πέπομφα, πέπεμμαι, ἐπέμφθην
 ἀποπέμπω: to send off or away, to dismiss
 παραπέμπω: to send past, dismiss
 προπέμπω: to summon
 προσπέμπω: to send for

πέτομαι: to fly πτήσομαι, 2 aor. -επτόμην
 διαπέτομαι: to fly, hasten

πήγνυμι: to fix, make fast πήξω, ἔπηξα, 2 perf. πέπηγα, 2 aor. pass. ἐπάγην
 καταπήγνυμι: to fix firmly
 συμπήγνυμι: to construct, frame

πίνω: to drink πίομαι, 2 aor. ἔπιον, πέπωκα, -πέπομαι, -επόθην
 καταπίνω: to gulp or swallow down
 συμπίνω: to drink together

πίπτω: to fall πεσοῦμαι, 2 aor. ἔπεσον, πέπτωκα
 ἐμπίπτω: to fall upon
 ἐπεισπίπτω: to fall in upon

πλάττω: to form ἔπλασα, πέπλασμαι, ἐπλάσθην
 συμπλάττω: to mould or fashion together

πλέκω: to weave ἔπλεξα, πέπλεγμαι, -επλάκην
    περιπλέκω: to enfold round, embrace

πλέω: to sail πλεύσομαι, ἔπλευσα, πέπλευκα, πέπλευσμαι, ἐπλεύσθην
    ἀποπλέω: to sail off
    ἐκπλέω: to sail out
    ἐπιπλέω: to sail upon or over
    καταπλέω: to sail down

πλήττω· το strike -πλήξω, -έπληξα, πέπληγα, πέπληγμαι, -επλάγην
    καταπλήττω: to strike down

πνέω: to blow πνεύσομαι, ἔπνευσα, -πέπνευκα
    ἀποπνέω: to breathe forth, to smell of

πράττω: to do πράξω, ἔπραξα, 2 perf. πέπραχα, πέπραγμαι, ἐπράχθην

πυνθάνομαι: to learn πεύσομαι, 2 aor. ἐπυθόμην, πέπυσμαι

ῥέω: to flow ῥυήσομαι, ἐρρύην, ἐρρύηκα
    καταρρέω: to flow down
    ὑπορρέω: to flow from under

ῥήγνυμι: to break -ῥήξω, ἔρρηξα, -έρρωγα, ἐρράγην
    ἀπορρήγνυμι: to break off
    περιρρήγνυμι: to rend

ῥίπτω: to throw ῥίψω, ἔρριψα, 2 perf. ἔρριφα, ἔρριμμαι, ἐρρίφην
    προσρίπτω: to throw at

σείω: to shake σείσω, ἔσεισα, σέσεικα, σέσεισμαι, ἐσείσθην
    ἀποσείω: to shake off
    ἐπισείω: to shake at or against

σκέπτομαι: to view σκέψομαι, ἐσκεψάμην, ἔσκεμμαι
    ἐπισκέπτομαι: to pass in review, inspect

σκώπτω: to mock σκώψομαι, ἔσκωψα, ἐσκώφθην
    ἀποσκώπτω: to banter

σπάω: to draw σπάσω, ἔσπασα, -έσπακα, ἔσπασμαι, -εσπάσθην
    ἀποσπάω: to drag away from
    κατασπάω: to drag down

στάζω: to drip ἔσταξα, -έσταγμαι, -εστάχθην
    καταστάζω: to drip over

στέλλω: to send, arrange στελῶ, ἔστειλα, -έσταλκα, ἔσταλμαι, ἐστάλην
    συστέλλω: to draw together

στρέφω: to turn στρέψω, ἔστρεψα, ἔστραμμαι, ἐστρέφθην
    ἀναστρέφω: to turn back

ἀποστρέφω: to turn
ἐπιστρέφω: to turn about, turn round

σύρω: to draw -έσυρα, -σέσυρκα, -σέσυρμαι
ἐπισύρω: to drag after, to write carelessly

σώζω: to save σώσω, ἔσωσα, σέσωκα, ἐσώθην
ἀποσώζω: to save away

ταράττω: to stir up ταράξω, ἐτάραξα, τετάραγμαι, ἐταράχθην

τάττω: to arrange, τάξω, ἔταξα, 2 perf. τέταχα, τέταγμαι, ἐτάχθην
προστάττω: to instruct

τείνω: stretch τενῶ, -έτεινα, -τέτακα, τέταμαι, -ετάθην

τελέω: to complete τελῶ, ἐτέλεσα, τετέλεκα, τετέλεσμαι, ἐτελέσθην
συντελέω: to accomplish

τέμνω: to cut τεμῶ, 2 aor. ἔτεμον, -τέτμηκα, τέτμημαι, ἐτμήθην
ἀποτέμνω: to cut off, sever
διατέμνω: to cut through, divide

τήκω: to melt τήξω, ἔτηξα, τέτηκα, ἐτάκην

τίθημι: to place θήσω, ἔθηκα, τέθηκα, τέθειμαι (but usually instead κεῖμαι),
ἐτέθην
διατίθημι: to arrange, dispose of
ἐκτίθημι: to set out, place outside
ἐπιτίθημι: to lay, place upon
κατατίθημι: to put down
προστίθημι: to put in addition, add
συντίθημι: to put together

τίκτω: to beget, bring forth: τέξομαι, ἔτεκον, τέτοκα, ἐτέχθην

τιτρώσκω: to wound -τρώσω, ἔτρωσα, τέτρωμαι, ἐτρώθην

τρέπω: to turn τρέψω, ἔτρεψα, τέτροφα, ἐτράπην
ἀνατρέπω: to overturn, upset

τρέφω: to nourish θρέψω, ἔθρεψα, τέτροφα, τέθραμμαι, ἐτράφην
διατρέφω: to sustain continually

τρέχω: to run δραμοῦμαι, ἔδραμον, -δεδράμηκα
ἀποτρέχω: to run away
ἐπιτρέχω: to run upon or at
προστρέχω: to run towards
συντρέχω: to encounter

τρίβω: to rub τρίψω, ἔτριψα, τέτριφα, τέτριμμαι, ἐτρίβην
διατρίβω: to spend time

142

ἐπιτρίβω: to crush, perish
συντρίβω: to rub together, crush

τυγχάνω: to happen **τεύξομαι, ἔτυχον, τετύχηκα. τέτυγμαι, ἐτύχθην**
ἐντυγχάνω: to encounter, read

ὑπισχνέομαι: to promise **ὑπο-σχήσομαι**, 2 aor. **ὑπεσχόμην**

ὑφαίνω: to weave **ὑφανῶ, ὕφηνα, ὕφασμαι, ὑφάνθην**

φαίνω: to show, appear (mid.) **φανῶ, ἔφηνα, πέφηνα, πέφασμαι, ἐφάνην**
ἀποφαίνω: to show forth, display, produce
ἐμφαίνω: to exhibit, display

φέρω: to bear **οἴσω**, 1 aor. **ἤνεγκα**, 2 aor. **ἤνεγκον**, 2 perf. **ἐνήνοχα, ἐνήνεγμαι, ἠνέχθην**
ἀποφέρω: to carry off or away
ἐπιφέρω: to bring, put or lay upon
καταφέρω: to bring down
παραφέρω: to bring towards
προσφέρω: to carry to

φεύγω: to flee **φεύξομαι, ἔφυγον, πέφευγα**
ὑπεκφεύγω: to escape

φημί: to say **φήσω, ἔφησα**

φθάνω: to anticipate **φθήσομαι, ἔφθασα, ἔφθην**

φθείρω: to corrupt: **φθερῶ, ἔφθειρα, ἔφθαρκα, ἔφθαρμαι**, 2 aor. pass. **ἐφθάρην**
διαφθείρω: to destroy, spoil
ἐκφθείρω: to destroy utterly

χαίρω: to rejoice at **χαιρήσω, κεχάρηκα, κεχάρημαι, ἐχάρην**

χαλεπαίνω: to be offended **χαλεπανῶ, ἐχαλέπηνα, ἐχαλεπάνθην**

χέω: to pour fut. **χέω**, aor. **ἔχεα, κέχυκα, κέχυμαι, ἐχύθην**
ἐγχέω: to pour in
ἐκχέω: to pour out

χράομαι: to use **χρήσομαι, ἐχρησάμην, κέχρημαι, ἐχρήσθην**

Glossary

A α

ἄγω: to lead or carry, to convey, bring
ἀεί: always
αἷμα αἵματος, τό: blood
αἰτέω: to ask, beg
ἀκούω: to hear
ἀκριβής –ές: exact, accurate, precise
ἀληθής, -ές: unconcealed, true
ἀλλά: otherwise, but
ἀλλήλων: one another
ἄλλος, -η, -ον: other
ἄλλως: in another way
ἅμα: at the same time
ἀμείνων, -ον: better
ἀμφότερος ἀμφοτέρα ἀμφότερον: both
ἄν: (*indefinite particle; generalizes
    dependent clauses with subjunctive;
    indicates contrary-to-fact with
    independent clauses in the indicative;
    potentiality with the optative*)
ἀνήρ, ἀνδρός, ὁ: a man, husband
ἄνθρωπος, ὁ: a person
ἄξιος, ἀξία, ἄξιον: worthy, deserving
ἅπας, ἅπασα, ἅπαν: all, the whole
ἀπό: from, away from (+ *gen.*)
ἀποδίδωμι: to give back; render; (*mid.*)
    to sell
ἀπόλλυμι: to destroy utterly, kill
ἄρα: therefore, then (drawing an
    inference)
ἄριστος, ἀρίστη, ἄριστον: best, noblest
    (*superl. of* ἀγαθός)
ἀρχή, ἀρχῆς, ἡ: beginning, rule
αὐτός, -ή, -ό: he, she, it; self, same

B β

βλέπω: to see, look
βούλομαι: to will, wish

Γ η

γάρ: for
γε: at least, at any rate (*postpositive*)
γίγνομαι: to become
γοῦν: at least then, at any rate
γράφω: to write
γυνή, γυναικός, ἡ: a woman, wife

Δ δ

δακρύω: to weep
δέ: and, but, on the other hand
    (*preceded by* μέν)
δεῖ: it is necessary
δεινός, -ή, -όν: awesome, terrible
δή: certainly, now (*postpositive*)
διά: through (+ *gen.*); with, by means of
    (+ *acc.*)
δίδωμι: to give
διηγέομαι: to describe in full
δοκέω: to seem, consider
δραχμή, ἡ: a drachma (*a coin*)
δύναμαι: to be able (+ *inf.*)
δύο: two

E ε

ἐάν: = εἰ + ἄν
ἐάω: to allow, permit
ἐγώ, μου, ἐμέ, ἐμοί: I, me
ἐθέλω: to will, wish, purpose
εἰ: if
εἶδον: to see (*aor.*)
εἰμί: to be
εἶμι: to go (*fut.*)
εἶπον: to say (*aor.*)
εἰς, ἐς: into, to (+ *acc.*)
εἷς, μία, ἕν: one
εἶτα: next, then
ἐκ, ἐξ: from, out of, after (+ *gen.*)

ἕκαστος, -η, -ον: each, every

ἐκεῖνος, -η, -ον: that, that one

ἐλπίς, -ίδος, ἡ: hope, expectation

ἐμός, -ή, -όν: mine

ἐν: in, at, among (+ *dat.*)

ἕνεκα, ἕνεκεν: for the sake of (+ *gen.*)

ἔνθα: there

ἔοικα: to seem, to be like (*perf.*)

ἐπαινέω: to approve, applaud

ἐπεί, ἐπειδή: since, when

ἐπί: at (+ *gen.*); on, upon (+ *dat.*); on to, against (+ *acc.*)

ἕπομαι: to follow

ἐραστής, -οῦ, ὁ: a lover

ἐράω: to love

ἔρχομαι: to go

ἔρως, ἔροτος, ὁ; love

ἐρωτάω: to ask, enquire

ἑταίρα, ἡ: a courtesan

ἕτερος ἑτέρα ἕτερον: the other (of two); other, another

ἔτι: still

ἔτος, ἔτους, τό: year

εὖ: well, thoroughly

εὐθύς, εὐθεῖα, εὐθύ: straight, direct

εὐθύς: (*adv.*) immediately

εὑρίσκω: to find

ἔχω: to have; to be able (+ *inf.*)

Z ζ

ζάω: to live

H η

ἤ: or; than

ἦ: truly

ἤδη: already, now

ἡδύς, ἡδεῖα, ἡδύ: sweet, pleasant

ἥκω: to have come, be present, be here

ἡμεῖς, ἡμῶν, ἡμᾶς, ἡμῖν: we, us

ἡμέρα, ἡ: day

Θ θ

θεός, θεοῦ, ὁ/ἡ: a god, goddess

θνήσκω: to die

θρίξ, τρίχος, ἡ: a hair

θυγάτηρ θυγατέρος, ἡ: daughter

θύρα, ἡ: a door

I ι

ἵνα: in order that (+ *subj.*)

ἵστημι: to make to stand, set

K κ

καθάπερ: just as

καθεύδω: to lie down to sleep

καί: and, also, even

καίτοι (καί-τοι): and indeed, and yet

κακός, -η, -ον: bad, cowardly

καλός, -ή, όν: good

κατά, καθ': down, along, according to (+ *acc.*)

κεφαλή, ἡ: the head

κομίζω: to take care of, provide for, escort

Λ λ

λαμβάνω: to take, catch

λέγω: to speak, say, tell

λυπέω: to cause to grieve

M μ

μακρός, -ά, -όν: tall, large

μάλα: very

μάλιστα; very much, especially

μᾶλλον: more, rather

μανθάνω: to learn

μάχη, -ης, ἡ: a battle

μέγας, μέγαλα, μέγα: great, large

μειράκιον, τό: a boy, lad

μείς, μῆνος, ἡ: a month

μέλλω: to be about to (+ *inf.*)

μέν: on the one hand (*followed by* δέ)

μένω: to remain, stay

μέσος, -η, -ον: middle, in the middle

μετά: with (+ *gen.*); after (+ *acc.*)

μεταξύ: between

μή: not, lest, don't (+ *subj.* or *imper.*)

μηδέ: but not or and not, nor

μηκέτι: no longer

μήν: truly

μήτε: and now

μήτηρ, μητρός *or* μητέρος, ἡ: mother

μικρός, -ά, -όν: small, little

μιμνήσκομαι: to remember

μνᾶ, ἡ: a mna (= *100 drachma*)

μόνον: only

μόνος, -η, -ον: alone, only

ὅμοιος, -α, -ον: like, same

ὅμως: nevertheless

ὄνομα, -ατος, τό: a name

ὁπότε: when

ὅπου: where, wherever

ὅπως: as, in such manner as, how

ὁράω: to see

ὅρκος, ὁ: an oath

ὅσος, -η, -ον: how many, whatever, whoever

ὅστις, ἥτις, ὅτι: anyone who, anything

ὅταν (ὅτε-ἄν): whenever (+ *subj.*)

ὅτε: when

ὅτι: that, because

οὐ, οὐκ, οὐχ: not

οὐδέ: but not

οὐδείς, οὐδεμία, οὐδέν: no one

οὐκέτι: no longer, no more

οὐκοῦν: therefore, then, accordingly

οὖν: so, therefore

οὗτος, αὗτη, τοῦτο: this

οὕτως: in this way

N ν

ναί: indeed, yes

ναύκληρος, ὁ: a ship-master

νεάνισκος, ὁ: a young man

νῦν, νυνί: now, at this moment

νύξ, νυκτός, ἡ: the night

O o

ὁ, ἡ, τό: the (*definite article*)

οἶδα: to know (*perf.*)

οἴομαι *or* οἶμαι: to suppose, think, deem, imagine

οἷος, -α, -ον: such as, what sort

ὀλίγος, -η, -ον: few, little, small

ὅλος, -η, -ον: whole, entire

ὅλως: (*adv.*) completely

Π π

παῖς, παιδός, ὁ: a child

πάλιν: back, again

πάνυ: altogether, entirely

παρά: from (+ *gen.*); beside (+ *dat.*); to (+ *acc.*)

πάρειμι: be present, be ready

πᾶς, πᾶσα, πᾶν: all, every, whole

πάσχω: to experience, suffer

πατήρ, πατρός *or* πατέρος, ὁ: a father

πείθω: to prevail upon, win over, persuade

πέμπω: to send, dispatch

πέντε: five

περί: concerning, about (+ *gen.*); about, around (+ *acc.*)

πίνω: to drink

πιστεύω: to trust, believe in

πλέων πλέον: more, larger (*comp.* of πολύς)

πλήν: unless, but

πλούσιος, -α, -ον: rich

πλουτέω: to be rich, wealthy

πόθεν: whence, from where

ποιέω: to make, do

πολύς, πολλή, πολύ: many, much

ποτε: sometime

που: somewhere

ποῦ: where?

πρᾶγμα, τό: a deed, matter

πράττω: to do

πρό: before, in front of (+ *gen.*)

πρός: to, near (+ *dat.*), from (+ *gen.*), towards (+ *acc.*)

προσβλέπω: to look at

προσέρχομαι: to approach

πρόσωπον, τό: a face

πρότερος, -α, -ον: prior, earlier

πρῴην: (adv.) earlier

πρῶτος, -η, -ον: first

πώποτε: ever yet

πως: in any way, at all, somewhat

πῶς: how? in what way?

Σ σ

στρατιώτης, -ου, ὁ: a soldier

σύ, σοῦ, σέ, σοί: you (*singular*)

συγκαθεύδω: to lie down with

σύν: with (+ *dat.*)

σύνειμι: to be together with, consort with

συνίημι: to perceive

Τ τ

τάλαντον, τό: a talant (*a measure*)

τε: and (*postpositive*)

τίθημι: to put, place, establish

τις, τι: someone, something (*indefinite*)

τίς, τί: who? which? (*interrogative*)

τοίνυν (τοί-νυν): therefore, moreover

τοιοῦτος, -αύτη, -οῦτο: such as this

τοῖχος, ὁ: a wall

τοσοῦτος, -αύτη, -οῦτο: of such a kind, so large, so great

τότε: at that time, then

τρόπος τρόπου, ὁ: way, manner, habit

τυγχάνω: to hit upon, happen

Υ υ

υἱός, ὁ: a son

ὑπέρ: over, above (+ *gen.*); over, beyond (+ *acc.*)

ὑπό, ὑφ': from under, by (+ *gen.*); under (+ *dat.*); toward (+ *acc.*)

ὑμεῖς, ὑμῶν, ὑμᾶς, ὑμῖν: you (*plural*)

Φ φ

φάρμακον, τό: a drug, dye

φάσκω: to claim, allege

φέρω: to bear, endure

φημί: to say

φιλέω: to kiss, to love

φίλος, -η, -ον: beloved, dear, friendly

Χ χ

χαίρω: to be happy; χαῖρε, (*pl.*) χαίρετε hello, goodbye

χάρις, χάριτος, ἡ: honor, favor, grace

χείρ, χειρός, ἡ: a hand

χθές: (*adv.*) yesterday

χράομαι: to make use of (+ *dat.*)

χρή: it is necessary

χρόνος, ὁ: time

χρώς, χρωτός, ὁ: skin

Ω ω

ὦ: oh! (*vocative of definite article*)

ὡς: (*adv.*) as, so, how; (*conj.*) that, in order that, since; (*prep.*) to (+ *acc.*); as if, as (+ *part.*); as ____ as possible (+ *superlative*)

ὥσπερ: just as

ὥστε: so that, and so

Made in the USA
Middletown, DE
18 March 2016